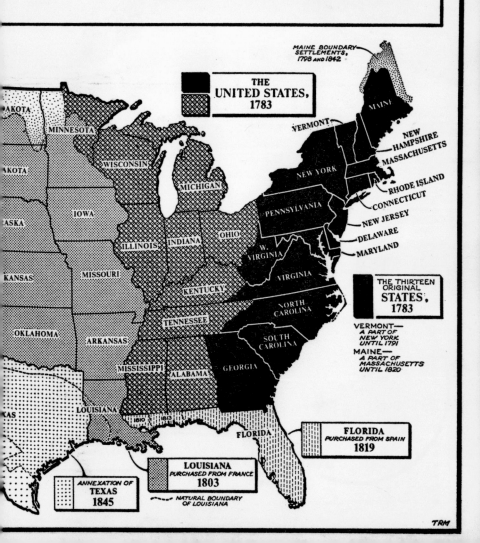

ADMISSIO[N]

1.	DELAWARE	1787	18.	LOUISIANA		1861
2.	PENNSYLVANIA	1787	19.	INDIANA		1863
3.	NEW JERSEY	1787	20.	MISSISSIPPI	1817	
4.	GEORGIA	1788	21.	ILLINOIS	1818	35. NEVADA 1864
5.	CONNECTICUT	1788	22.	ALABAMA	1819	36. NEVADA 1864
6.	MASSACHUSETTS	1788	23.	MAINE	1820	37. NEBRASKA 1867
7.	MARYLAND	1788	24.	MISSOURI	1821	38. COLORADO 1876
8.	SOUTH CAROLINA	1788	25.	ARKANSAS	1836	39. NORTH DAKOTA 1889
9.	NEW HAMPSHIRE	1788	26.	MICHIGAN	1837	40. SOUTH DAKOTA 1889
10.	VIRGINIA	1788	27.	FLORIDA	1845	41. MONTANA 1889
11.	NEW YORK	1788	28.	TEXAS	1845	42. WASHINGTON 1889
12.	NORTH CAROLINA	1789	29.	IOWA	1846	43. IDAHO 1890
13.	RHODE ISLAND	1790	30.	WISCONSIN	1848	44. WYOMING 1890
14.	VERMONT	1791	31.	CALIFORNIA	1850	45. UTAH 1896
15.	KENTUCKY	1792	32.	MINNESOTA	1858	46. OKLAHOMA 1907
16.	TENNESSEE	1796	33.	OREGON	1859	47. NEW MEXICO 1912
17.	OHIO	1803				48. ARIZONA 1912
						49. ALASKA 1959
						50. HAWAII 1959

THE UNITED STATES, 1783

MAINE BOUNDARY SETTLEMENTS, 1798 AND 1842

THE THIRTEEN ORIGINAL STATES, 1783

VERMONT—A PART OF NEW YORK UNTIL 1791
MAINE—A PART OF MASSACHUSETTS UNTIL 1820

FLORIDA PURCHASED FROM SPAIN 1819

LOUISIANA PURCHASED FROM FRANCE 1803

ANNEXATION OF TEXAS 1845

NATURAL BOUNDARY OF LOUISIANA

TRM

THE STORY OF
AMERICAN STATEHOOD

THE STORY OF
AMERICAN STATEHOOD

BY

DANA LEE THOMAS

WILFRED FUNK, INC., NEW YORK

Copyright © *1961 by Wilfred Funk, Inc.*

Library of Congress Catalog Card Number 61-6626

Printed in the United States of America

1

Preface

THIS BOOK is being written at a time when the word "imperialism" is charged with greater emotional intensity than it has ever had. Not so many years ago a vast empire symbolized power and glory, and revolt against king or emperor would have been immoral if, indeed, it had been possible. Today, the idea of imperialism is universally repugnant, not only to idealists, but to those demagogues who practice it in thinly disguised form. The supremacy of the people, rather than of king, emperor, or "Parliament," is universally acclaimed to be the only morally right form of government, even by those who distort or misunderstand the meaning of democracy.

In Asia, the Middle East, and Africa the last vestiges of classic colonialism are disappearing; the old-time colonial powers are relinquishing their hold on distant peoples in still-primitive lands. At the same time, a new kind of remote control is replacing the old: the ideological persuasion of new nations is as important to the entire world

v

today as religious allegiance or economic support was to the imperial powers of old.

In a republic like the United States it is natural to think that any government which modeled itself according to a resilient constitution like our own would surely succeed in achieving a stable, progressive government. But the way in which the United States developed from a string of unrelated colonial trading posts into a unified world power is unique in history. A group of colonies in an environment of absolute power wielded from above would have been unready for the "independence" achieved by the Revolutionary War. The system of government which the colonies had already developed was, however, so well advanced by 1776 that it made feasible the adoption of a federal constitution that would bind together, without overpowering, the thirteen sovereign states. For those eager but unschooled people who have not learned self-government by the time they have its burden thrust upon them, we can only hope that our own experience and achievement may be an example of the way men may prosper under a constitution based upon the inherent right of the individual to life, liberty, and the pursuit of happiness.

After the Revolutionary War, the thirteen states—acting under the Articles of Confederation and through their representative body, the Continental Congress—proved their faith in the form of government they had won by enacting the Northwest Ordinance to solve the problem of how to deal with the new lands won from England. The Ordinance they passed provided for the ultimate achievement of statehood "on an equal footing with the original States in all respects whatever" by settlers of the Northwest Territory. Each of the new states (not less than three nor more than five were to be carved out of the said territory) was to be "at liberty to form a permanent constitution and State government: provided, the constitution and government so to be formed, shall be republican, and in conformity to the principles contained in these articles [the six articles of the Ordinance]."

The territory for which the Northwest Ordinance provided a government extended from the west side of the Alleghenies to the east bank of the Mississippi, and from the north bank of the Ohio to the present Canadian border. The principle upon which the Ordinance was founded, however—that unsettled lands be administered as states-in-preparation and be oriented as such from the very beginnings of settlement—was so sound that it was to serve for all other territories acquired by settlement or annexation up to, and in, the Pacific. As statehood moved westward it became more flexible; west of the Alleghenies constitutions were framed for a society of pioneers, farmers, and other rugged individualists very unlike the aristocratic society which was long influential in the East.

Suspicious of strong executive government, the people of western states delegated the bulk of power to their legislative assemblies, confining their governors to mere administrative functions. But even as they yielded increasing authority to the executive over the years, they evolved devices for retaining control where it belonged—at the grass roots. It was in the West that the first provisions for initiative and referendum were put into state constitutions. Female suffrage was first enacted in Wyoming and Oklahoma. The West fostered free enterprise on the one hand, and the eight-hour work day, workmen's compensation laws, and regulation of public utilities on the other.

It took the American public almost two hundred years to achieve independence in thirteen colonies along the coast. In less than that amount of time they were to raise thirty-seven additional territories to full participation in the family of states. How the instruments of the United States government, devised by the elected representatives of the people, enabled this republic to grow in size and power without allowing it to neglect its first principles, is the theme of this book.

Contents

Illustrations appear at page 116 and page 148

THE STORY OF
AMERICAN STATEHOOD

Introduction

THE WAY in which a nation governs itself is always a fascinating study. Whether a government will stand or disintegrate depends on so many factors that it is probably impossible to foresee how any apparently sound structure will hold up through the years. While the Articles of Confederation was not a success as an instrument of national unity, the foundation on which it rested was already so firm that it was possible to scrap the old and build the new Constitution without causing more than a brief tremor.

The first foundation stone was laid on July 30, 1619, in a church in Jamestown, Virginia, when the first legislative assembly on the continent held its first meeting. The cornerstone was the Constitution of 1787, ratified by all of the original thirteen colonies between 1787 and 1790, which formally rendered the foundation complete. In the years between the first and last steps in this construction of a government, it was the English colonies which pro-

1

vided the genius for self-rule. The French colonies were under despotic, if not unenlightened rule; their function was chiefly commercial. The French came not to settle the land, but to take its fish and furs for France. Spain's Conquistadors used the Indians to provide the coffers of kings and nobles with mineral wealth. Like the French, the Spanish were not (excepting, by and large, the missionaries) migrants to the New World but colonial satraps. Even the Dutch, in their tiny settlement in Manhattan, never achieved a vestige of self-government. In every case, the government of Europe's colonies reflected the political picture at home.

The beginnings of English colonization in America were also commercial in purpose, but the principles of self-rule were already known to the Englishmen who came to Virginia and Massachusetts at the beginning of the seventeenth century under the aegis of chartered trading companies. The king granted the charters and had the final word on all colonial matters, but the companies' private stockholders—whose investments made colonization possible—had a voice and a vote in the administration of the overseas colonies. As private trading ventures the colonies were failures, but the people who had come over on the companies' ships stayed on after the charters were revoked. In the case of the Massachusetts Bay Company, its Puritan stockholders bought all the stock and sailed to America—with the charter—to found a commonwealth free of all obligations to a commercial office in London and to establish a life free from religious persecution.

Aside from the trading-company charter, the royal colony and the proprietary grant were the chief vehicles of English sovereignty in America. None of these was excessive in its demands on the settlers once a colony became firmly established, though the early days of trading-company operations were marred by the general mismanagement of local affairs in the Virginia colony. In 1618, however, when the success of the tobacco crop had made emigration attractive to Englishmen, the Virginia company devised "head rights," which gave fifty acres of land free to each emigrant to Virginia who had paid his own passage, and ordered the introduction of English common law and a representative assembly empowered to make by-laws. The first meeting of this assembly—twenty-two burgesses elected by all males over the age of sixteen in the settled districts—was not only the first building-block of democracy in America, but was to have no parallel in non-British colonial history for nearly three centuries. Even when the company lost its charter and Virginia became a royal colony, she did not lose such local democratic institutions as the assembly and courts of justice, though the governor and his council were no longer elected by stockholders large and small, but were appointed by the king. At the time, this was Charles I, and he was pleased enough with the customs revenues pouring in from the tobacco crop to give his colony wide latitude in running its internal affairs.

As for the proprietary grant, which the king made to a gentleman or noble as a gift, the recipients of such grants in America were given considerable power in the setting up of a local government. Pennsylvania, Maryland, and the Carolinas were such grants, and their settlers were not slow about winning from the proprietors the right to legislative assemblies. William Penn took the initiative in his own colony, and called for elected representatives of the people to enact the democratic "Great Charter" in 1682.

By this date, democracy was already well established in New England. The Fundamental Orders of Connecticut of 1639 was the first written constitution devised by a commonwealth for itself in the Western world, and provided for the popular election of a governor and a bicameral legislature. The charter Roger Williams secured for Rhode Island gave full self-governing powers to the little colony, and the second charter in 1663 gave Rhode Island, like Connecticut, the status of a tiny republic within the British Empire. The Crown's one stipulation was that no laws be made contrary to those of England.

At the beginning of the eighteenth century certain forces were in operation which were to lead to the development of an American nation. France held a huge empire in the New World, an empire calculated to cut off British expansion westward past a line drawn from Quebec to New Orleans, and a struggle between herself and England was inevitable. While England's string of colonies was stronger and far better populated than the scattered and poorly organized colonies of her adversary, the French made use of the Indians to harass and intimidate the English settlers. England went to war with Spain in 1739 over her depredations on English trading vessels in the Caribbean; thousands of American volunteers were lost in this war, which lasted about three years and ended inconclusively. Between 1744 and 1748 the British and French were at war in America, and once again—as was the case in nearly all wars fought on American soil until after the War of 1812—the colonists were drawn into a New World extension of a European war; they fought now until an inconclusive truce was drawn.

The French, however, did not give up. In 1753 Governor Dinwiddie of Virginia sent George Washington, a 22-year-old lieutenant-colonel of Virginia militia, to prevent a French advance into the Ohio Valley. The expedition failed, and the French built Fort Duquesne in Pittsburgh. War was not officially declared until 1755, although the English colonists in America were as eager to rid themselves of their French antagonists as England was, and were already all but officially at war. While England and the colonists were thus occupied in America, war broke out in Europe, and by 1762 England found herself at war with France, Spain, Austria, Russia, Sweden, and most of the German states. As allies, she had Portugal and Prussia.

Had England lost this costly war, France would have become natural heir to all North America west of the Alleghenies, but in 1758 England's new foreign minister, William Pitt, devised the strategy that was to bring victory to England: concentrate British power on victory in America, help finance the allied operations of Prussia in Europe, and, with Britain's superior navy, paralyze the French at sea. The heroic young James Wolfe won Canada on the Plains of Abraham on September 13, 1759. Montreal surrendered in 1760. France had lost the war, and with it her vast claims in the American West. (The Indians continued fighting until Pontiac's rebellion collapsed in 1766.)

Spain was also on the losing side in the Seven Years' War (called the French and Indian War in America), and she gave up Florida to Great Britain, just as France gave up Canada, by the peace treaty of 1763. The sovereignty of the region west of the Mississippi was not yet settled, however. To her former ally, Spain, France secretly ceded Louisiana and all her other claims to the West.

The colonists, who had fought for England better than the English themselves in some areas, now shared an awakening experience: they had united in battle, and they had won. They began to look beyond their chartered or proprietary horizons, and saw that despite nagging sectional differences from North to South and between the seaboard and back country—religious, economic, cultural differences—they had much in common with their sister colonies: the English language, a form of local government based on English common law, a keen sense of colonial rights.

It is significant, from the standpoint of constitutional development, that the great majority of the early colonists were English. They paved the way for Catholics, French Huguenots, Jews, Scotch-Irish, Dutch, German and Swiss, Swedes and Italians, who, as individuals and as communities, came to the New World in the great waves of migration that began in 1628, and swelled the population of the British colonies. Minorities who didn't know the English language and law learned them. With intermarriage, Old World customs and attitudes gave way to an Anglo-American culture. Even solid communities like the Germans in Pennsylvania adapted themselves to the political climate of this English land, though they might hold to their own language and social customs.

There was much in favor of a union of the colonies, and it had been thought of more than ten years before the war's cohesive effect. In 1754 Benjamin Franklin's Albany Plan of Union provided for a president-general to be appointed by the king and a Grand Council which was to be chosen every three years by the colonial assemblies. But it was not democratic enough for the colonial assemblies—

who saw no need to relinquish any of their power to a central body—and it was too democratic for the Crown, so it was never adopted. But this was before the French and Indian War—before the colonists had discovered that united they were strong and England had decided that the colonies' arrogant evasion of her excises was a weakness that must be corrected with firmer handling.

Loyalty to England was unquestioned even after the War, and new thoughts of union did not include independence. Though she had been extremely liberal in her administration of the royal provinces and proprietary colonies, England had always considered these possessions as extensions of herself. She was primarily interested in their value as traders and as a market for her own products, and as long as they made a good showing in this regard she had not troubled herself particularly with their internal affairs. After the treaty of 1763, however, she found herself with a greatly expanded empire to administer; she decided that a general overhaul of the Crown's colonial affairs was in order, and that the colonies must be made to share the ever-increasing costs of administration and defense.

The American colonies were blithely ignoring the Navigation Acts that had long been in effect for the protection of British-American trade. These acts must now be enforced. The Declaratory Act of 1766 reasserted in strong terms the supremacy of Parliament. The colonies were forced to support ten thousand British soldiers sent for the "protection of the colonists" against Indian attack. Import and export taxes were levied and strictly enforced. "Writs of assistance" were invoked by the Crown to search and seize wherever smuggling operations were suspected to exist, even in private homes.

Perhaps the most provocative of George III's new or renewed measures, however, was the closing off of the western lands to colonial expansion. This was done by the Royal Proclamation of October 7, 1763, and was bitterly resented in a land where men had just given their lives to rid themselves of the French barrier to western settlement. The reason for the Proclamation was that the Indians must be mollified by their conqueror before it would be safe to move into the territory. Another logical reason was that an American migration westward would make the business of royal administration far more difficult, and would put many colonists out of reach of the British goods they were supposed to buy. The Proclamation went so far as to forbid any purchase of these lands—between the Alleghenies, the Floridas, the Mississippi, and Quebec—from the Indians, and to warn all who may already have "inadvertently" settled upon the land that they must remove themselves forthwith. This automatically canceled all the western land claims of the Thirteen Colonies—for the most part valid claims to a natural extension of their present settlements. To make men's tempers even shorter, times were hard after the ravages of the French and Indian War.

Riots broke out at scattered points in 1765. At first there was no organization of forces, only disorderly local protests against abuses; the Stamp Act was one abuse. Responsible citizens and merchants next took more effectual action in boycotting English imports on which taxes had been levied, thus forcing Parliament to repeal the Townshend Act—except for the tax on tea—in 1770. What might be called the first concerted act of revolution, however, was the formation of a Committee of Correspondence, on November 2, 1772, in Massachusetts. Its reason for being was the news that henceforth governor and judges were to be paid by the Crown and would therefore be under its control. Its function was to set up communication between the towns so that they could collaborate on deciding the course of action to be taken on matters which concerned them all; no longer would a little province protest in isolation. Its impact lay in its statement of the rights of colonists "as men, as Christians, and as subjects," which was printed and circulated with explosive effect.

Similar committees and similar declarations sprang up in other colonies, and in 1773 the Virginia Burgesses appointed the first of the intercolonial committees, a network which quickly spread to the farthest reaches of American settlement.

In May of 1774, the Virginia House of Burgesses—eighty-nine men among whom Jefferson, Richard Henry Lee, and Patrick Henry were numbered—was dissolved by the royal governor for proclaiming a day of prayer and fasting in protest against the Boston Port Act, a severe retaliatory measure for the Boston Tea Party. In a body, the Burgesses marched to the Raleigh Tavern and continued their meeting. On August 1, Speaker Peyton Randolph summoned the members of the legally defunct House of Burgesses; this now revolutionary legislature, the first Provincial Congress, "caught on," and other colonies quickly followed suit. Of monumental importance was an enactment of the Virginia legislators at their Raleigh Tavern meeting: a call for an annual congress to discuss "the united interest of America," which, vigorously championed by the Massachusetts Assembly on June 17, brought delegates from every colony except Georgia to Philadelphia on September 5, 1774, to the first Continental Congress.

The foundation of an American government was taking form. It might still, at this stage, have been demolished. It had built-in weaknesses—the slavery controversy, the early and sometimes violent rumblings of sectionalism, an overall "shakiness" resulting from Tory loyalty to the king opposing the radical philosophies of such men as John Locke and Tom Paine. It was the first Continental Congress that set off the War for Independence, though its petition to the king to abolish the recent grievances contained the words: "Your royal authority over us, and our connection with Great Britain, we shall always carefully and zealously endeavor to support and maintain." The incendiary action of the Congress, however, lay in its declarations approving Massachusetts' opposition to certain acts of Parliament and supporting the principle that any attempt to force submission of any or all of the colonies to despotic control should be met with "resistance and reprisal." Measures of non-importation, non-exportation, and non-consumption were enacted to give force to the Congress' demands. The most important work of the Congress at this time, however, was the declaration of the rights of the colonists, which brought all the colonies onto common ground although it was Massachusetts in particular that was most deeply at odds with Parliament.

The crux of the dispute had become the matter of supremacy. It no longer mattered as much whether the taxes were paid as whether the American colonies could be made to acknowledge the ultimate authority of Parliament. On this point the Congress was clear: The colonies were not represented in Parliament and were therefore being taxed without representation; the colonies were entitled to "a free and exclusive power of legislation in their several provincial legislatures . . . in all cases of taxation and internal polity, subject only to the negative of their sovereign." They would consent to Parliament's regulating their external trade for the benefit of the mother country and of the empire as a whole, but they excluded "every idea of taxation, internal or external, for raising a revenue on the subjects in America, without their consent."

A deadlock had been reached. Neither side would, or could, withdraw from its position. Massachusetts organized a Provincial Congress and a Committee of Safety late in 1774 and began stockpiling arms and supplies at Concord and Worcester. By January 1, 1775, there were thirty-five hundred men garrisoned at Boston, with another five hundred in service on guard details. England promised reinforcements to General Gage, and sent Generals Howe, Clinton, and Burgoyne to join him in Massachusetts. On April 18, 1775, Gage marched to Concord to destroy the military stores. The Committee of Safety was alerted. Joseph Dawes, Samuel Prescott, and Paul Revere were dispatched to warn the people in towns and on farms. At Lexington Green, Gage found "a body of country people drawn up in military order, with arms and accoutrements." A shot was fired. The American Revolution had been all but effected; the war had just begun. All the colonies rallied behind Massachusetts.

The Second Continental Congress had already been elected, and became, for lack of any other centralized authority, the government of the Thirteen Colonies. It convened at Philadelphia on May 10, 1775, and formed a Federal union. Each colony was to retain the right to run its internal affairs according to its constitution, and Congress was to have the power to make peace or war, enter into treaties and alliances, and legislate on such matters as concerned the security and welfare of the whole community. Congress promptly enlisted an army and set about readying the new confederacy for full-scale war. Currency was issued, forts were built, and George Washington was unanimously elected by Congress as commander-in-chief of the Continental Army.

While the Continental Congress was acting in the quite limited capacity it had assigned itself—cautiously, it took upon itself practically no power over the individual colonies but simply offered them recommendations—the colonies were independently strengthening their executive and legislative departments. The forms of royal government were discarded in Virginia and New Hampshire in 1775, and a constitution and plan of government was adopted by the legislatures of each; both colonies declared for independence and instructed their delegates to Congress accordingly. The more conservative colonies hesitated, but on July 4, 1776, when the Second Continental Congress executed the Declaration of Independence, the thirteen united colonies became, by unanimous consent, a single sovereign state, the United States of America.

The Articles of Confederation—proposed in June, 1776, presented to Congress on July 12 of that year, adopted with extensive modifications in November, 1777, ratified at last in 1781—tried to solve the difficult problem of sovereignty which had now been transferred from the lap of England to that of the United States. The individual states were as jealous of their rights under their own Congress as they had been as colonies under Parliament and the king's governors. Even during the Revolutionary War their cooperation with the aims of Congress was far from adequate;

France's help had been indispensable—she provided credit, arms, ships, and, finally, direct intervention—since one of the Congress' most serious weaknesses was that it had not had the power to enforce taxation of the colonies. The important thing to all concerned was that the thirteen states should establish governments for themselves, and in 1776 Congress recommended that this be done. By April of 1777 all thirteen states had ratified constitutions, in many cases based on their charters from the king, and in some cases unchanged except for the substitution of "the people" for "the king" in their wording. All thirteen constitutions were essentially alike: none permitted hereditary privilege; nearly all contained a bill of rights; most formally adopted English common law as part of the law of the land; all had a strong legislature as compared with the executive arm of government. Certain religious limitations for holding office were common, as were property qualifications for voting rights.

On October 19, 1781, Lord Cornwallis surrendered to "the Combined Forces of America and France" at Yorktown, Virginia. The treasury of the United States was empty; the young country was deeply in debt—even her army had long gone unpaid. When the treaty of peace between Great Britain and the United States was signed at Paris on September 3, 1783, Americans by the thousands had already begun the long migration westward. Pack trains—men, women, children, cattle, axes and rifles—and flatboats set out for Kentucky and Tennessee, and settlers who staked out "cabin claims" in this hostile Indian territory eventually set up civil governments for themselves. Tennessee was then the western land claim of North Carolina, and Kentucky was Virginia's "West," but neither of these hard-won settlers' lands wished to be considered part of the states to the east. Also before the War had ended— in June of 1783—Congress was asked for land grants to the territory north of the Ohio River which England had closed to settlement twenty years before.

On March 1, 1786, a group of American officers and soldiers organized the Ohio Company for the purchase and settlement of western lands ceded by England or purchased from the Indians, and acquired from Congress some million and a half acres. The Northwest Ordinance, which settled the question of how these lands were to be governed, was the most permanent work effected by the much abused and distrusted Continental Congress.

There was little disagreement with the fact that the Articles of Confederation had serious shortcomings, and that the Second Continental Congress had been ineffectual in many areas of national concern. The weakness of the Articles—which rendered the Congress weak in turn— could be traced to the states' jealousy of their individual sovereignty, so recently and bitterly won. The Articles provided only for a league of states, without an executive head or a judiciary, in which all members had an equal voice regardless of their population. Unanimous consent was necessary to amend the Articles.

This "firm league of friendship" placed state sovereignty above that of "the United States in Congress assembled" in all matters except those which were necessarily national and international. By Article I of the Articles of Confederation, each state retained "its sovereignty, freedom, and independence, and every power, jurisdiction, and right . . . not by this Confederation expressly delegated to the United States in Congress assembled." Congress was given apparently broad powers—to make war, conclude peace, send and receive ambassadors, make treaties and alliances, resolve interstate disagreements, regulate coinage, weights, and measures, manage Indian affairs, raise an army and equip a navy, requisition the states for men and money, establish a post office, and borrow money on the credit of the United States—but no measure in the areas of making war and peace or alliances, coinage, borrowing money and making appropriations, or determining the cost or extent of national defenses, could be passed without the assent of nine states. Less weighty matters could be passed on by a simple majority. What rendered many of the Congress' seemingly wide powers ineffectual, however, was that no power to enforce any of its measures was provided. Moreover, the states reserved to themselves the specific, meaningful powers: complete control over taxation and the regulation of foreign and interstate commerce. So it was that, while Congress was empowered to raise an army and to borrow money on the credit of the United States, it had no enforceable means of raising revenue to pay the army or repay the debt.

The individual state had grown so strong, so jealous of its independence, that for a time it seemed that lack of a centralized government would destroy the new nation. For this reason, Hamilton and Washington urged that the Articles of Confederation be strengthened. Even these powerful voices were lost in the wrangling of the thirteen sovereign states, but in September of 1786 delegates from five of the Middle States met at the Annapolis Convention and recommended that another convention be held at Philadelphia in May of the next year. Congress approved, by resolution, and on May 25, 1787, delegates from

every state except Rhode Island met. Instead of revising
the old, they devised a new, federal constitution.

The delegates to this convention—at which was framed
the document called by British Prime Minister Gladstone
"the most wonderful work ever struck off at a given time
by the brain and purpose of man"—included some of the
most illustrious men in American history. Fifty-five delegates, representing twelve states, were chosen by the state
legislators, though only thirty-nine were to sign the completed work. Numbered among the signers of the Constitution were George Washington, planter, of Virginia; Benjamin Franklin, philosopher, of Pennsylvania; Alexander
Hamilton, lawyer, of New York; James Madison, lawyer,
of Virginia. Washington was unanimously elected president of the convention.

Not long after the convention opened, on May 25, 1787,
it became apparent that a mere revision of the Articles of
Confederation was not what many of the nationalist-
minded delegates had in mind. On May 29, the Virginia—
or large-state—plan was submitted by Edmund Randolph,
and two weeks later the New Jersey—or small-state—plan
was offered by William Paterson of that state. The plans
differed in many respects, but the most sensitive matter at
issue in the beginning was representation: the first plan
based state representation in the legislature on population;
the second provided for an equal number of delegates from
all states regardless of size. Bitterness arose between the
advocates of the two plans; the first was considered unfair
to the small states, and the second to the large states. Weeks
of wrangling ended when a committee appointed for the
purpose brought in a compromise, called the Connecticut
or Great Compromise. Their solution was a two-house

legislature, with an equal vote for all states in the Senate, and representation on the basis of population (using the "federal ratio" of free population plus three fifths of the slaves) in the House of Representatives.

The Great Compromise was the first of the many compromises which inevitably evolved out of philosophical and sectional differences: the nature and role of the executive, the terms of office for executive and legislature and their manner of election, the proportion of votes necessary to pass laws of various types in Congress, the areas of jurisdiction of the state and federal governments, the "balance of power" between non-slave and slave states.

With the example of the ill-fated Confederation before them, the delegates were able to see where strength would be needed in the new government, and to work out their blueprint accordingly. Under the Articles, the states had had the power to immobilize the Continental Congress. The new Congress, therefore, was given—in addition to the traditional ones—the all-important powers its predecessor had lacked: to levy and collect taxes, duties, imposts, and excises; to regulate interstate and foreign commerce; to provide for calling forth the militia to execute the laws of the union, suppress insurrections, and repel invasions; and to make all laws "necessary and proper" for carrying into execution all its powers under the Constitution. The Constitution obliged all state officials to take an oath to support it, and the difficult question of how Congress was to enforce its laws on the state governments was admirably resolved by the convention in Article VI of their handiwork: The Constitution, the laws of Congress, and all treaties made under the authority of the United States "shall be the supreme Law of the Land; and the Judges in every State shall be bound thereby, any Thing in the Constitution or Laws of any State to the Contrary notwithstanding." By this provision, the laws of Congress were made binding upon the people and were enforceable not only through the federal, but through the state courts.

In order to insure the preservation of popular sovereignty, a clear line was drawn between the areas of jurisdiction of the federal and state governments, and the federal government itself was divided into three branches—executive, legislative, and judicial—all equal in strength and independent of the others in operation, but each subject to certain restrictions by the other two branches.

The foresight of the delegates was plainly indicated in Article IV, which provided that Congress should have the power to admit new states into the union, and to "dispose of and make all needful rules and regulations respecting the territory or other property belonging to the United States." This provision was to call for interpretation before long, but one of the most admirable features of the Constitution is its flexibility in the matter of interpretation as times and conditions change.

On September 17, 1787, the Constitution was engrossed and signed "By unanimous consent of the States present." To this day it remains something of a miracle not only that the document was completed to the satisfaction of so many different interests, but that it has remained a living body of laws through nearly two centuries of rapid and unforeseeable changes in the country and in the world. And so the cornerstone was laid. The structure could be raised. Modifications could be made; new "wings" could be added. The foundation was sound.

CHAPTER I

The Northwest Territory

NOWHERE WAS THE American pioneer more successful in conquering his environment than in the American Northwest, a territory extending southward from the Great Lakes, and from the west bank of the Ohio River to the east bank of the Mississippi. This was a land of luxuriant natural resources, richly forested except in the fertile grasslands of what is now Illinois. Deer, elk, and buffalo abounded; Indians raised squash; at the edge of the surrounding waters herons cried shrilly.

The Northwest Territory had been a prize for its first European explorers, the French, who sent missionaries and fur-traders to the Indians as early as the sixteenth century. To the British—who wrested this land from the French in 1763 as a result of the French and Indian War—it was a buffer against westward expansion of the American colonies. In furtherance of this end, George III provided no government for this part of his territorial acquisition, thus leaving it in legal possession of the Indians. The seem-

ingly benign policy of England was: "Let the Savages enjoy their deserts in quiet."

For the American colonists, however, the Northwest was
a land of opportunity, a place to move on to if one failed,
or grew restless, in the East.

In 1494 Pope Alexander VI divided the heathen lands
of the world between Spain and Portugal; Spain received
the western half, containing North America. Neither England nor France was deterred, however, from exploring
and laying claim to the New World. The King of France
sent Giovanni da Verrazano to explore the North American coast in 1524, and Jacques Cartier furthered his country's claim to Canadian territory ten years later, but the
first French explorers to penetrate the American Northwest Territory were Jacques Marquette and Louis Joliet,
in 1673.

Seventeenth-century missionaries had received reports
from the red men about the great "Messipi" River that
flowed through fertile lands where snow rarely fell, and
where two crops of maize a year were harvested. The Spaniards had christened it the *Rio del Espiritu Santo* (River
of the Holy Ghost), and had calculated that it ran south of
the Great Lakes. But whether it meandered into the Gulf
of Mexico or into the Pacific, no European knew. The fact
was that no white man had as yet explored it to its source.

In June, 1672, France took a decisive step. Colbert,
Louis XIV's minister of finance, wrote to Jean Baptiste
Talon, financial administrator in New France, directing
him to launch a new exploration. If this proved successful,
it would open the American West to French commercial
interests and make feasible the construction of a network

of colonies that would seal the English off on the Atlantic coast.

Talon suggested to Count de Frontenac, governor of New France, that Louis Joliet be the leader of the expedition. Joliet, the son of a wagon maker, was a trader and trapper on the Great Lakes. Tall, blue-eyed, bronzed by continual contact with the outdoors, Joliet had traveled widely among the savages and knew their dialects.

The French authorities decided to appoint a companion for Joliet—a spiritual leader capable of winning the friendship of the Indians who would be encountered en route. When the head of the Jesuits in New France was asked to suggest a missionary, he promptly replied, "The ideal person is Father Jacques Marquette."

A happier choice could not have been made. Marquette had been in the New World only six years, but he was already greatly respected for his accomplishments among the Hurons and Ottawas. Moreover, he had mastered a variety of Indian tongues. And he had shown abundant capacity for withstanding physical hardship.

Marquette and Joliet requisitioned the assistance of five French-Canadian woodsmen and two canoes for this exploration that would take them thousands of miles through uncharted regions. The canoes were strongly built of birchbark and ribs of spruce veneered with yellow-pine pitch, yet they were so light four men could haul them over the portage paths, and in calm water they could be paddled at a speed of about four miles an hour. In these canoes guns and ammunition and extra clothing were stored, as well as sails to exploit friendly winds and presents for the Indians to be encountered on the way. The food supply consisted of Indian corn and smoked meat.

From every quarter the explorers received warnings. The Indians were especially foreboding in their prophecies. They did not expect the explorers to reach the river. One chief declared gloomily, "We have heard that the heat that steams up from its banks will roast your flesh. The river teems with monsters who will topple your canoes. Should you escape these perils, you will be murdered by hostile tribes."

On the seventeenth of May, 1673, when the ice melted at Michilimackinac, the party set out. Priests, trappers, and Ottawa and Huron braves gathered at the rim of Lake Michigan. Joliet, jauntily attired in a blanket coat and brightly colored sash, and Marquette, in his priestly black robe and broad hat, waved good-bys and entered the canoes. As they were about to round Point Barbe, the men glanced back. Then they disappeared from view.

They paddled past the lowering stone of the Point. Now they were lifted up by the current that catapulted through the Strait of Mackinac and swept along the northern shore of Lake Michigan, moving into an expanse of water the French had named "Putrid Bay" because from its slimy bottom rose vapors that blended with the odor of a salt spring with dreadful effect. The air was cold, and spasmodic squalls whipped the waters. Kneeling on birchbark rushes, the explorers paddled into Green Bay through the "Door of Death," so named because of the crosscurrents that had shipwrecked many a sailor.

The men inhaled the pungent air of Green Bay, scented by the tamarack and pine growing on the shores. Occasionally they bathed their faces in the chill, refreshing waters. On Fox River they encountered water so shallow that the canoes crunched against the bottom, and the men frequently had to carry their vessels into deeper currents, bruising their feet on the rocky riverbed as they walked.

One month out of Michilimackinac, on June 17, the two canoes came out at last into the Mississippi. The river was recognizable by its depth, its current, and its great width—a mile at this point. Having entered it, there was no choice but to proceed wherever it would take them.

As the party continued down the Mississippi, the bottom lands teemed with herds of buffalo, an animal totally unfamiliar to the explorers. Marquette made a sketch in his journal of this strange, bellowing creature.

Entering the lower Mississippi, the air was hazy with tormenting clouds of mosquitoes. Indians living in the area dealt with the problem by sleeping on raised platforms with fires underneath. The system was effective at night, but in the daytime there was no escaping the maddening insects. The white men fashioned their sails into a tent, but this provided small comfort.

One day, while rounding a densely wooded bank, they encountered the trouble they had feared from the beginning—the menacing clubs and warlike cries of a band of Indians on the shore. Throughout the trip down the river they had met and even visited with the different Indian tribes living along the shores, but these encounters had until now been more or less friendly. They managed to elude the hostile savages, but that night the voyagers held serious council.

According to their calculations, they had gone over a thousand miles down the river, and were now at latitude 33° 40'. They had not reached the sea, but it was Joliet's opinion that they had obtained the information they were after and should now start back. "Unquestionably the Messipi does not debouch into the California ocean—or into the Atlantic by way of Virginia. Its mouth can only be the Gulf of Mexico. Therefore," he concluded, "we have fulfilled our mission."

Father Marquette and the Canadians agreed with him. The priest did not wish to take the risk, by venturing further downstream, of losing their valuable journals and maps in an Indian attack or having them fall into the hands of the Spaniards who controlled the Gulf.

Therefore, on July 17, 1673, at the mouth of the Arkansas River, seven hundred miles north of the Gulf of Mexico, the explorers started on their return journey.

One day, toward the end of September, seven men staggered into the Mission of St. Francis Xavier, along the De Père Rapids of the Fox River. The mission was thrown into a tumult. Indians and missionaries crowded around the travelers as if they had returned from the grave, rather than from a four-month voyage. There was far more justification for celebrating than they knew. One of the most extraordinary explorations in recorded history had been accomplished.

The immediate significance of Marquette and Joliet's achievement was that it gave France a claim to the Northwest Territory, which she held until the end of the French and Indian War in 1763. When she ceded this territory to England, complications quickly followed.

The Indians—Ottawa, Potawatomi, and Wyandot—had lived on friendly terms with the French. They had fought on their side in the war, and were bitterly disappointed at the cession to Britain. Their resentment was heightened by the fact that the English were far less friendly than the French, who sometimes took native brides and generally showed respect for the red men. Also, the English were settlers, and when they moved into Indian territory they took, and defended, large tracts of the best land available. Even King George's Proclamation of October 7, 1763, prohibiting settlement of the territory between the Mississippi and the Ohio, did not quell the Indian rebellion which had begun in May. Only after hard fighting were the red men finally subdued late in 1764. By the time the colonies revolted, however, the Indians had become the allies of the British sovereign.

In the War for American Independence, the Northwest again became a battleground. Now British agents furnished the Indians with arms to use against the settlers. Help for the frontiersmen came in the person of George Rogers Clark, a soldier of fortune, who captured the British forts in the Illinois and Wabash territory. His victories provided the new American government with its claims for territory lying between the Mississippi, the Ohio, and the Great Lakes. Rather than have this disputed land seized by either France or Spain, Britain reluctantly recognized the American claim and ceded the land in the Peace Treaty of 1783. This sprawling "back country" was now an American problem.

Before the problem of organizing the Northwest Territory was met face to face, pioneers south of the territory had already started their own westward push. In 1767, Daniel Boone had explored the Kentucky valleys, laying out the Wilderness Road. For the next ten years only the hardy and adventurous undertook to fight the Indians for the land, and in 1776 Kentucky became a county of Virginia. By 1784, after the War's end, the population had grown to such an extent that Kentucky began agitation for separation from Virginia as a separate state. Not until June of 1792, however, was she admitted to the Union as the fifteenth state.

Daniel Boone played a part in the formation of another state, because his Wilderness Road brought settlers not only into Kentucky, but into Tennessee. Originally part of North Carolina, Tennessee was separated from the mother colony by a rugged mountain region. In 1769, the first permanent settlers came to the banks of the Watauga River and thought they were in Virginia. When a survey proved them to be in North Carolina, and they realized that they were not, after all, under Virginia law, and that North Carolina was occupied with troubles of her own, they were shocked into organizing a civil government for themselves. The result of the labors of some fine citizens was a commonwealth which, through the efforts of two young men named John Sevier and James Robertson, formed the first written constitution west of the mountains. They elected a representative assembly of thirteen members, of which a committee of five had judicial and executive power. In 1776 the Watauga Association petitioned North Carolina for annexation, for the sake of protection, and in 1784, when the General Assembly of North Carolina ceded this territory to the United States, the Wataugans were so indignant that they called a convention for the purpose of organizing a separate state. North Carolina repealed the cession, which gave the Wataugans the impression that they now "belonged to nobody." As an independent group, therefore, they formed a state which they named Franklin; John Sevier was its governor, and it had a constitution and an elected legislature. The state of Franklin had a short life and a not very happy one; factions sprang up between pro- and anti-Sevier elements, and settlers refused to pay taxes to either Franklin or North Carolina. In February, 1788, the ill-fated state ceased to exist; the area reverted to North Carolina, which again ceded it to the United States. Tennessee was promptly organized as the Territory Southwest of the Ohio, and six years later the state of Tennessee was formed, with John Sevier as its governor. The first representative of this sixteenth state in the House was Andrew Jackson.

To keep the chronology straight, the northeastern state of Vermont, fourteenth to enter the Union, must be accounted for at this point.

Vermont, curiously enough, had been an independent republic. Occupying the eastern portion of land claimed by New York, Vermont settlers—who were actually trans-planted Connecticut Yankees—met in convention in 1777 and declared their independence. The Vermont constitution was the first in the United States to prohibit slavery. Although the opposition of New York and other states who had claims on her territory prevented Vermont from being admitted to the Union for a number of years, the plucky little republic remained vigorously loyal to the principles of the American nation. British agents tempted Vermont to become a British province. One general, in 1780, sent a letter to Ethan Allen (of "Green Mountain Boys" fame), delivering it by way of a British soldier dressed as an American farmer. It was an invitation to collaborate with the Redcoats. When no reply was received, the British sent a second message. Allen mailed both to the Continental Congress. Finally, New York withdrew its opposition to Vermont and the republic was admitted to the Union on

February 18, 1791, the fourteenth American state, and the first to achieve statehood since the ratification of the United States Constitution.

By the cession of the Northwest Territory, the area of the United States was enlarged by some two hundred million acres. The original thirteen colonies, now free and independent states united under the Articles of Confederation, were faced with a common responsibility: to determine a policy for the disposition of these public lands and to provide a form of government for them.

The Northwest Territory did not pass directly into the hands of the United States government. Virginia, the Carolinas, Georgia, New York, Massachusetts, and Connecticut revived old colonial claims to an extension of their boundaries beyond the Appalachians, and it was not until 1780 that New York's claim was ceded to the United States. The Continental Congress—anticipating the Revolution's success—now passed a resolution that lands thus ceded to the United States would be "disposed of for the common benefit of the United States, and be settled and formed into distinct republican States, which shall become members of the Federal Union . . . ," and Connecticut, Massachusetts, and Virginia soon surrendered their own claims.

After the treaty of 1783, then, Congress had to face squarely the question of how to administer the western lands, and committees on land and government were appointed to solve the problem. The Land Ordinance of 1785 successfully settled one aspect of the problem by providing for a rectangular survey of the public domain into six-mile-square townships, each to consist of thirty-six sections of 640 acres (one square mile) each. Land offices were established for sale of these lands at not less than one dollar an acre. Excepted were four sections of every township to be reserved for the United States government and one section for the maintenance of public schools. A stipulation that favored private land companies was that not less than a 640-acre section could be sold, and the Ohio Company of Associates succeeded in acquiring a million and a half acres along the banks of the Ohio and Muskingum Rivers for a fraction of its value in 1787.

The committee on government, headed by Thomas Jefferson, began an intensive study toward recommending a system of administration, one which would ultimately enable this territory to be divided into states that would enter the Confederation on an equal basis with the original members. The plan Jefferson's committee submitted called for the territory's division into ten new states, with names drawn from Latin, Greek, and Indian: Sylvania, Cherronesus, Michigania, Assenisipia, and Metropotamia were among the names suggested. Congress adopted the Jefferson report in April, 1784, and the policy it outlined later formed the basis of the Northwest Ordinance—except, obviously, for the number and names of the states-to-be.

In the meantime, the impatience of land-hungry pioneers was typified by a meeting of ex-Revolutionary War soldiers in Boston in March, 1786, which set up a plan for the ultimate division of the Northwest Territory into not less than three nor more than five states, all to have served apprenticeship as organized territories before assuming statehood. Each district of the territory (the entire Northwest Territory was designated as a district, subject to division into two) was to be administered by a governor, a secretary, and a court of three judges, all appointed by Congress. When the population grew to 5,000 free adult males, a bicameral legislature was to be elected by them and designated a General Assembly. As soon as the population reached 60,000 free inhabitants, the territory would qualify for admission to the Union as a state "on an equal footing with the original States in all respects whatever"—provided its government and constitution were "republican, and in conformity to the principles contained in these articles." Slavery and involuntary servitude, other than for the punishment of crimes, were banned, and the inhabitants were to be guaranteed the writ of habeas corpus and trial by jury.

Landed estates were to be divided equally among the children of a deceased property holder, to avoid the concentration of property holdings characteristic of Europe, where, by the laws of primogeniture and entail, entire estates commonly passed from the father to the eldest son.

The territory was to "forever remain a part of this confederacy of the United States of America, subject to the Articles of Confederation, and to such alterations therein as shall be constitutionally made; and to all the acts and ordinances of the United States in Congress assembled, conformable thereto." Further, the inhabitants and settlers in the territory were to be subject to federal taxation, which would be "apportioned on them by Congress according to the same common rule and measure by which apportionments thereof shall be made on the other States . . ." As soon as a legislature was formed in a territory, the upper council and the House were to have authority by joint ballot to elect a delegate to Congress who would have the right to debate, but not to vote, during the period of territorial government.

In 1788, a year after the passage of the Ordinance, Arthur St. Clair was appointed the first governor of the Northwest Territory. But although legal title had passed to the American nation it was to take thirty more years of war with the Indians before the land became "American soil."

The utmost good faith shall always be observed towards the Indians; their lands and property shall never be taken from them without their consent; and, in their property rights and liberty, they shall never be invaded or disturbed, unless in just and lawful wars authorized by Congress.

So, in part, reads Article 3 of the Northwest Ordinance. But the American frontiersman wanted land, and after the war's end he began moving into the fertile lands of the Miamis, the Scioto, and the Muskingum, despite the law.

The Indians grew increasingly sullen at these depredations—although they were known to claim more than their share of the land. The British, too, were a problem. Despite the Treaty of 1783, they refused to give up possession of a number of forts in the Northwest Territory. They had lost control of the land south of the Lakes, but they intended to safeguard their influence over the rich fur trade of the north.

As the Indians stepped up their attacks on Americans, the United States government retaliated. President Washington chose "Mad" Anthony Wayne to take command of the American armies in 1792. General Wayne's recklessness—from which the epithet "Mad" was derived—was looked upon with some apprehension by his fellow officers. But although subject to gout, Wayne loved a hard fight, and this was a quality of character the Northwest needed.

Wayne's first task was to rebuild and train an army that had recently suffered bloody defeat at the hands of Indians in the Wabash country. He sent out a call for recruits, and was deluged by a motley crowd of unlikely candidates, many of whom were deportees from the eastern cities. Those who survived a year of Wayne's intensive discipline, however, were transformed into the best-trained fighting machine ever turned against the Indians in the West.

In 1793, Wayne's army broke camp at Cincinnati and advanced northward in the direction of the Maumee. News of their advance traveled ahead, and many of the Indians living in the northern villages fled. When the troops arrived at the junction of the Maumee and Auglaize rivers, they built a fort they named "Defiance."

Next, Wayne moved his army to the left bank of the Maumee; from here they proceeded downstream toward the British Fort Miami—the point to which the Indians had retired. In a day the troops reached "Fallen Timbers," a site so named because of the piles of trunks and branches lying about as the result of some violent storm. Here, from behind the natural breastworks of logs, the Indians—with arms popularly believed to have been supplied by the British—launched an attack on Wayne. They turned loose a thunderous fire, pushing back Wayne's first line of mounted Kentuckians. But the infantry behind them, infected with their general's recklessness, rushed the breastworks and dislodged the red men. With Wayne's men in pursuit, the Indians made a run for the British fort—but the British refused to open the gates. Cut off from their line of supplies, the British themselves subsequently gave up the fort.

Thanks to this decisive victory at Fallen Timbers in

1794, followed by the Treaty of Greenville (by which, in 1795, peace was ultimately established), America at last held the upper hand in the Northwest Territory. By this treaty, two thirds of the present state of Ohio was ceded to the United States government by the Indians. Settlers poured into the area almost on the heels of Wayne's triumph. In the vanguard were the investors and the speculators, who, individually or corporately, purchased burgeoning tracts of land to resell at a profit. Pamphlets describing the opportunities of the West deluged the East. Not only farmers whose lands were heavily mortgaged, and men overburdened with debts, but people of means pulled up stakes and moved westward. To the consternation of many New England communities, some of the "best citizens" packed their belongings. The emigrants reached such numbers that many Eastern factory owners grew alarmed that their labor force would be seriously depleted. Anti-West pamphlets began to appear, and protests were voiced at town meetings. One widely publicized cartoon illustrated a well-dressed individual astride a fleshy horse meeting a skeleton of a man dragging along a skinny steed. "I'm going to Ohio," exulted the rider. "I've *been* to Ohio," muttered the skeleton.

The colonizing of the West was above all the work of the homeseeker, who moved into the new country on his own initiative and settled wherever he wished. In addition to the New Englanders, emigrants poured in from Pennsylvania, Virginia, and Kentucky. A month before Wayne launched his campaign to crush the Indians, a native of Connecticut named Moses Cleaveland, leading a party of fifty neighbors, founded a settlement in Ohio which he rather immodestly named after himself. The spelling of this name was subsequently modified to "Cleveland."

Ohio, the first region of the Old Northwest to be densely settled, became the gateway to the Mississippi. The favorite pathway into the Ohio Valley was initially the Cumberland Gap, at the southeastern corner of the present state of Kentucky. As other routes were discovered, the lines of travel spread from Maine to Georgia. But all converged on the Ohio River—La Belle Riviere, as La Salle had called it—located midway between the Northeast and the Northwest.

The majority of emigrants had to travel long distances before they reached this waterway. The very poor went on foot, pulling their possessions in carts. The more affluent traveled in horse-drawn covered wagons, packing their furniture, household utensils, seed, and medicines into the roomy interiors.

When the migrants arrived at the Ohio, they had to build boats to cross it with their possessions. The flatboat became the most popular vessel for the downstream journey to the promised land, giving place in the years to come to steamboats and even ocean-going vessels. The trip from Pittsburgh to Cincinnati took about eight days. Upon reaching its destination, the flatboat was either converted into a floating store or broken up so that the wood could be used for building cabins.

Before the introduction of sawmills, wood, ironically enough, was hard to come by even in the midst of plenty. Oaks, poplars, and sycamores had to be cut by hand for every use. But though the forests yielded up their treasure reluctantly, the earth readily provided food to those who made some effort to get it. "Johnnycake" and "pone," favorite varieties of cornbread, and game, fruits, wild grapes, and garden vegetables kept the frontiersman healthy.

Hard work was the only possible way of life. While the men hunted and farmed, the women spun thread for their own simple linsey dresses and sewed buffalo-hair hunting shirts, deerskin trousers, and moccasins for their husbands. Children went barefoot in the summer; they were taught the three R's by itinerant pedagogues who were paid for their services in produce. Although textbooks were rare, shale for blackboards and soapstone for pencils were abundant.

One specter continued to haunt this new world—the deteriorating relations between the white man and the Indian. The country was overrun by traders who demoralized the natives with alcohol. Wherever Indians and white men lived as neighbors, there was a degeneration of the dignity of both. After weeks in the wilderness, an Indian party would arrive at a settlement to trade its pelts for alcohol. Brandy was available by the kettleful, and the Indians bought it that way. On the morning after, dejected, their blankets burned and new shirts torn, the Indians would start off again down the river, bereft of hope and profits.

In addition to vitiating his spirit, some of the emigrants violated the red man's territorial rights. "Long Knives" from Virginia cut through boundary lines and took possession of lands barred by treaty. Hunters and traders penetrated deeper and deeper into the forbidden woods.

The more isolated tribes of the North and West watched this activity with mounting alarm. To the Indians, the implications were clear. The white conquest had to be rolled back or the Indians were doomed to extinction. But the contest was unequal; the scattered tribes were outnumbered by an opponent that was unified, well armed, and determined.

Serious crises breed great leaders. This instance was no exception. The stage was set for the appearance of a man who was probably the greatest leader produced by his race. He was to point out to his people a road to salvation.

Tecumseh—"Shooting Star"—was a Shawnee. He had a brother named Tenskwatawa, who later became known as The Prophet. Tecumseh grew to be a superior person in intelligence and physical appearance. He was straight and hard-muscled, and his eyes had a habitually merry expression. His manners were courtly. A mighty warrior, he nonetheless scorned violence and opposed the custom of torturing prisoners.

As a child he had listened to tales of Pontiac's rebellion. His own father had been killed in battle against the white man, and he had seen Indian refugees pouring from their villages at the advance of American armies.

When Tecumseh was twenty-three, he became head of a band of spies who performed their duties so efficiently for the chief Little Turtle that in 1791 Little Turtle gave St. Clair's American army the worst beating in the history of Indian warfare. And Tecumseh was present at Fallen Timbers when "Mad" Anthony Wayne scattered the Indians to the four winds. Through experience, Tecumseh learned one lesson well: In unity there is strength.

At Fallen Timbers in 1794, Tecumseh met for the first time the man who was to be his greatest white adversary— William Henry Harrison. Harrison was about Tecumseh's age (twenty-six), and an aide-de-camp to General Wayne. Both young men were in subordinate positions, but each was destined to rise to a position of leadership and for twenty years contest the bitter issue of race supremacy.

As a chief, Tecumseh evolved a logical and formidable plan for solving the Indians' dilemma. He conceived the idea of binding together all Indian tribes from the Lakes to the Gulf and from the Alleghenies to the Rockies into a single nation like that of the Americans to the east. A central government would be established that would own all the Indians' lands, and the cession of territory by petty chiefs would be halted.

Tecumseh traveled the length and breadth of the Northwest to convert the tribes to his "communal socialism." With him went his brother and co-worker, The Prophet, a man of very different character but—for a time—valuable in his own way. Possessed of a sinister countenance from which an eye had been lost, The Prophet worked on the superstitions of his people. He claimed to be the recipient of visions sent by the Great Spirit. Under Tecumseh's influence, he exhorted the Indians to abstain from alcohol and to dwell in peace.

While The Prophet prayed, Tecumseh worked assiduously to further his plan. It was not an easy task to convince the far-flung, individualistic tribes to accept the principle that land should be held in common. However, his concept slowly gathered adherents. One tribe after another, bewitched by his eloquence, united with the rest to form a single community centered at the junction of the Tippecanoe and Wabash Rivers, where the vast system of waterways to the South and West was easily accessible.

The strategic implications of this confederacy were not lost upon the frontiersman. Although Tecumseh professed peaceful intentions, the white settlers grew wary as reports came in that his agents were prowling the land preaching rebellion. Harrison bombarded Washington with a plea for troops. In July of 1811 he informed the Secretary of War:

> If it were not for the vicinity of the United States, Tecumseh would . . . become the founder of an empire that would rival in glory Mexico or Peru. No difficulties deter him. . . . You see him today on the Wabash . . . you hear of him on the shore of Lake Erie or Michigan, or on the banks of the Mississippi; and wherever he goes he makes an impression favorable to his purpose. He is now upon the last round to put the finishing stroke to his work.

To complicate matters, trouble was brewing between the United States and Great Britain, trouble that was to lead to the War of 1812. British agents were once again rumored to be supplying the Indians with firearms and ammunition, and Harrison was convinced that Tecumseh was secretly working with them. Alarm mounted as acts of violence increased; farms were abandoned, and many settlers left the Northwest.

At this point, when he might possibly have regained the West for the Indians, Tecumseh made a fatal error. Leaving the Tippecanoe region to travel south and persuade the tribes of Tennessee and Alabama to join forces with the northern tribes, he directed The Prophet to continue to build up the confederation, maintaining peace at any cost.

On his return home, he found that his orders had been disobeyed. Itching for a fight, and aroused by Harrison's encampment on the outskirts of the Indian village, The Prophet had—in November of 1811—attacked the American troops at Tippecanoe. The white men, taken by surprise, had rallied their forces, driven back the Indians, and burned Tecumseh's settlement—by now abandoned.

When Tecumseh returned, he found that not only the homes of his people, but his dreams of a confederation had gone up in smoke. The Indians under his leadership—thousands of them—had been scattered like leaves.

In June, 1812, the United States declared war on Great Britain, and Tecumseh desperately played his last card. He joined the British and donned the uniform of a brigadier general. For a time Fortune seemed to smile on his people. Potawatomie Indians fell upon Fort Dearborn in Chicago, massacring soldiers and civilians. The Indians surprised settlers in Pigeon Roost (Indiana) and threw their bodies into the burning cabins.

At first the untrained American volunteers were no match for the British regulars and their Indian allies, and seemed destined for certain defeat. But, as in the earlier case of General Wayne's recruits, the rawness was hammered out of these novices, and Americans turned defeat into victory on land while Commodore Perry won a decisive engagement on Lake Erie.

Tecumseh reluctantly accompanied the British on their retreat up the Thames. Faced with the demise of his hopes, he would have preferred to die fighting. As Harrison's pursuing army came nearer, he pleaded with the British commander to halt. The Englishman finally consented, posting his men on the left bank of the Thames while the Indians stationed themselves in swamps on the right.

Tecumseh announced to his Indian aides a prophecy of his own death. He unbuckled his sword and handed it to a chieftain. "When my son becomes a warrior, give this to him." Then he took off his British uniform and arrayed himself in the battle-dress of a native warrior. Once again the solitary black and white feather adorned his hair.

On October 5, 1813, Harrison struck with his mounted militia. The British broke and ran. But the Indians, led by Tecumseh, stood their ground. They fought until they realized that they no longer had a leader. When they found Tecumseh dead on the field, they buried him where he had fallen—the exact spot is no longer known—and along with this "noblest savage of them all" they buried their last hope of regaining their hunting grounds and their homes.

With the conclusion of the war, the Northwest drew a deep breath of relief. The intrepid pioneers had not waited for the land to be cleared of the Indian menace, but now settlers would be able to come in in great numbers without fear. On May 7, 1800, an act of Congress had divided the Northwest Territory into two sub-territories. The reason for this was that the eastern part was filling up far more rapidly than was the western, and would be ready for statehood soon if a dividing line were drawn. So the area west of a line beginning at the Ohio opposite the mouth of the Kentucky River, and running to Fort Recovery and thence north to the Canadian border, was designated the Indiana Territory. The eastern part was organized as the Territory Northwest of the River Ohio, with its capital at Chillicothe; it was this territory which became the state of Ohio in 1803—the first state to enter the Union under the terms of the Northwest Ordinance.

As first organized in 1800, the Indiana Territory included the county of St. Clair on the upper Mississippi, the county of Knox on the Wabash, and the county of Wayne on the Detroit River. The Wayne County settlements were organized into the Michigan Territory in 1805, with its capital at Detroit. By the end of 1808 the Indiana Territory east of the Wabash had reached a population of 5,000 free adult males, so in February of 1909 Congress set off this populated area and authorized a territorial legislature. The area west of the Wabash was then organized into the Illinois Territory. Eight years later Congress authorized the election of a convention to frame a state constitution for the Indiana Territory, and the state of Indiana was formally admitted into the Union on December 11, 1816. Two years later, on December 3, 1818, Illinois entered as the twenty-first state of the Union and the third state to be carved from the Northwest Territory.

The fourth state (twenty-sixth in the chronology of American statehood) was Michigan, which entered on January 26, 1837. Before she was able to reach this stage, however, a boundary dispute had to be settled with the state of Ohio. Michigan claimed that under the Northwest Ordinance and the Act of Congress which constituted her a territory in 1805, she was entitled to the area including the lake port of Toledo and the mouth of the Maumee River. President Jackson put the question before Congress, which offered Michigan instead the upper peninsula. Acceptance of these terms was made a condition of statehood, and though the first state convention called to decide the matter turned down the proposal in September, 1836, a second convention approved it two months later. In this way the state of Michigan acquired her present boundaries.

Although Michigan, like her sister states of the Northwest Territory, devised a constitution that was highly democratic in every respect, she outdid herself in the matter of public education. A million acres of land were set aside for schools, a public school was required to be kept in each school district for at least three months in every year, a superintendent of public instruction was appointed, and the state was pledged to preserve all donations for schools or for the university as permanent funds not to be diverted to any other purpose. Michigan was thus the first state in the nation to recognize specifically the state's obligation toward the education of all its citizens. A state university was established in March, 1837. Though this approach to education was not actually translated into effective action for almost a century, because of legislative squabbles and insufficient appropriations, the principle, at least, was indelibly written for all to see.

The fifth state to enter the Union from the old Northwest Territory was Wisconsin. From 1805 until 1809 it had been part of Indiana Territory. From 1809 to 1818 its territory was incorporated into the Territory of Illinois, except for a small projection at the northeast which was unassigned to any territory. When Illinois became a state, all country north of Illinois' present boundaries (including Wisconsin) was joined to Michigan Territory. Finally, in 1836, the year before Michigan became a state, the present-day area of Wisconsin, together with a large territory west of the Mississippi embracing the present states of Iowa, Minnesota, and part of Dakota, was detached from the Michigan Territory and organized under the name of Wisconsin. Subsequently, the area of Wisconsin was reduced by creating from the trans-Mississippi sector the Territory of Iowa, thereby giving Wisconsin what are substantially her present limits, except that her western boundary was still set at the Mississippi River to its source, and a line drawn due north to the international boundary. Wisconsin was admitted as the thirtieth state of the Union on May 29, 1848, with her present limits.

The opening of the Northwest Territory not only provided opportunities for American citizens in the East, but also for immigrants coming from Europe eager for a new life. The constitution framed by the state of Wisconsin was exceptionally congenial to foreigners. Taxes were minimal, and cheap timberlands attracted the industrious Germans who streamed into the territory beginning in the 1830's. Milwaukee, the chief city of Wisconsin, eventually took on the character of a German city. By 1860, Germans constituted sixteen percent of the total state population. Swiss immigrants also came to Wisconsin in large numbers. In fact, an organized migration from the canton of Glarus, Switzerland, turned Glarus, Wisconsin, into a miniature Swiss community. Scandinavians came to represent the second largest group of immigrants—the Germans ranking first—and the state of Wisconsin became one in which foreign-born population outnumbered the American-born three to one.

Five states had been carved from the Northwest Territory, the first in 1803 and the last in 1848. This forty-five-year period saw changes which were to affect the entire continent's economic future; their effect on the Old Northwest was almost immediate.

Robert Fulton's development of the steamboat, shortly after 1803, made the central river system a fabulous network of trade routes. By 1810, the Industrial Revolution was under way in New England; cast-iron ploughs replaced wooden ones, and textile manufacture moved from home to factory. Farm production went up, as population did, and many a young farmer set out for the West to establish himself on a wide, cheap farm or cattle range. Here he had a natural advantage in that the forest line ended in the Ohio River area; west of that point lay the prairies, which were fertile and far easier to prepare for cultivation.

The Erie Canal, opened in 1825, made an artificial waterway between the Hudson River and Lake Erie, and five years later the first successful locomotive, the "Rocket," had been constructed and the Pontiac and Detroit Railway Company incorporated. This railroad did not materialize, but in 1836 the Erie and Kalamazoo Railway Company began its run between Toledo, Ohio, and Adrian, Michigan. With transportation an ever-lessening problem, as the new reapers and harvesters increased the production of wheat in the West, the railroads and the Erie Canal brought the produce to an expanding eastern market. Return trips brought eastern manufactures to the West.

Between the second census of 1800 and the seventh census of 1850, the population of the Northwest Territory increased from about fifty thousand to more than two and a half million. The nation as a whole was growing at a fantastic rate—not only economically and numerically, but also in geographic size. In the year that Ohio became a state, Napoleon sold to the United States government the Louisiana territory.

CHAPTER II

The Louisiana Purchase

THE HISTORY of Louisiana was a drama enacted in two parts of the world: the chancelleries of Europe and the American wilderness. To the nations of the Old World, the Louisiana territory, stretching from the Canadian border to the Gulf of Mexico, was a major strategic stronghold in the struggle for colonial power in America. In New Orleans, the most developed point in the entire area, a civilization existed that was both a re-creation of France and a New World outpost. *Nouvelle Orléans,* the capital of the French colony (named after the Duc d'Orléans), was a city of Creoles and Cajuns, pirates and speculators, and elegant French ladies. Its architecture, the garbled streets and interior gardens of the Vieux Carré, breathed Parisian elegance, but a medley of incongruous sounds filled the air: brisk French, mellifluous Spanish, and the blurred, liquid music of the "gombo" spoken by the Negroes.

Although Spanish explorers were the first to discover the region—de Pineda sailed along the Louisiana Gulf Coast in 1519—no attempt was made to settle it for Aragon or Castile. One hundred years after de Soto reached the Mississippi—near Memphis—in 1539, French explorers came upon the scene. Marquette and Joliet navigated the Mississippi in 1672; La Salle completed the river's exploration, reaching its mouth in 1682 and claiming all lands drained by it for France. He called the territory Louisiana in honor of King Louis XIV. In 1699, Pierre Le Moyne, Sieur d'Iberville, established the first French settlement on the Gulf. Natchitoches, Louisiana's pioneer city, was founded in 1714 by Louis Juchereau de St. Denis.

But the French court was too deeply immersed in financial problems to pay much attention to the new territory. At the conclusion of the Seven Years' War in 1763, France ceded to England all the Louisiana province east of the Mississippi. A year earlier, in a secret treaty with Spain, she had ceded the Isle of Orleans and all land west of the river, the exact extent of which cession was undetermined at the time and in dispute for years afterward.

The French settlers of New Orleans were passionately attached to their motherland, and deeply resented the cession. They considered themselves as French as the citizens of la patrie, and blamed Choiseul, Louis XV's foreign minister, for using Louisiana like a chip in a game of chance. To make matters worse, Spain forbade the colonists to trade with any country other than herself, and banned the importation of French wines.

A frosty atmosphere greeted the Spanish governor, Antonio de Ulloa, when he arrived in 1766 to take over Louisiana, and the indignant settlers refused to surrender their nationality. A French garrison of about three hundred soldiers rebelled at entering the service of Spain. Eventually Spanish authority prevailed, and continued in effect for the next thirty years. No evidence of moderation or even generosity on the part of Spain could, however, reconcile the Louisiana French to the "crime" of cession.

New Orleans continued to grow in importance, not only as a key port, but as a seat of culture. The descendants of the French and Spanish settlers were called "Creoles." Rubbing shoulders with them were the "Cajuns," or Acadians, French farmers who had been driven from their homes in Nova Scotia by the English in 1755. A network of plantations was established along the Mississippi, operated by the wealthier settlers who imported African slaves to till the soil and pick the cotton. A new race was thus added to the spectrum of peoples along the Mississippi.

Life in New Orleans was in marked contrast to that of other American cities. While the New England Puritans considered pleasure to be a snare of the devil, the Creoles devoted themselves to the art of having a good time. In every phase of life, their varied heritages peeped through. Louisiana inherited the French system of civil law, and from the Spanish came the name "parishe," which in New England was called the "county."

While New France throve, important changes were taking place in Old France. Napoleon Bonaparte came to power, and he set about creating a spirit of jingoism. The nation, once apathetic to Louisiana, now demanded its return. Napoleon negotiated its retrocession by the secret Treaty of San Ildefonso in 1800. When the news became known a year or so later, Frenchmen at home and abroad rejoiced. But their exuberance was short-lived. The First Consul, like the king before him, waved the flag as a device to beguile the people. Loyalties were to him merely pawns to be exchanged with cool detachment. The fortunes of the game demanded that France once again rid herself of Louisiana. Napoleon had been planning to expand his empire by the sword. England alone stood in his way. War was inevitable. But to launch an invasion across the channel would require substantial funds. The treasury was already drained by his military preparations. How better to collect cash than by selling Louisiana—not again to Spain, but to a new party, the infant United States?

One of history's most extraordinary declarations of war took place on a Sunday evening in Paris, in March, 1803. The Tuileries was ablaze with lights; Napoleon's wife, Josephine, was giving a reception for the diplomatic representatives stationed in Paris. The guests were paying their respects to the future Empress of France and exchanging amenities with one another when a stocky figure entered the room. All eyes followed Napoleon as he made the rounds. To some he bowed briefly. To others he spoke a few words.

But on greeting the American Resident Minister, Robert R. Livingston, Napoleon stopped to chat, ignoring the British Ambassador standing close by. Everybody wondered at the motive for this signal attention.

They were not kept long in doubt. Napoleon fixed his eye on the Englishman. An ominous hush blanketed the room. "England will give me Malta or I shall declare war!"

The guests were stunned. Rarely had international good manners been violated in such brutal fashion. But to Livingston, Napoleon's outburst provided the opportunity he had been waiting for since coming to France twenty-four months before.

In 1802, the Spanish intendant at New Orleans, still in control despite the transfer to France, suddenly decided to rescind the three-year guarantee permitting American settlers in Kentucky and Tennessee to deposit their goods at New Orleans for shipment through the Gulf of Mexico. President Jefferson had sent Livingston to France to purchase the Isle of Orleans and the Floridas; he was authorized to offer up to fifty million francs. If this offer was rejected, he was to try for the Isle of Orleans alone at a lesser price, or space for an American port on the east bank of the Mississippi. If all else failed, he was to obtain a perpetual guarantee of the rights of American navigation and deposit at New Orleans.

Although these were relatively inconsequential concessions for Napoleon to make, all of Livingston's efforts had ended in failure. His notes to the foreign office went unanswered. Livingston's pride was mortified by Jefferson's growing impatience. When he attended Josephine's reception, he had just learned by letter that Jefferson was sending James Monroe as envoy extraordinary to work with him. Apparently Washington felt that Livingston was incapable of handling the office by himself.

Now, only a miracle could avert the disgrace that seemed in the making. When Napoleon turned upon the British Ambassador with such ferocity, Livingston sensed intuitively that his hour had come. War with England would take money, so the United States' offer was bound to receive more serious consideration. Upon returning to his quarters that night, Livingston sent Jefferson a report on

Napoleon's behavior toward the British Ambassador, together with the implications as he saw them.

During the weeks that followed, while Monroe was crossing the Atlantic, Livingston worked tirelessly to press his advantage. He had made many important friends in Paris, and he worked through them to influence Napoleon. But a month slipped by and the First Consul remained adamant. Monroe's vessel was due to arrive at any moment; Livingston's recently revived hopes sank.

And then Luck smiled. What all of Livingston's persuasiveness failed to do was accomplished by Talma, a celebrated actor of the day. Parisian society had been eagerly awaiting the première of Talma's *Hamlet* at the Comédie Française. The announcement that Napoleon would attend the opening heightened the anticipation. Thousands of Parisians poured into the theater, not only to applaud the distinguished actor, but to cheer their First Consul. The susceptible Napoleon was intoxicated by this demonstration. It was all the proof he needed of the people's support in any venture he undertook—even war.

If Napoleon himself was not fully convinced of the wisdom of selling the province, the opposition of his family (his brother Lucien's *Memoirs* give evidence of this) decided him. His determination was further strengthened by the news that England had decided to take up his challenge and was arming herself for war. He ordered Barbé-Marbois, Minister of the Treasury, and Talleyrand, the Foreign Minister, to negotiate immediately with the American Minister for the sale, not of the Isle of Orleans, but of the whole of Louisiana.

In the meantime, however, Robert Livingston abandoned all hope of success. Weeks passed, and Monroe arrived in Paris. There was nothing to do but accept the inevitable. Livingston welcomed Monroe and invited him to dinner with members of the embassy the night of his arrival.

Just as the guests were rising from the table after dessert, Livingston's servant announced that Barbé-Marbois was waiting to see him. The Frenchman entered and, after greeting Monroe and the other guests, drew Livingston aside. "I have something to say to you in private. Can you come to my office after your friends have left? It is a matter of urgency."

Livingston's prayerful anxiety could not move the hands of the clock any faster. It was not until midnight that he was free to join Marbois in his office. He listened in amazement while the Frenchman explained that he was authorized to offer America the whole of Louisiana for one hundred million francs. (Marbois had been authorized to ask only fifty million francs. He took it upon himself to double the figure.)

Livingston was stunned and, experienced diplomat though he was, could not help showing it. The opportunity of buying the entire territory from the Mississippi to the Rocky Mountains had not even been contemplated in Washington. Yet the sum asked by Marbois was much more than the United States government would ever dream of offering.

Livingston mentally reviewed the alternatives. It would take weeks to communicate by mail with Washington. By then the opportunity might slip away. There was no telling what new mood might seize the little Consul; he might suddenly withdraw his extraordinary offer.

And so Livingston, patriot and gambler, took a chance.

He did haggle price with Marbois until it reached sixty million francs, to which was added twenty million for American assumption of earlier claims against France. Going far beyond his authority, Livingston agreed to these terms. The negotiations were conducted in the small hours of the morning of April 14. The following day Monroe officially presented his credentials to the First Consul at the Tuileries. By then a report of Livingston's negotiations was on its way to Washington.

Jefferson, confronted with a totally unexpected situation, found himself in a dilemma. The Constitution made no provision for the purchase of foreign territory, but if he were to wait for a constitutional amendment, this splendid opportunity might be lost.

And so Thomas Jefferson, a President who strongly advocated limiting the powers of the federal government to a minimum, embraced a "loose constructionist" view in the case of Louisiana. The Federalist Party, which ordinarily favored a broadening of federal powers, opposed the territorial acquisition out of fear that the balance of power would veer from New England to the new area. In Congress, however, both parties agreed that the federal government did have the right to acquire new territory, either by conquest or treaty, and the Senate immediately ratified the treaty by a vote of 24 to 7. The constitutional question was settled long after the purchase was consummated. In 1828, Chief Justice John Marshall of the Supreme Court, in a case pertaining not to the Louisiana Purchase itself but to another matter, expounded the doctrine that the power to govern territory flowed naturally from the right to acquire it, and this interpretation was used as a legal foundation for later annexations of foreign territory within and beyond the continent's shores.

The treaty was concluded on April 30 for fifteen million dollars. Robert Livingston came home a hero, thanks to a gifted tragedian and the headstrong nature of a dictator who was "feeling his oats."

On October 31, 1803, Jefferson signed the law authorizing the occupation of the territory and transferred all civil, military, and judicial powers exercised by the previous government to his own appointees. The people were guaranteed the protection of their property, liberty, and religious practices.

The Louisiana Purchase was a giant step forward in America's march to the Pacific Coast. This most important act of Jefferson's administration secured for his country a territory of 828,000 square miles out of which all or parts of fifteen states were to be created.

Jefferson and his ministers were not the only ones to realize the historical implications of this act. Napoleon himself wryly remarked: "This accession . . . affirms forever the power of the United States, and I have . . . given England a maritime rival that will sooner or later lay low her pride."

The Treaty of Paris which ended the Revolutionary War had extended the boundaries of the United States at one fell swoop to the Mississippi River; the Louisiana Purchase extended them to the Rocky Mountains. By a stroke of a pen, the territory of the United States was doubled.

This historic Purchase embraced thirty-six hundred square miles of the southern part of the present state of Mississippi, on the Gulf of Mexico; twenty-three hundred square miles of the present state of Alabama, west of the

Perdido; the whole of the present states of Arkansas, Louisiana, Missouri, Iowa, Nebraska, and the Dakotas; Minnesota, west of the Mississippi; much of Colorado, Wyoming, and Montana; and all but the southwest corner of Kansas.

At the time of the purchase, the boundaries of the territory were extremely ambiguous. While the Gulf of Mexico was definitely fixed as the southern end of the territory, and the Mississippi River was designated as the eastern end, there was no clear understanding by the United States or other nations as to whether the cession included West Florida and Texas. The northwestern limits as well were vague. While it was understood that the territory extended west to the Rocky Mountains, some American interpreters placed its boundary at the Pacific. (In addition to inheriting the French claims to the Far West, the United States had an independent claim created by the discovery of the Columbia River by Captain Robert Gray in 1792 and the subsequent overland explorations in the Northwest by Lewis and Clark.)

The acquisition of Louisiana presented an even more serious problem than had the annexation of the Northwest Territory. The area in and around New Orleans was inhabited by civilized white men of foreign allegiance. Now they had been handed over by Napoleon without a plebiscite. Their customs were essentially different from those of the Anglo-Saxon culture of the Eastern seaboard.

The United States now found itself facing the ticklish job of incorporating the Spanish and French inhabitants of Louisiana into the American Union. This was to be a major test of the adaptability of the Constitution: Could the infant American republic, which had itself so recently thrown off the shackles of a foreign government, bring under its jurisdiction peacefully the government of a very dissimilar foreign population?

With the Northwest Ordinance serving as precedent, on March 26, 1804, Congress divided the new province into two parts, separated at the thirty-third parallel. The area to the north, which was still virtually a wilderness, was organized as the District of Louisiana and attached to the Territory of Indiana, and the lower portion, the home of the French and Spaniards, was formed into a separate government and designated as the Territory of Orleans. (In 1805 the upper region was organized as a territory of the first grade, and renamed the Territory of Louisiana.)

But although the United States now "owned" New Orleans and governed it with an appointee of the President, the Americanization of the territory was a long, tortuous process. After the acquisition, large numbers of frontier Americans poured into the city of New Orleans, which was the seat of government and the financial headquarters of the territory. Their aggressiveness antagonized the refined, sensitive Creoles. A gulf of mutual suspicion separated the groups.

Riots were common. Yanks and Creoles fought in ballrooms over whether New England jigs or French cotillions should be danced. Whatever the Americans were opposed to, the Creoles automatically supported.

This, more than any other factor, is responsible for the career of that incredible story-book phenomenon, the pirate Jean Laffite, who added a touch of romance to the already lively history of New Orleans.

Laffite sailed to America from France with his brother Pierre. He wanted to make money, and it seemed to him that smuggling was the quickest way to do so. He came to

Louisiana in 1810, surveyed its network of islands, bayous, and passages, and established himself on the tiny Island of Grand Terre, off the coast between the Gulf and the Bay of Barataria.

From these headquarters, Laffite's ships plied the seas, using faked letters of marque to board vessels and seize cargoes of goods and slaves. Laffite accumulated gold aplenty, but he himself was for the most part a landlocked pirate. He usually permitted his captains, Dominique You and Ray ne' Beluche, to handle the hazardous "sea duty."

To dispose of his prizes, Laffite rented a shop in New Orleans and hung up the sign, "Blacksmith." As his business expanded, he opened a "brokerage" shop in Royal Street. To these apparently respectable establishments the rich plantation owners of the South wended their way to buy slaves and other luxuries at bargain prices. In those days smuggling was accepted by the Creoles as a necessary evil. Ships bearing legitimate imports were few and far between, and, during the time of Spanish control, tariff rates were formidably high. So deeply rooted was the smuggling habit that when the United States bought Louisiana, its attempts to abolish the practice were totally unsuccessful.

From time to time there were skirmishes with the United States government which left the self-confident Jean unperturbed. On one occasion—after an officer had been killed attempting to stop a slave auction—Governor Claiborne of Louisiana set a reward of five hundred dollars on the head of Laffite, who retorted by offering six times as much for the head of the governor!

This impudence outraged the governor. He indicted Laffite and his Baratarians and managed to capture Pierre, whom he jailed without bail. But Jean, with his enormous wealth, enlisted the services of two of the ablest attorneys in Louisiana, and Pierre was acquitted.

At one point in his career, Laffite turned from pirate to patriot. This was during the War of 1812. Laffite offered his services and a secret cache of arms to the United States. At first he was rejected. Governor Claiborne scoffed at this "display of loyalty." But Laffite sent the governor a copy of a contract which had been offered to him by the British, according to which he would be paid thirty thousand dollars and guaranteed a captain's commission in the British Navy for leading a British expedition through a maze of inlets, channels, and bayous to an attack on New Orleans.

Laffite's refusal of the British bribe succeeded in impressing the governor and the administration in Washington. The buccaneers of Barataria demonstrated their loyalty to the United States in the most concrete way. They fought valiantly beside the American soldiers. Afterward Jackson wrote in a report to Washington: "The General cannot avoid giving his warm approbation of the manner in which these gentlemen have uniformly conducted themselves while under his command, and the gallantry with which they redeemed the pledge they gave at the opening of the campaign, to defend the country."

President Madison, in his message on the Battle of New Orleans, publicly forgave the offenders when he declared, "Those who have aided to repel the . . . hostile invasion of the territory of the United States can no longer be considered an object of punishment but as objects of generous foregiveness."

Jackson's warm feeling toward Laffite became the talk of the town, putting the pirate in a predicament. While he was grateful for the acknowledgment shown him, he was not willing to give up his lucrative business of piracy. Yet how could he continue to flaunt the laws of the land which was so effusively praising him? With uncharacteristic tact, he decided to withdraw from United States territory completely.

Bidding adieu to Louisiana, the Baratarians boarded their vessels and headed for another island in the Gulf. Campeachy—or Galveston Island as it is called today—was low and marshy, much less attractive than Barataria. Its only other inhabitants were a few Indians and rattlesnakes. Nevertheless, it enjoyed the advantage of lying between American and Spanish territory, while belonging to neither nation.

At first Laffite lived on his ship. As business prospered, he built a house, which he called La Maison Rouge, and furnished it with valuable paintings and furniture from Europe. The "Red House" became a haven of hospitality along the Gulf. Within its walls a cosmopolitan group of guests was entertained.

In 1818 the United States government decided that Laffite's piracy could no longer be countenanced. He was sent an ultimatum to desist. Obediently, he disbanded his men, set fire to the Red House, placed a few valuables aboard his ship, and was last seen sailing toward South America—where, no doubt, new opportunities existed.

Ever since the United States took title to the original Louisiana territory, emigrants from the states to the east had been moving into New Orleans. It was the War of 1812, however, that succeeded in doing what years of commerce between Creole and Yankee had failed to do: it

brought their two worlds together in spirit as well as politically.

The War of 1812 came about chiefly as a result of the
indignities the United States was subjected to in the struggle between England and France in the Napoleonic Wars.
A second major cause of this war, however, was the American frontiersman's insatiable—and understandable—desire
for land. The Louisiana Purchase had doubled the area of
United States territory, but millions of acres of the new
country were in legal possession of the Indians by treaty,
and other millions lay within the semiarid region of
the West. The humid lands of the Northwest were far
more attractive to the frontiersman, but under the Ordinance of 1787 the red men's rights to their hunting
grounds in Indiana and Illinois were protected. To the
north, England held choice fertile lands in upper Canada,
in the Lakes region.

The Indians of the Northwest presented a problem the
frontiersmen settled by force or purchase; but Great Britain's lands were not so accessible. Seizing upon England's
depredations of the neutral United States' merchant fleet
and her impressment of American seamen—though many
Americans thought Napoleon's sins against these merchants were greater—a group of young Congressmen,
dubbed the "War Hawks," advocated an invasion of Canada in "retaliation." Henry Clay and John C. Calhoun
were the leaders of this faction, and President Madison
was unable to withstand their pressures. On June 18, 1812,
just two months after the state of Louisiana was admitted
to the Union, the United States declared war on Great
Britain.

The first American invasion of Canada was badly organized, and Tecumseh's confederacy sided with the British at the first sign of American weakness—the surrender of the garrison at Michilimackinac. At this juncture, and fearful of the Indian confederacy, General Hull surrendered. Fort Dearborn, in Chicago, was lost.

At sea the United States made up for its failure on land; the *Constitution,* the *Wasp,* and the *United States* shocked England with their victories. On Lake Erie, Commodore Perry ("We have met the enemy, and they are ours") was victorious. General William Henry Harrison won the Battle of the Thames, in which Tecumseh was killed.

In the spring of 1813 the war on land became more violent. The Americans again invaded Canada and lost. By the end of the year Canada had cleared out the American invaders; the frontiersman was never to fall heir to her soil. The next year saw Napoleon's abdication, leaving England free to carry on the American war more vigorously than before. She planned a massive invasion of the United States, to operate out of the Lakes area. Her efforts here were unsuccessful, but the British navy harassed the Atlantic coast throughout the summer, and in August the British army burned the White House and Capitol at Washington.

Although the British managed to run up a streak of victories, they were unable to push matters to a conclusive decision, and a compromise treaty was signed at Ghent on December 24, 1814. None of the United States' objectives had been achieved in this war, but a final irony was still to come. America won her most spectacular victory in a battle that took place three months after peace was concluded—the battle of New Orleans.

The distance between the national capital and New Orleans was formidable in 1815. A rider bearing official news from Washington had a journey of many weeks ahead of him. Accordingly, news of the peace treaty which ended the War of 1812 failed to reach Major General Andrew Jackson, in command of the U. S. Army expedition in New Orleans, until three months after it was signed. The only important news Jackson had received previously was the information from Jean Laffite that the British were preparing to launch an invasion of Louisiana.

It was a curious battle for another reason. Backwoodsmen, armed mainly with rifles and overwhelmingly outnumbered, put to rout a professional, highly disciplined British army.

Early on the morning of January 8, 1815, at Chalmette —a few miles down the eastern bank of the Mississippi— Jackson rose at dawn to inspect his troops. The morning light was shut out by an enveloping fog. As he walked behind the breastworks, by the campfires that were now being smothered, the figures of his men appeared ghostlike. Jackson moved among them in his easy-going but dignified way. He knew almost all of the pioneers from Tennessee and Kentucky by name.

Suddenly two rifles barked out. Jackson turned quickly. "My Indian scouts have sighted the British." Shortly afterward, the head of the British column appeared. According to one of Jackson's officers, who later gave the details to a newspaper, the column appeared to be about 200 files long, formed four ranks deep. "They were 600 to 650 yards away; too long a range for our small-bore rifles, which . . . were not effective more than 400 yards at the outside. In a minute or two, the enemy began to march. Two rockets were fired."

General Jackson ordered his men not to answer until word was given, and then aim above the cross-belt plates.

The men were tense and very cold. A buzz of low talk ran along the line. When the enemy's front line was within 500 yards—boom! went our first gun. Then all of us opened up. The British batteries, formed in the left rear of their storming column, were still concealed by the fog, but they replied, directing their fire by the sound of our guns. It was a grand sight to see their flashes light up the fog—turning it into the hues of the rainbow.

Suddenly a rifle cracked to the left. A mounted officer a little in front of the British column toppled to the ground. The officer's account went on:

What followed can hardly be described. The British had kept on, apparently not minding the artillery fire much. They were used to it. But now, when every hunter's rifle was searching for their vitals, they couldn't stand it. In five minutes the entire front of their formation was split asunder, as if by an earthquake. Not one officer was left mounted. Either rider or horse, or both, were down—dead or dying, or fleeing the field in panic. I had been in battles with Indians in the northwest frontier under Harrison. But I had never seen anything like this.

Incredible as it may seem, this whole column, numbering I should say 2,500 or 2,600 men, was literally melted away by our rifle fire. And it was done in less than twenty minutes from the first rifle shot. No such execution by small arms was ever accomplished before.

The battle of New Orleans represented more than a major, though "unofficial," military triumph. It brought Creole and Yankee together as comrades-in-arms in a war that had at least two positive results: a strengthening of national unity and a new prestige in the world's eyes.

The political consolidation of the Territory of Orleans had been completed in the first year of the war. By 1810, the territory—exclusive of the Florida parishes—had grown to more than 76,000 people. The city of New Orleans itself had a population of 25,000. On February 11, 1811, Congress had authorized the election of a convention to adopt a constitution preparatory to the admission of the Territory of Orleans as a state. Sixty delegates from the original parishes met and framed the compact, and the state of Louisiana was admitted into the Union on April 8, 1812, on an equal footing with the original states. A few days later Congress extended the boundaries of the new state by the addition of the Florida parishes. Louisiana's laws, even today, stem from the Napoleonic Code and its customs from Old France, but the physical traces of the state's colonial origins are chiefly in its buildings and historical monuments.

At the time of the admission of Louisiana, most of the northern part of the original Purchase was still a wilderness and, designated as the Territory of Louisiana, was still a territory of the first, or lowest, grade. In June of 1812, it was advanced to the second grade of territories—that is to say, it had achieved a population of 5,000 free adult males (it had, in fact, many more) and could now elect a legislature—and its name was changed to the Territory of Missouri, with its seat of government remaining at St. Louis.

Out of the Territory of Missouri six states were carved whole: Missouri (1821), Arkansas (1836), Iowa (1846), Nebraska (1867), and the Dakotas (1889). Although some of the boundaries of the original Purchase had been vague, all these states lay clearly within its limits. It was not until after the annexation of Texas in 1845 and the Mexican Cession of 1848 that the western edge of the Purchase ceased to be of any concern, and four states are composed at least partly of the former Mexican lands and partly of the Purchase lands: Kansas in 1861, Colorado in 1876, Wyoming in 1890, and Oklahoma in 1907. The acquisition of the Oregon country, by a treaty signed with Great Britain in 1846, gave Montana her western boundary as a state—which she became in 1889—and also gave Wyoming most of her present western edge.

Minnesota, admitted to the Union on May 11, 1858, was formed from the northwestern corner of the old Northwest Territory and the northeastern part of the Louisiana Purchase—that is, the area west of the St. Croix River and that west of the Mississippi which had previously been included in the Iowa Territory.

When Louisiana was purchased in 1803, many American voices had been raised in opposition—particularly since President Jefferson had concluded the negotiations without consulting Congress. Even aside from the problems of the constitutionality of the purchase and the distinct "foreignness" of most of the New Orleans population, the nature of much of this vast territory was absolutely unknown. Also, the very vastness of the acquisition was worrisome from the standpoint of its defense: it might still be tempting to a foreign power, it was argued. New England, the stronghold of Federalism, so bitterly resented the incorporation of Louisiana into the American nation that she planned to secede from the Union and form a Northern Confederation. The chief grounds for her displeasure were that the annexation was unconstitutional, and therefore the states were not obligated to accept it; that the North could no longer be fairly represented once the western and southern interests of Louisiana won a voice in Congress; and that since much of the territory lay within the latitudes of slavery, this blight would be extended. This New York and New England confederacy plan was dropped when Aaron Burr, its apparent champion, was defeated in the election for governor of New York and killed Hamilton in a duel.

New Orleans had also been unhappy at having been sold to a nation which sent to preside over it a young man— Governor Claiborne—who neither understood nor had much interest in the local laws, languages, and customs.

By and large, however, most Americans agreed with Jefferson that the purchase of Louisiana had been a highly advantageous move. The United States gained possession of the entire central river system of the continent. The importance of the fertile Mississippi Valley was universally recognized, although it was not until Lewis and Clark reported to Jefferson on their exploration of the northwest region that the extent of the Plains region became known.

The issue of slavery, which reawakened old dissensions at the time of the Purchase, was destined to face its ultimate challenge in this new territory. The plantation system, and the slaves needed to maintain it, had been introduced into Louisiana by the French in the early eighteenth century. To the east, the colonies of the Carolinas had had slaves at work in the cornfields and on the dairy farms by the year 1700. Even Georgia, which had begun its colonial existence in 1732 as a refuge for Europe's "deserving poor" and for persecuted Protestants, and had from the beginning banned slavery, succumbed to the lure of the slave-traders by 1740. The Mason and Dixon Line, determined by the two English surveyors after whom it was named, was ratified by the crown in 1769 as the boundary between the colonies of Pennsylvania on the north and Delaware, Maryland, and West Virginia (then still part of Virginia) on the south. Until the Civil War, this line, and a natural extension of it provided by the Ohio River, was popularly recognized as the boundary between slave and free states.

By 1803, then, the North-South agricultural pattern was well established in the United States, and the traditions of the plantation system existed "ready made" in the southern end of the Louisiana Purchase. The nature of this system accounts for the westward movement from the original Southern states, which began in earnest shortly after the War of 1812. Cotton and tobacco, the plantation's most profitable crops, have a ravaging effect on the soil, but because they were profitable the practice was to grow them year after year with never a season's intermission. As the overworked land's fertility steadily declined, the plantation owner had to cast about for fresh territory—preferably a pioneer community where the soil was already broken for cultivation by small farmers willing to sell their property and move on.

As the South—with its retinue of slaves—was expanding westward, gaining statehood for Kentucky in 1792, Tennessee in 1796, Louisiana in 1812, Mississippi in 1817, and Alabama in 1819, the North was matching its progress with Vermont in 1791, Ohio in 1803, Indiana in 1816, and

Illinois in 1818. Including the original thirteen states in the roster, the year 1819 saw eleven states each for North and South. By 1820, the most populous region of the Missouri Territory was ready for statehood, and Arkansas had recently won territorial status. The South had taken the lead in bringing its population and its institutions across the Mississippi, into the Purchase lands. The North, however, had a population of over five million—giving it 105 Representatives in Congress—while the South had slightly under four and a half million, and 81 Representatives.

When a bill for the admission of Missouri to statehood came before the House in February of 1819, Representative James Tallmadge of New York offered an amendment prohibiting the further introduction of slaves into the state-to-be, and providing that all children of the present slave population would become free at the age of twenty-five. The bill, with this amendment, passed the House, but the Senate, fearing the North's increasing power in the House, rejected it. When Congress adjourned in March, the debate continued among the people. Threats of secession were heard from North and South, the North maintaining that Missouri lay well within the latitudes of the free states east of the Mississippi, and the South insisting that the right to their human property could not be taken from slave-owning citizens of a state. This right had gained new economic significance in 1793, when Eli Whitney's invention of the cotton gin made it possible to increase enormously the output of the valuable fiber.

The important point at issue was not that the state of Missouri be permitted to keep its slaves, but that an even balance between slave and free states be maintained in Congress—in the Senate, at least—so that neither section would win a position of dominance over the other.

The road toward settlement of the issue was paved by admitting an avowedly free state along with Missouri. Maine, which was a part of Massachusetts, had been asking for statehood ever since the end of the Revolutionary War. Poor roads made it difficult for its residents to reach the seat of government in Boston. Many sections had no representation in the legislature, and the tax system was onerous. Discontent reached a climax when Massachusetts failed to come to the defense of Maine during the War of 1812. In 1819 Maine formally separated from Massachusetts, and began the preparation of a state constitution.

The "Missouri Compromise" provided for the admission of Maine as a free state and of Missouri as a state "with no restriction on slavery." The long-range significance of the Compromise, however, rested in an amendment prohibiting slavery in that part of the Louisiana Purchase which lay north of the line 36° 30′ north latitude.

For thirty-four years the Missouri Compromise remained in effect. Within that time, seven new states entered the Union: Arkansas, Florida, and Texas in the South; Michigan, Iowa, and Wisconsin in the North; and California, which excluded slavery by a unanimous vote at its constitutional convention in 1849. The Kansas-Nebraska bill of 1854, which repealed the Compromise of 1820 (see Chapter VII), set the stage for the Civil War.

CHAPTER III

Texas

AT THE TIME of the Louisiana Purchase, no definite boundaries had been established for it except the Mississippi and the Gulf of Mexico, although it was generally agreed that the Rockies and the Canadian border were its western and northern limits. The fact that France had had a claim to the Texas region by right of La Salle's discovery of it and France's seventeenth-century colonization, and that she had never relinquished her Texas claim to Spain, led many Americans to believe that the Louisiana Purchase should include this region right down to the Rio Grande.

Spain, however, had an undisputed claim to Florida at the time of the Purchase, though for years West Florida was a bone of contention. By a treaty of amity concluded between Spain and the United States on February 22, 1819, the King of Spain ceded to the United States "all the territories which belong to him, situated to the eastward of the Mississippi, known by the name of East and West Florida," and established, finally, a boundary line between

American and Spanish lands which began at the Sabine River and extended, in a series of northward and westward steps, to the forty-second parallel, and then west to the "South Sea" (Pacific Ocean). This boundary line—now agreed upon and no longer open to interpretation—left to Spain the entire area of the present states of Texas, New Mexico, Arizona, California, Nevada, Utah, and parts of Oklahoma, Kansas, Colorado, and Wyoming not included in the Louisiana Purchase.

To many Americans, these terms were highly unsatisfactory. Too much had been signed away. A southern boundary of the Rio Grande could no longer be claimed. Florida had been won, but Texas was lost—and to make matters worse, Spain got a settlement amounting to many millions of dollars. The King of Spain, for reasons of his own, delayed ratification of the treaty for two years, and shortly after the ratification was announced Mexico won her independence from Spain. In a new treaty with the United States, the boundaries which had been Spain's became Mexico's. The United States of Mexico now incorporated the provinces of Texas and Coahuila into a state, which framed a constitution in 1827.

The United States, and particularly the Southern states, were not willing to abandon Texas. She lay south of the 36° 30′ line recently established by the Missouri Compromise as the northernmost boundary for slaveholding, and she was large enough to provide five new states to the Union. Shortly after ratification of the new treaty, then, Secretary of State Henry Clay proposed the purchase of Texas from Mexico. This was not accomplished. In 1829, President Andrew Jackson authorized an offer of five million dollars, which Mexico declined.

What negotiation could not do, however, was being accomplished by the ever-moving tide of American emigration, which ignored "legal" frontiers wherever choice land was to be had. So far as emigration was concerned, the extension of slavery was not the point. Slaveholders brought their property with them, but many migrants came unencumbered with it.

Mexico had no objection to such emigration. Strangely enough, in fact, she encouraged it with huge and valuable land grants to American colonizers—one of whom was Stephen F. Austin in 1821. By 1830, more than 20,000 Americans had built homes amid the mesquite and yucca flowers that stretched over a greater area than that of Iowa, Illinois, Wisconsin, and Indiana combined.

A major lure to immigrants was the profits to be earned from cattle-raising. Feeding on the vast unfenced plains were herds of longhorns—wild cattle descended from the stock introduced by Coronado in 1541.

In Texas, the American pioneers built themselves simple dwellings of adobe or wood. From the beginning they were concerned with the education of their children, who were taught at home by traveling teachers. At these "cornfield schools," the teachers were paid in farm products.

Life was far from easy. For one thing, the Comanche Indians roamed the southern plains from Kansas to Mexico. One never knew when they would come swooping down on the ranches, waving blankets to stampede the horses. The Comanche Indian had a unique way of riding horseback. He kept a loop of horsehair braided into the animal's mane so that he could protect himself from enemy arrows by throwing his body into the loop and riding against the horse's side, or even underneath the animal, keeping one heel on the horse's back for support. Even in this position he could aim his deadly weapon straight to its mark.

Even more difficult to cope with than the Indians was the erratic Mexican government. Slavery was abolished throughout the Republic of Mexico, but an exception was made in the case of Texas when the numerically superior American colonists threatened insurrection if their property was taken from them. Difficulties also arose, and increased, over tariffs and immigration, and over the matter of political representation. Also, Texas was quite Americanized as compared to Coahuila, and agitation for their separation was a gadfly to the Mexican government.

In 1835 President Santa Anna proclaimed a federal constitution that all but abolished states' rights in Mexico, and the American settlers gave up their hope of an amicable solution of their problems and set up a provisional government for Texas. On March 2, 1836, Texas declared her independence.

The colonists, in their rebellion, had two leaders of overpowering personality. One was Stephen Austin, who brought three hundred American families to a colony on the Brazos River beginning in 1821. The other was Samuel Houston.

Before emigrating to Texas, Houston had had a career that reflected the ups and downs of life on the frontier. Born in Virginia in 1793, he lost his father when he was thirteen. His mother, to forget her grief, took her nine husky sons from Virginia into the Tennessee wilderness. Sam, the tallest of these young giants, learned only to read and write. When he came upon an English translation of

Homer's *Iliad,* he exulted over the sonorous verse. He read and reread the volume until its leaves were ready to fall out.

To prepare him for a livelihood, Sam's older brother apprenticed him to a storekeeper. But Sam couldn't bear the long hours of confinement, and he ran away to join a tribe of Cherokees in East Tennessee. He lived among them for several years, learning their woods lore and absorbing the oratory of their chiefs around the council fire. Many of their traits became part of Sam's own moral fiber —a lasting gratitude for favors rendered, a delight in bright colors, an affection for small children, an uncomplaining fortitude.

Still in his teens, Sam left the Cherokees to become a schoolteacher. Attired in a gaudy calico shirt, his hair dressed in a long queue, he enthralled the youngsters. When the War of 1812 broke out with Britain and President Madison called for volunteers, Sam joined up with Andrew Jackson's Tennessee volunteers. He was injured at Horseshoe Bend in the battle against the Creeks.

Upon returning from service, Sam decided upon the law as a career. He passed his bar examinations after six months of study—instead of the usual eighteen—and hung out his shingle in the town of Lebanon, Tennessee. As a lawyer, Sam succeeded from the first day. His brisk speech and colorful appearance won widespread admiration. Soon he was persuaded to enter politics, and his ascent in public life was swift. He dominated every group not only by force of personality, but by his sheer hugeness. At all times he remained a staunch admirer and friend of Andrew Jackson.

Sam's adopted state sent him as Senator to Congress. His

farewell speech to his neighbors was characteristically sin-
cere—and over-dramatic. "I was naked, and ye clothed me.
I was hungry, and ye fed me." Sam served three terms in
the Senate and then returned to Tennessee to run for governor. He won easily, in 1827, and he brought to that office
his unique brand of aggressive zest.

Then a strange thing happened. After two years in office,
Houston married a beautiful young woman named Eliza
Allen, and three months later he resigned his office without explanation and, alone, took a boat into the wilderness. Speculation ran riot, of course; some time later Mrs.
Houston won a divorce on the grounds of abandonment.
Not until years later was this mystery, never explained by
either Sam or his wife, apparently cleared up by some un-
covered correspondence which indicated that Eliza had
loved someone else.

At any rate, Sam Houston returned to the Cherokees in
what is now Oklahoma, and became a member of their
nation. As a government post trader and adviser, he became very familiar with the underhand dealings of the
government's Indian agents, and in 1830 and 1832 successfully represented the Indian cause in Washington. He
married a handsome half-breed woman at about this time,
and remained with her until he returned to civilization;
she refused to return with him.

It was President Jackson who brought Houston back
into government service. He commissioned Houston to go
to Texas late in 1832 to negotiate treaties with the Indians
there. This was almost a personal service to Sam at this
time, since he had fallen into the habit of drunkenness to
such a degree that the Indians who had called him Colon-
neh ("the rover") now called him the equivalent of "Big

Drunk." The Cherokee chief Oo-loo-tee-kah, whom the whites called "John Jolly," explained to the tribe that this man had been a great chief among his own people, "but a dark cloud fell upon the path he had been walking."

At first sight of Texas, Sam fell in love with that vigorous, youthful land, and Texas fell under Sam's spell. His past did not cause raised eyebrows in Texas. Here a man was judged by his present deeds, not by his past. Sam came on a brief mission and remained for good, throwing himself into life again with his old-time gusto.

When Houston arrived in Texas, the American colonists were in heated controversy with Mexico, the mother country. In 1821, when Mexico had thrown off the Spanish yoke, she adopted a republican form of government that embraced a confederation of independent states known as the United States of Mexico. Despite the promise of democracy, however, the Mexican leadership fell into the hands of Santa Anna, a general of the army who made life as difficult for the American settlers as he did for his own nationals.

One of the first Americans Houston encountered when he arrived in Texas was Stephen Austin, the champion of greater autonomy for Texans. Austin and Houston laid the basis for a lifelong friendship as they joined forces in what was to become a campaign for Texan independence. It is important to note that until this time—and for several years afterward—most of the settlers wanted a redress of grievances rather than annexation to the United States or independence.

Shortly after Sam's arrival, on October 1, 1832, the two men called together a council of citizens. The council wrote a petition containing a list of complaints which it sent to Coahuila, the seat of government for the Texas province. One cause of irritation was Mexico's recent imposition of a law prohibiting further colonization of Texas by American immigrants. This law had been motivated by Mexico's not unjustified fear of growing American domination. The Council asked that the law be repealed. It also requested separation from Coahuila, to which Texas was joined for purposes of administration, and it asked that the English language be used in all administrative affairs involving Texans. The petition was ignored in Mexico City, the national capital.

A year later the colonists met again in San Felipe and drew up another, more insistent, petition. Still thinking that conciliation with Santa Anna was possible, Austin undertook the dangerous task of personally conveying the document to the capital. His reward for this effort was eight months in a Mexican prison, and when he returned to Texas he found it overrun with Santa Anna's troops. It didn't take much urging on Sam Houston's part to make Austin see that there was no longer any choice left but open revolt.

Into the battle Sam Houston threw himself, in 1835 becoming commander-in-chief of the Texas forces. A provisional government was established at Washington-on-the-Brazos. Its first constitutional convention met there on March 1, 1836. Despite its imposing name, the town had a population of only a hundred people.

The first obstacle confronting the infant government was the lack of a building large enough to seat the fifty-eight delegates. A patriotic blacksmith offered them the use of his newly built shop. The warm hospitality of this individual compensated somewhat for the freezing blast of a Texas "norther" which whistled through a flapping curtain.

Texas has always been proud of these delegates to its first convention, and several counties have been named after them. Most had had legislative experience in other states, and their advice was of inestimable value to Texas.

The Texas constitution, based upon that of the United States, was accepted by the convention in an hour, after only one reading. But tense moments were spent in composing it. The authors worked under the threat of approaching war. They learned that the Mexicans were preparing to launch an attack at any moment.

On the second day of the convention, an urgent letter arrived from Colonel Travis, besieged in the Alamo since February 23. Spurred, the delegates rushed through their work. The Texas Declaration of Independence was completed on March 2, and on March 6 the Alamo fell.

The battle of the Alamo was the "Thermopylae" that aroused all Texas. But unlike the ancient Spartan disaster, no one survived. One hundred eighty-seven Texans inside the Franciscan mission at San Antonio were massacred. The decisive moment in the revolution belongs to those men huddled in the mission's little adobe chapel, firing their last round of ammunition against three thousand Mexicans.

"Remember the Alamo!" To this battle call was soon added another cry: "Remember Goliad!" For shortly after the capture of the Alamo, the Texans suffered another catastrophe.

Colonel James W. Fannin was billeted at Goliad, a mission originally founded by Franciscan monks, when the word came from Colonel Travis that he was surrounded in the Alamo and desperately in need of reinforcements. But Fannin never reached Travis. Mustering as many men as he could, he set out for San Antonio, more than a hundred miles away. A heavy fog prevented him from learning, until too late, that the Mexicans were surrounding him. Outnumbered, he was forced to surrender. The terms of capitulation stated that he and his men would be treated as prisoners of war and, in time, returned to the United States.

The Texans were marched back into Goliad. Their mood was cheerful. They were, after all, to have their freedom. When word came that they were to be released on Palm Sunday, the men gathered in the chapel, praying and singing "Home Sweet Home."

On the morning of Palm Sunday, the Texans were awakened before dawn and given orders to form into three divisions. They had marched only a mile down the road from Goliad when they received the command, "Halt!" Then the Mexicans turned their rifles on them and fired.

Fannin was the last to die. The Mexicans teased him with promises of mercy if he would go down on his knees and beg for his life. Fannin's answer was that he would rather die. Just before he was shot, he snatched the handkerchief from the guard who tried to tie it over his eyes.

Goliad, unlike the Alamo, had a few survivors; several of Fannin's men escaped the first volley of fire. Two physicians who had been ministering to wounded Mexicans were among the survivors. From the mission they heard the cries of their friends over the cracking of the rifles. For one of the physicians, a Dr. Shackelford, the agony was particularly great; his son and nephew were among the massacred. A huge funeral pyre was ignited that Palm Sunday night, March 27, 1836. More than three hundred bodies were burned in the flames that were to sere the memory of Texas forever.

With the fall of the Alamo and the massacre at Goliad, the lot of the Texans seemed hopeless. Sam Houston faced a colossal task in attempting to whip his fellow citizens into an orderly army. Most of the men had no military experience, and there were few officers to train them. Houston, however, created an arm of victory.

Understanding the psychology of Santa Anna, Houston planned to lure the Mexican into a trap and let his arrogance be his undoing. At San Jacinto, on April 21, 1836, this aim was accomplished. Houston enticed Santa Anna into a cul-de-sac and descended shouting: "Remember the Alamo!" In a battle that lasted eighteen minutes, five hundred Texans killed, captured, or put to rout about twelve hundred Mexicans, with little loss on their own side. Sam was shot in the ankle.

The Texans celebrated that night, but early the next morning they set out to hunt the fugitives who had escaped from the battle. Chiefly, they were determined to capture Santa Anna. As Sam had predicted, they found the Mexican hero dressed as one of his subordinates. The encounter between the two leaders was melodramatic. Sam sat against a tree, resting his injured leg, as Santa Anna was brought before him. Completely deflated, the vanquished hero pleaded for generosity.

"You might have shown some at the Alamo," Sam replied.

Before Santa Anna was returned to Mexico, he was

forced to sign a treaty providing for the independence of Texas. The treaty was later disavowed by the Mexicans, but in the meantime Texas assumed a *de facto* sovereignty. It tore down the eagle, cactus, and serpent of Mexico and raised the Lone Star of the Texas Republic. Sam Houston was elected president.

With almost five hundred miles of coastline to defend, and a territory that took in part of the present states of Colorado, New Mexico, Kansas, Wyoming, and Oklahoma as well as Texas, the new republic organized a navy. In fact, the first ships were put into service during the Texas Revolution. It was a navy of outmoded vessels with white sails and seamen more notable for their daring than for their nautical skills. Frequently the vessels were accosted by foreign ships who did not recognize the Lone Star flag, never having heard of the country of Texas. The little navy, with ships bristling with weapons and flags flying, bore down on all suspicious craft along the coast, seizing contraband goods and routing all enemies.

While the rules and regulations of the Texas navy were identical with those of the United States, many of the officers preferred to be guided by their own ingenuity in conducting cruises, rather than to wait for orders. As a result of their exploits, the republic was constantly involved in lawsuits and controversies, and was the butt of jokes as well as accusations. To many outsiders, the Texas sailors were "pirates."

There were only four ships in the first fleet, but they bore courageous names—*Liberty, Invincible, Independence,* and *Brutus*—and they played an important role in the revolution. A number of Mexican prisoners, including

Santa Anna, were sent home on the *Independence,* and it was she who brought the Texas envoy to New Orleans to negotiate with the United States for recognition of the new republic.

In April, 1836, the *Independence* and *Invincible* were anchored in Galveston harbor, hopefully waiting for good news from the battle front. The sailors broke into loud shouts when at last they saw a rowboat coming out, and the Commodore of the fleet's flagship *Independence* stood stiffly ready to welcome the messenger.

But the messenger, forgetting protocol in his exuberance, completely ignored the waiting Commodore and made a beeline for the *Invincible* to tell the news to his good friend, who was captain of that ship.

"What news?" the captain bawled.

"We've won! It's over! Sam Houston licked the Mexicans at San Jacinto!"

Without waiting for orders from his superior officer, the patriotic captain cried: "Fire the gun!"

As three ear-splitting cannon shots resounded in the harbor, the captain realized he had overstepped his authority. "Hold off," he yelled, "or I'll be put in irons!" But the Commodore ignored the discourtesy and joined in celebrating the joyous event.

These fearless little vessels went down for their country during its first year of independence. When a windstorm destroyed the last survivor, the *Brutus,* Texas immediately negotiated for a new navy. Seven vessels were purchased from the United States, and the republic swelled with pride. With this new fleet it could trade with foreign countries and command the respect of the world.

The adventures of this second navy were even more colorful than those of the first. In 1840, President Mirabeau B. Lamar, who followed Sam Houston as chief executive of Texas, ordered the fleet to Yucatan, a province of Mexico which, following in the footsteps of Texas, was in revolt against Mexico. Yucatan had promised to finance the Texas fleet in return for assistance in its uprising against Mexico. To the Texans, handicapped by lack of funds, the offer was tempting. The treaty was signed on September 17, 1841, and the Texas navy made three cruises to Campeachy, routing the Mexicans, capturing their ships, and setting up blockades.

Then came an event which infuriated Sam Houston and reverberated through the republic. The Texas fleet had put in at New Orleans to undergo repairs when a Yucatan envoy arrived and offered the Commodore a new subsidy of $8,000 if the Texas navy would again sail to the aid of the revolutionists, who were experiencing rough going. The Commodore signed the agreement without informing Houston, who had again been elected president. Now that Texas had won her independence, Houston was striving to cement relations with the outside world, including Mexico, and the navy's acts of piracy were a source of embarrassment to him. He dispatched a message to the maverick Commodore, accusing him of treason. The Commodore set out for Galveston to answer the charges.

On the high seas he was intercepted by a ship from Yucatan bringing news of that province's impending defeat and the rumor that Mexico was planning an invasion of Texas by way of retaliation. The Commodore boldly swung the fleet about and proceeded to Yucatan, where he engaged the Mexican navy and inflicted severe losses on it. Yet the fleet was frustrated as it was about to strike a final blow. On June 1, 1843, a proclamation from President Houston disavowed responsibility for the actions of his Commodore, and suspended him. Houston accused him of piracy, and asked the nations whose good will he was wooing to seize the ships at sea. This was a shock to die-hard Texans. They felt themselves humiliated before the world.

A month later the fleet sailed into Galveston harbor. Houston decided that if it were ever to be admitted into the family of nations, the republic must get rid of its madcap navy despite all sentimental considerations. He announced that the ships would be sold at auction to the highest bidder. Texas patriots were enraged. To sell the navy by auction, they thought, was the most shameful kind of transaction. As the day of the sale approached—July 25, 1843—actual threats were made against the government. Nevertheless, Houston went ahead with his plans.

When the day arrived, throngs gathered at the auction place. First the navy was offered as a unit. Then the individual ships were put up for sale. High prices were asked; then low ones. But there were no takers. No bid was offered, and the navy remained the property of the Republic of Texas.

The conflict was over. Houston bowed to the pride of the people. The gallant vessels continued to sail the Gulf of Mexico, but their free-booting days were over. Then, on December 29, 1845, when Texas was admitted to the Union as the twenty-eighth state, the little men o' war proudly entered the service of the United States.

On March 3, 1837, the day before his term of office ended, President Andrew Jackson had recognized the Lone

Star Republic; Congress had approved the day before. By this time, the subject of annexation had already been long under consideration, both in Congress and in the new republic. In the United States, the old matter of the balance of power between North and South was the most important one to be considered; in Texas, Sam Houston was first in acknowledging that the little republic was in a precarious position in regard to Mexico, and needed far greater protection than it could provide for itself.

North-South power was still in balance, with thirteen free and thirteen slave states in the Union, at the end of 1837. Future prospects, however, were that three free territories—Wisconsin, Iowa, and Minnesota—would soon be ready for statehood in the North, while only one—Florida—would be entering as a slave state. If Texas were annexed, America reasoned, its territory might provide as many as five new Southern states. The republic was less than a year old when its first application for annexation was received by the United States government, but for nearly a decade afterward the matter remained unsettled.

Van Buren managed the defeat of the resolution on annexation in 1838. Tyler, the Virginian who succeeded the short-lived William Henry Harrison as President in 1841, got as far as the preparation of a treaty of annexation in 1844—but the Senate rejected it. Van Buren, on the basis of his opposition to annexation, lost the 1844 Democratic nomination to James K. Polk, who favored it; and Henry Clay, Whig candidate, lost the antislavery vote—and the election—because of his indecisiveness on the subject.

While political fortunes were rising and falling at home on the annexation issue, Texas was involved in a series of negotiations with Britain and France to act as mediators in obtaining recognition of the republic by the Mexican government. This would be an alternative to annexation so far as Texan security was concerned—particularly since European guarantees were to be part of the "deal"—but the hope of annexation was more popular in Texas. These maneuvers came to nothing, however, for Mexico refused to recognize the independence of Texas. The shadow of slavery was in this picture, too: Great Britain clearly stated her hope for "the general abolition of slavery throughout the world," a sentiment which made the Southern states doubly fearful of British influence in Texas.

The election of 1844, so crucial in the history of Texas, was won by the Democrats on an issue other than slavery or abolition. The slogans of their campaign—"Reoccupation of Oregon and reannexation of Texas" and "Fifty-four forty or fight"—were summed up in the phrase, "manifest destiny," which first appeared in a Democratic publication in the summer of 1845. According to this philosophy, it was "our manifest destiny to overspread the continent allotted by Providence for the free development of our yearly multiplying millions." The nation was bound to expand, and Texas was as natural an extension of the American South as Oregon was of the Northwest. ("Manifest destiny" was later stretched to include the acquisitions of Alaska and Hawaii.)

Before Polk's inauguration, a joint resolution providing for annexation was introduced into the House of Representatives; it provided that up to four new states, besides Texas proper, should be carved from the new territory (an authorization which has not yet been used), and that slavery be prohibited north of the line 36° 30′—a meaningless provision, since the state of Texas did not extend that far north. On February 18, 1845, Congress passed the resolution, and on his last day of office President Tyler—eager to make the achievement clearly one of his administration —dispatched a messenger to Texas with the news that her admission to the Union was secured. Washington offered Texas the most generous terms of admission yet given to a state. In December, 1845, a joint Congressional resolution permitted her to keep title to all her public lands; in every other case but that of Hawaii, the federal government took title.

On February 10, 1846, a convention of Texans gathered at Austin to take the momentous action of ratifying the agreement. The hall of delegates was hushed as Anson Jones, the last president, lowered the Lone Star flag and announced: "Gentlemen, the Republic of Texas is no more."

As for old Sam Houston, who has been considered the George Washington of the Texas Revolution, in his remaining years he was to touch off a few more sparks. He went to Washington as Senator from Texas and held the capital spellbound. Then he returned to the state to become its governor in 1859, but at the outbreak of the Civil War, when he fought to have Texas remain in the Union, he was driven into political exile by the popular sentiment for secession.

His last years were spent in poverty and obscurity in a log cabin. Occasionally the skies cleared. One such time was when he was asked to review his old regiment. He appeared in the uniform in which he had defeated Santa Anna. It was in rags now. At his side hung his sword, fastened with the original buckskin thong. Throwing aside his cane, Sam hobbled forward, bellowing orders. The young soldiers responded perfectly, thrilled by the presence of their hero.

Sam Houston died in 1863, soon after the fall of Vicksburg.

CHAPTER IV

California

LIKE TEXAS, California was part of Mexico before becoming an American state, but it had a considerably briefer existence as an independent republic before joining the American family. Unlike Texas, the bulk of California's settlers were not slaveholders. The magnets that lured them over the Rockies to the Pacific Coast were an overland trail through the mountains, cheap land for sale, and the prospect of finding gold.

These were sufficient causes for migration. But the catalyst that brought about the annexation of California was war.

Committed to the doctrine of "manifest destiny," the United States government was expanding its borders in both North and South. In the North it ran headlong into a dispute with Great Britain over the Oregon boundary. In the South it quarreled with Mexico. Shortly after the annexation of Texas, a dispute arose over the southwestern limits of this new state. The United States insisted that they extended to the Rio Grande, taking in all land west of the Sabine. The Mexicans claimed that the boundary was the Nueces River.

It is not within the scope of this book to go into detail about the war that followed. Suffice it to say that the American march from the Alleghenies had now entered a new phase. For the first time, the United States waged war with a sister republic, a nation much smaller than herself. However, while California and, as we shall see later on, New Mexico and Arizona were won by conquest, their people were admitted as full American citizens.

On a crisp, cool day in September, 1849, forty-eight men assembled in a two-story yellow sandstone building in Monterey, California. They were a mixed group, ranging from wealthy landowners from rancherías as far south as San Diego to scrubby-handed Forty-niners from mining camps on the Oregon border. There were engineers, doctors, lawyers, printers, saloon politicians, adventurers. Six were Mexicans; one was a Scotsman who had married a *mestiza*. They were of a dozen blood ties, united by a single tie of dedication to the fortunes of California. On this fall afternoon, the heterogeneous assembly moved expectantly into the hall built with local taxes collected from gamblers and used as a community schoolhouse.

Robert Semple, the chairman (who ran a ferryboat for a livelihood) rapped sharply for order.

"Gentlemen," he declared through an interpreter who spoke the various languages of the group before him, "we have been chosen by the voters to draw up a constitution for the territory of California. I needn't remind you that Congress in Washington has been reluctant to admit us as a state because of the pressure of Southern senators who oppose our desire to ban slavery—but we will hammer on the door until it swings open. . . ."

For twenty-eight days these descendants of three civilizations—American, Spanish, and Indian—wrestled mentally and verbally with a problem that could wait no longer. This magnificent land of giant forests, mineral-studded mountains, and endless cattle ranges had been desired by Americans since the time of Jefferson. Now Mexico's rule was ended, and a United States military governor had a loose grip on the administrative reins as California's delegates pondered its future.

By day the delegates diligently studied the constitutions of the thirty other states, and from them drew their own blueprint for statehood. For recreation, when the day's work was done, they were entertained by wealthy citizens of Monterey at garden parties given on the patios of charming Spanish-style dwellings.

Gold had recently been wrested from the veins of California, and the delegates (thirty-eight of whom had come West from other states), in an exuberant mood paid themselves handsomely for their services. Each member received sixteen dollars a day plus sixteen dollars a mile for travel. Ten thousand dollars was appropriated for the convention clerk to print the assembly's final report in English and Spanish. The delegates assessed themselves twenty-five dollars each for a gala costume ball that was held at the convention at the windup of their deliberations.

The momentous event, the signing of the constitution, took place on October 13. When the last of the delegates had put his name on paper, Robert Semple addressed the assembly: "Gentlemen, this is the happiest day of my life."

The names of most of the delegates to this historic convention have been forgotten, but their work, after all, only put the finishing touch on a development that had been brought about by giants—two giants in particular.

One was John Augustus Sutter, a man whom gold made poor; the other, Junípero Serra, who was rich in his poverty. One was an amasser of real estate; the other a fisher for souls. Both gave their lives for California, for entirely different reasons. But both had one thing in common. They towered over their fellow men.

Fray Junípero was enrolled in the order of Franciscan missionaries who had originally arrived in America with Cortés and Pizarro, and who had helped mitigate the harshness of the Spanish conquest. He might be called one of America's founding fathers, although his contributions have been comparatively neglected by posterity. At the very time that George Washington was winning independence for the colonies on the Atlantic seaboard, Junípero Serra was directing the colonization of the Pacific Coast.

Serra was a remarkable fellow. Not only did he teach the Indians native to Mexico City, but he preached among the outlying peoples, journeying hundreds of miles over mountains and rocky mesas. During one journey he was bitten by a poisonous insect, which left him permanently lame. This did not deter him from his travels.

In his fifty-fifth year, Serra—as head of all the Spanish missions in Baja California (an area that is currently part of Mexico)—focused his attention on Alta California for the purpose of developing new missions. His interest was sharpened by the political situation. In the spring of 1768, José de Gálvez, the Viceroy appointed by the Spanish monarch Charles III to govern the colony of Mexico, arrived at Santa Ana and sent a messenger to fetch Serra.

"Vital information has reached His Majesty that Russia, eager for the fur trade of North America, is infiltrating the Aleutian Isles from Siberia. It is feared that even now she may have sent expeditions to seize the coast of the mainland."

Fray Junípero acknowledged that such activities would not be in the best interests of Spain.

"To keep this territory from the Russians," Gálvez went on, "I am ordered to march north immediately to fortify San Diego and Monte Rey. We want you to go with us, Father, to win the allegiance of the Indians by your missionary work."

Serra accepted the new assignment willingly, and preparations were immediately begun. To provision the expedition, cattle were slaughtered, pepper and cocoa were stored in quantities, and an assortment of seeds from Spain was requisitioned for planting at their destination, five hundred miles to the north.

The party was split into two groups; one was to travel in two ships by sea; the other was to march overland. Father Serra set out overland with the column under Gaspar de Portolá, commander of the expedition, on May 16, 1769.

The column struggled over blistering hot prairies and up tortuous mountain slopes. The climbing seemed endless. When one summit was gained, the agonized travelers were plunged into despair to see another mountain range directly ahead. Water was unbearably scarce. All too frequently the shovels digging for water turned up nothing but mud.

Despite such hardships, the morale of the travelers remained unflagging. At night around the campfires, the

Spanish soldiers polished their rifles and dreamed of the gold to be found at San Diego. And so, with the indomitability of the troops of Coronado who had sought the Seven Cities of Çibola before them, they struggled on, entering country that grew continually more verdant, ablaze with poppies and juniper trees. One dawn they stumbled on a flower well known in Spain as the Rose of Castile; for the first time, their mood became joyous.

At last, on a morning in July, forty-six days after their departure, the pungent odor of the ocean pervaded the air. Hurriedly they climbed the last hill and descended to San Diego Bay. The two ships assigned to the expedition had preceded them into San Diego, bringing alarming news. An epidemic of dysentery had broken out among the crew. It was into a devastated area that the column marched.

The dysentery, which spread rapidly among the foot soldiers, was checked only after all the afflicted were removed from the area of pestilence and vigorous methods of sanitation were instituted. But by this time, half of the expedition—over a hundred men—had been wiped out. Sorrowfully, Father Junípero conducted a Requiem Mass for the dead as the militia fired their rifles skyward, substituting the resonance of gunfire for a church organ.

In the meantime, the expedition which had set out from Mexico in soaring spirits had become utterly demoralized. Decimated by the epidemic, the Spaniards faced further difficulties. Their provisions were running dangerously low, and a ship scheduled to arrive from Mexico laden with food and supplies was overdue. Panic mounted as days passed and the vessel failed to appear.

Gaspar de Portolá and his fellow officers decided to

abandon camp and start back for Mexico before their food ran out altogether. The soldiers cheered this decision, but Father Serra dissented. He calmed his colleagues and urged them to stiffen their spines. They must remain at San Diego at all costs; the ship would shortly arrive. The stakes were high. If the Spaniards abandoned Upper California, the Russians might well move in, and the whole Pacific Coast would be lost.

Daily, Father Serra limped to the headland to look for the vessel and kneel in ardent prayer for its arrival. Finally, on November 25, 1769, his prayer was answered. The ship hove into sight, bringing provisions essential to the Spanish occupation of Upper California.

From San Diego the expedition pushed further north, into the wilderness, to carry out the second part of the assignment—the fortifying of Monte Rey. Once this settlement was found, Father Serra decided to make it the headquarters for his missionary activities.

The priest felt that if the Indians were to be effectively dealt with, the mission must be free of military control. Therefore he selected a site five miles from the garrison and the sea, on the bank of the Carmel River. "Carmel" means "garden" in Hebrew. Here the air was fragrant with rosemary and lavender spiced with sea-scent. Giant cypresses towered above, and in the background loomed the Santa Lucia Mountains, shimmering green in the haze that swept in from the sea. Serra called his mission San Carlos Borromeo. It comprised a chapel and a warehouse for agricultural tools, all enclosed in a stockade for protection against hostile Indians.

When word of the Spanish priest's arrival got around, swarms of natives were lured to the spot by their curiosity.

They were extremely primitive. According to their religious teachings, God was a coyote who lived in a cave in heaven. A young man was not admitted to the status of brave until he had submitted to being flogged into unconsciousness and placed on a bed of insects which, goaded by sticks, crawled all over him. Only if the candidate survived this hardship was he enrolled in the company of warriors.

Such were the savages Father Junípero Serra hoped to educate in his determination to turn the California wilderness into a civilized community. To entice the Indians into his classroom he had one potent lure—food. It was much easier for a savage to feast on Spanish tortillas than to chase game through the wilderness. Curiously, the squaws were attracted in even greater numbers than the males. Large numbers of females, won over by the gentleness of Serra and the dignity afforded them by mission life, remained in the mission to bring up their children as Christians.

Father Serra's plans for Upper California were extremely ambitious. He set about to erect a network of missions along the coast, following the trail of the Spanish occupation known as the Camino Real, or "King's Highway." Each mission was but a day's journey from the next. Serra's motive for spacing them in this way was: "I'd like to guarantee a traveler a good night's rest and a tasty supper."

For each mission he established he assigned two Franciscan fathers to provide companionship for each other. These padres performed marriages, baptized Indian converts, and supervised all labor around the missions. They trained the more resourceful of the converts to become carpenters, mechanics, and skilled blacksmiths. And they provided children from the age of five up, in daily classes, with the rudiments of a practical education.

Over the years Serra's missions grew in political and social influence. More enlightened than his contemporaries, he planted the seeds of new ideas in the minds of his superiors—ideas that were to influence the shape of history. It was he who campaigned for Spanish families to move into the wilderness around his missions, and organized permanent settlements. He wrote to the Spanish Viceroy in Mexico City, pointing out that military outposts alone were not sufficient to colonize the New World. He urged the Viceroy to send out married farmers, mechanics, and workmen, and wives for the soldiers. "Only when Spanish children are born on the land can it truly belong to Spain."

Serra's counsel was given thoughtful consideration. A call went out for families, with an offer of land and cattle for all volunteer settlers. A further inducement, a chronicle of the time informs us, was ample yards of ribbon for hats "as grand as any worn in Spain."

As a result, in 1776 thirty-six colonists, under the leadership of Don Juan Bautista de Anza, a dashing *hidalgo,* were gathered in Spain for the journey to the new country. Their destination was the *Estero de San Francisco.* The señoras and señoritas in the group were a major attraction. When the travelers stopped off to rest at various *presidios* along the way, soldiers rushed from their quarters to ogle the ladies. A white woman had never before been seen in the wilderness.

Their first glimpse of the San Francisco Bay overwhelmed the party. "This is the harbor of harbors; nature's masterpiece," Anza wrote home.

Other migrations followed this one. The wilderness south of San Francisco was cleared, and in 1781 forty-two Spanish pioneers and their wives, tempted by government allotments of cash and cattle, settled the *pueblo de la Reina de los Angeles*. In the same year, thirteen colonies three thousand miles eastward were engaged in the fight for independence. Within the span of a lifetime, California and Massachusetts would be sister states under a common government.

As for Serra, his work was about over. He had established nine flourishing mission settlements where four thousand converts lived and worked. There was San Juan Capistrano, with its palm groves, and roses clinging to the mission walls; gracious San Gabriel Arcángel; San Antonio de Padua, San Diego de Alcalá, and San Buenaventura; San Carlos Borromeo, Santa Clara de Asís, San Francisco de Asís; and, finally, San Luis Obispo de Tolosa, with its celebrated vineyards from which were pressed the finest wine in America.

With the intuition of inspired artists, the missionaries built structures that blended so perfectly with their natural surroundings that, although some of them suffered deterioration and are today restorations, they continue to delight painters and tourists.

In August, 1784, at the age of seventy-one, Serra completed his own mission in life. After his death, his successors, faithfully carrying out his policies, increased the number and influence of the missions. At their height, over forty thousand converts were productively employed in them. So well had the Spanish padres done their work that when Americans entered California they found irrigated fields, cultivated vineyards, and communities of peaceful

Indians who lived by industry and trade. In a very real sense, Fray Junípero, although he would have been astonished to know it, founded, settled, and saved California for the United States.

Some part of Father Serra's extraordinary story, written in the very trees and architecture around them, must have passed through the minds of landowners, miners, and Indians who assembled in the yellow sandstone schoolhouse that afternoon in September, 1849, and debated whether to sign a constitution that would transform California into a state.

There were other spirits presiding over this assembly besides that of the Spaniard who was buried at the mission of San Carlos Borromeo. There were the spirits of the Mountain Men who had learned every inch of the Rocky Mountain passes and river routes in the beaver-trapping orgy that had begun in the twenties; of the Yankee traders whose ships brought home fantastic profits in California hides and tallow and glowing descriptions of the golden West; of the pioneers who left the panic-stricken Mississippi Valley in the late thirties and started a series of heroic migrations that brought American vigor to the decadent Mexican West. There was the spirit of the "Pathfinder," John Frémont, American explorer and impetuous patriot, and Thomas Larkin, the American Consul at San Francisco, who led a military uprising to set up a "Republic of California" in 1846.

But perhaps the most compelling of all was the spirit of a man whom destiny had capriciously chosen to play a towering role which, though it was the very antithesis of that played by Junípero Serra, was a critical one in the epic of California.

John Sutter was the son of a printer, a man of limited means, and at an early age he became obsessed with a longing for power. He wanted land—more land than any other man in his town, in his country, in the whole world. By the 1830's the westward migrations were beginning to get under way in America, and tales of plentiful cheap land echoed to the realms of Europe. So John Sutter left his family and his debts behind in Switzerland, and sailed for New York in 1834.

The crowded East was no place for this aspiring thirty-one-year-old, so he set out with a handful of fellow immigrants for St. Louis. This was the eastern terminus of the Santa Fe trail, and the tales of the traders soon convinced Sutter that his destiny lay in the Far West. First he joined the company of those American Bedouins who started off each spring in covered-wagon caravans stuffed with eastern manufactures and returned from Santa Fe laden with gold, silver, furs, and sundries. He next joined an American Fur Company outfit, then traveled to Hawaii and to Alaska before his journeyings ended at last on the California coast. He arrived at Monterey in July, 1839.

John Sutter could not have found another place on earth as well suited to his aspirations as California in 1839. Spain's hold on the Far West had been weak; Mexico's was weaker. The impossibility of keeping a firm grip on the reins of distant provinces without means of communication was clearly foreseen by the Mexican government. Spain had used the missions and presidios in her colonial organization, but largely through the pressure of powerful landowners, the Indian missions were secularized by the Mexican government in 1833. A chaos of looting, cattle slaughter, and desecration followed. The education of the Indians was abandoned, and these onetime charges of Father Serra and his fellow missionaries quickly sank into near-slavery, laboring from morning to night just for their keep on the vast ranchos of mission-cultivated land now available to Mexican citizens.

Sutter had winning ways, and had little trouble securing a grant of nearly fifty thousand acres on the Sacramento River from California's Governor Alvarado. Now thirty-six years old, Sutter was on his way at last. Starting with eight Hawaiians, three white men, and an Indian, he set about recruiting more Indians into his service, building a massive fort and a mansion, and borrowing seed and livestock to start his own farms and herds. He named this western empire of his New Helvetia, after the Latin name of Switzerland, and devoted himself and his increasing army of laborers to the business of its expansion. He set his men to trapping, fishing, tanning, and making whiskey out of the wild grapes that grew in great abundance on his land. In 1840 he became a Mexican citizen, and was given the authority of governor over his northern frontier country. Whatever he acquired, and he steadily extended his holdings, he held with an iron fist. At the peak of his fortunes, Sutter lived like a feudal lord in an adobe castle, master of an empire of forty thousand square miles, an empire five times the size of Massachusetts and bigger than Belgium and Holland and Switzerland combined.

Sutter's Fort became not only a landmark of its time, but a stopping place for fur trappers, traders, and land-seeking pioneers. The man himself had a reputation for hospitality and good relations with the Indians, although no European king was more absolutely the ruler of his people and no general more strict with his soldiers.

And then came the discovery of gold, and the ruin of Sutter's empire.

The discovery of gold was practically simultaneous with Mexico's cession of California to the United States, a result of the Mexican War. War had broken out in 1846 over the boundary of the southwestern end of Texas, but previously, tension between the two countries had extended to other areas where Americans were settled side by side with Mexicans. This applied notably to California. As early as 1844, two years before actual hostilities began, American troops were dispatched to California under the command of Captain John C. Frémont. In 1846, another band of Americans attacked a Mexican fort at Sonoma, unfolded a homemade flag bearing a single star and a grizzly bear, and announced that they had formed the independent republic of California. But before they could push their scheme further, President James Polk, on May 11, 1846, sent his war message to Congress. The Treaty of Guadelupe Hidalgo in 1848, which ended hostilities and fixed the boundary of Texas, provided the United States not only with California but all other Mexican lands north of the Rio Grande and Gila Rivers, all for $15,000,000. The cession included the present states of Texas and New Mexico, and parts of Utah, Nevada, Arizona, Wyoming, and Colorado.

War had won California, but it was the discovery of gold that populated it. Shortly after the peace treaty with Mexico, a man by the name of James W. Marshall, a worker on Sutter's land, found a wealth of yellow dust which was to give the United States a return of about fifty thousand percent on the purchase price of California. Marshall was supervising the building of a sawmill. As he inspected the excavation for the millrace, he observed several glistening particles in the soil. Gathering them up, he washed them out in a tin plate, and he weighed them. Gold!

Through a violent rainstorm, Marshall hurried down to Sutter's residence and told his employer about the discovery. Sutter, fearful of a sudden stampede on his property, sent a trusted associate to Colonel R. B. Mason, provisional governor of California, requesting that the government guarantee his claims to his land. He also petitioned his workers to keep silent about the discovery.

But these efforts were useless. Silence about such a "find" was impossible, and once the news had leaked out it spread quickly. In the beginning, people were doubtful, and only a few gold-seekers filtered in by vessel or through the mountain passes. Soon, however, one after another of Sutter's employees started drifting away. Why labor for someone else when they could be rich merely by scooping up handfuls of gold? Then, too, it was impossible to police such a vast stretch of land. There was no one to catch them if they dug out the gold. With these sentiments, a reign of lawlessness began. Whenever an individual came upon a piece of Sutter's land bearing gold, he "squatted" on it and readied his rifle. A bullet moved faster than a legal debate.

Before long, the trickle of gold-hunters turned into a flood. From every part of America, and from practically every country in Europe and Asia, came wave on wave of prospectors into the valley of the Sacramento. From there the madness spread as new discoveries were made, until the mine sites were strung through one hundred and fifty miles of hills. When the mother lode was struck in early '49, the six-hundred-mile-long belt wasn't big enough to accommodate the rush.

Farmers stored away their plows, factory workers left their jobs, clerks deserted their counters, saloon keepers abandoned their bars to seize a boat for Panama or for the long trip around Cape Horn, or set out over the mountains for California. Debtors grabbed at the golden opportunity to cancel their debts at a stroke; unattached ladies bought tickets to San Francisco, following the gold by way of the men; vagabonds, rich men, gamblers, beggars, mothers with young children, all rushed off to the goldfields. Thousands of individuals sank their money into heavy mining equipment which they carried with them, in some cases for several thousand miles.

People who had retained their reason cautioned their relatives and friends about heading for an unknown country by way of the unmarked desert of the Humboldt Sink and the Sierra Nevadas, noted for the harshness of their winters. The majority of amateur miners had had no experience in outdoor living. Nevertheless, the stampede West continued undeterred.

The journey Easterners made via Cape Horn was long and rough, and the cross-country trek through Panama left many Americans behind in tropical cemeteries, but the overland trail was an ordeal of the damned. Those who arrived in California were no longer the same people who had started from the East; suffering changed many personalities into a different mixture of elements.

Upon arriving at the gold diggings, many cheery survivors of every hazard of travel drank at last the dregs of disillusionment. They had expected to find gold lying on or near the surface of the earth, but the first-comers had stripped the top layers in '48. The Forty-niners had to dig for it, and digging among the boulders and gravel, under the intense California sun, was hell. No matter how rich the diggings averaged—short of an actual bonanza—the individual miner was almost invariably chagrined at the results of his grueling labor. Easterners who had never done a day's work as laborers stood immersed to their waists in the icy waters of high Sierra snows, their heads exposed to the sun, cursing at the slim pickings they wrested from the streams.

But perhaps the most disillusioned Californian of all was a man who, far from seeking gold, had tried desperately to dodge it. Long before the peak of the Gold Rush was reached, despair had entered John Sutter's heart.

Sutter did not bow to his fate submissively. He converted his factories into warehouses and his home into a saloon. For a time he continued to thrive. But the streams of human locusts kept pouring in, taking over his fields and his horses. They killed his livestock, robbed his stores, and finally set fire to his property, confiscating the deeds that supported his claim to New Helvetia. John Sutter was left as bare and afflicted as Job.

The story of the Gold Rush is in many ways one of unspeakable tragedy. John Sutter was only one of its thousands of victims, but his losses had no parallel. He paid hundreds of thousands of dollars for the services of lawyers, and when the Supreme Court eventually invalidated his claims to the bulk of his land, he brought his case before Congress. All that he ever received in return for his vast holdings was a pension of two hundred and fifty dollars a month, granted some years later by the California legislature. Thirty-one years after James Marshall first discovered a few strands of yellow dust in a millrace, John Sutter died in a Washington hotel room, fighting for restitution until the end.

The positive results of the Gold Rush were many. After a hundred thousand aggressive Americans took hold of California, it was no longer possible for Congress to postpone action in favor of political maneuvers—the United States legislators had not even gotten around to giving California the status of an organized territory. Gold made possible a very rapid development, once the mining camps succeeded in organizing something like civilization in their midst. By the mid-1850's, San Francisco had more newspapers, more schools, and more libraries than all the rest of the country west of the Mississippi. It became the one spot in provincial mid-century America that was to give Lola Montez, the celebrated dancer and amoureuse of the King of Bavaria, a welcome as tumultuous as any she had received in Paris. It wined and dined her and set her up as the hostess of a salon.

Bohemia flowed through the veins of San Francisco. Journalism was gaudy and uninhibited. The *bon vivant* flourished. *Hamlet* strode across the boards of the Jenny Lind theater when Seattle and Dallas and Denver were still cow pastures. Opera took hold against one of nature's most imaginative backdrops.

And the hapless John Sutter played a key role in this transition from the old to the new. For it was the discovery of gold on his land that had turned California from a territory of transient traders, trappers, and soldiers into a populous social community qualified for entrance into the American family of states.

The fact that this family was given to squabbling had become apparent thirty years earlier, when Missouri had presented her petition to Congress. A compromise had settled the problem then, and a compromise was needed now—on the same problem: slavery. Henry Clay was still on the scene, a mediator through eight months of wrangling, a feeble, aged man scolding and cajoling pro- and antislavery senators alike. Old John Calhoun was there, too, opposing the admission of California with a die-hard speech that had to be read for him because he was too ill (near death, in fact) to deliver it himself. Webster's famous "7th of March" speech was the most vigorously delivered, and probably the decisive one in winning the conservative support and effecting the great Compromise of 1850, which admitted California as a free state and established territorial governments for Utah and New Mexico with no reference to slavery. Other parts of the Compromise dealt with the Texas-New Mexico border, the abolition of the slave trade in the District of Columbia, and the compulsory return of fugitive slaves who escaped into free states. During the interminable negotiations President Zachary Taylor died, and it was left for Millard Fillmore to sign the bill admitting California to the Union on September 9, 1850.

News traveled slowly in those days. The short-lived pony express was not to come into being until ten years later, and the telegraph did not yet span the vast unsettled plains which lay between California and the Mississippi. No railroad line extended westward beyond the boundary of Illinois; the Panama Canal was half a century away.

So California awaited the arrival of a ship that would bring the good news round Cape Horn. On October 18, a windmill-like contraption atop Signal Hill, which indicated the arrival of ships into San Francisco Bay, raised its arms to inform the people that the *Oregon* had been sighted. Twelve thousand San Franciscans rushed up to the hills. The ship rounded Clark's point, flying the flags of a dozen nations, and towering above all the rest was the Stars and Stripes. At the top of the mast a large streamer, erect in the wind, carried the message, CALIFORNIA ADMITTED.

The cannon in Portsmouth Square spoke out, followed by artillery from the Presidio. The ships in the harbor rang their bells and whistled. Eleven days later, San Francisco officially celebrated its admission as the thirty-first state of the Union with the most brilliant parade in its history. Led by officers of the American army, the procession included a representative of California's last Mexican governor leading a troop of *caballeros,* followed by fifty Chinese attired in lavish brocades and carrying gaudy ensigns. The procession halted in Portsmouth Square, where an Ode of Admission was sung by a choir to the strains of the *Star Spangled Banner.* That night merrymakers danced a French quadrille.

The spirit of fiesta which erupted typified the spirit of mid-century California with its heritage of riches, its fields of gold—not only mineral wealth, but magnificent fields of wheat and herds of fine cattle. This earthly paradise had its fallen angels, and a period of lawlessness sullied California's early years as a state, but her glory was by no means ended. When the Civil War accounts were tallied,

Californians could boast of their record of battle against Confederate troops, Indians, and secessionists at home.

The Golden State had come into her own, but sixty-two years would pass before the United States closed in against her last strip of eastern border.

CHAPTER V

The Far West

By THE ANNEXATION of the Northwest and the Louisiana
Purchase, the United States had acquired territory extending as far west as the Rockies, south to the Gulf of Mexico, and north—in theory—to the Canadian border. The
act of acquisition provided only the opportunity to advance. First, the wilderness had to be explored and
mapped.

The explorations of Meriwether Lewis and William
Clark opened the way into the Far West. In 1803, under
Congressional authorization, they descended the Ohio,
crossed the Missouri, spent the winter in the present North
Dakota, crossed the Rockies, and, on November 7, 1805,
came within sight of the Pacific Ocean. The following
year they returned to St. Louis and reported on their travels.

Their favorable report whetted the appetite of every
manner of American. Some visualized huge profits in real
estate. Impoverished laborers saw an opportunity to begin

life anew "out West." As time went on, more and more began to be heard of America's right to all the territory to the Pacific Ocean.

Interpreting its powers along ever-broadening lines, Congress began lacing together the old and new territories. As late as 1792, neither Kentucky nor Tennessee—to say nothing of the Northwest—had a single post office, but in the ensuing years the federal government steadily expanded the mail routes and reduced the postage rates. Post roads burgeoned from 5,000 miles in 1794 to over 100,000 miles in 1829, and by 1838 the rates had shrunk to half of what they had been in 1815. Toll turnpikes stretched from eastern cities to Illinois, and the Erie Canal —financed by the State of New York—linked the Hudson River to Lake Erie in 1825. In 1844 a message was successfully transmitted by telegraph. Eleven years later New York was connected with Chicago by a continuous line of railroad track.

The most important permanent stimulus to settlement of the frontier was, of course, the availability of land. The Land Ordinance of 1785 had provided a system for the distribution of public lands, and by 1800 the officers and legal machinery for such sales were well established. The fact that not less than a 640-acre section could be purchased was, however, a deterrent to many a would-be pioneer farmer, and the land laws were gradually modified. In 1804, for example, the minimum acreage purchasable was reduced to a quarter-section, or 160 acres, and a credit system was introduced. This proved unfortunate in that many settlers lost their land through inability to make the payments, and by the Act of April 24, 1820, "cash on the line" became the rule, $1.25 instead of $2 an acre the minimum price, and 80 acres the minimum unit of sale. In 1832, with Andrew Jackson in the Presidency, it became possible to purchase a quarter-quarter-section (40 acres).

Congress in 1785 had forbidden settlement on the public domain, and in 1807 "teeth" were added to the law in that civil and military force could be used to remove illegal settlers. As time went on, however, the right of preemption came gradually to be recognized, until in 1841 the Preemption Act provided that any person who was the head of a family, a widow, or a single man over the age of twenty-one, and was a citizen or had filed application for citizenship, and who had made or would make "settlement in person" on surveyed public land and improve the same, might enter a tract not exceeding 160 acres and after six months' residence purchase it at the minimum price of $1.25 an acre. Only one entry was permitted each qualified settler, and no one who already owned 320 acres of land was eligible.

While cheap land was a great inducement to the American farmer who saw new western lands being opened up to settlers (in 1862 the Homestead Act was to provide land free), other lures brought adventurers of many kinds. In California and the Southwest, for example, some of the earliest "pioneers" were Spanish missionaries sent to convert the Indian, while later arrivals came in a mad rush for gold and silver. In the Pacific Northwest, fur was the magnet that drew the white man in the eighteenth century. Traders from Russia, England, and the American East coast vied with each other to secure from the Indians the valuable sea-otter pelts which in those days were plentiful. Spain had an old claim to the Northwest coast, but for some reason—the rigorous climate, perhaps—she was never active there.

England's claim to the Pacific fur trade dated from 1778, when Captain Cook nosed his ship along the coast in search of the Northwest Passage. He didn't find it, but in his journal of the trip he described how sea-otter pelts were gotten from the natives for almost nothing and sold in Canton, China, for fabulous prices. Inspired by Cook's writings, a group of Boston merchants sent Captains Robert Gray and Benjamin Kendrick around the Horn in 1787. They returned with a staggering profit in oriental cargo, and when Captain Gray discovered the Columbia River on his next trip, in 1792, America's claim to the area was established. By now the sea route to the Oregon coast was alive with traders, and by 1800 England was busy with the Napoleonic wars at home and the Yankees were left in control of the coast.

Inland, beyond the coastal ranges, it was a different story. Here England had the upper hand. Alexander Mackenzie, an agent of a Canadian fur company, pushed his way to the Pacific across the continent in 1793, and the Hudson's Bay Company had spread its network of trading posts to include Oregon in the early 1800's. Inland, beaver was the prize—and the technique of getting it was the same as that used on the coast: swap trash and liquor for pelts the Indians secured.

When the Lewis and Clark expedition returned in 1806 with glowing accounts of plentiful beaver easily accessible in the Far West, American traders quickly set out to contest England's claim to this happy hunting ground. John Jacob Astor, the German-born wizard of the American Fur Company, founded Astoria at the mouth of the Columbia River in 1811. From here he planned to direct a chain of trading posts that would stretch from the Great Lakes to the Pacific, a perfect outlet to the Orient trade. His dream was short-lived. He had no sooner gotten under way when the United States and England became embroiled in the War of 1812, and Astor sold out to Canada's North West Company a year later.

This left the Canadian traders in undisputed control of the inland regions, and the British monopoly became complete when the Hudson's Bay Company (merged with the North West Company in 1821) established itself in Fort Vancouver, on the north bank of the Columbia River. Dr. John McLoughlin, who supervised the giant trading operation, not only kept a firm grip on its fur interests but built up a highly successful agricultural sideline and "public relations" outpost of the British Empire.

With English traders, trappers, and now farmers solidly entrenched (Spain relinquished her claim in 1819, Russia in 1825), Oregon appeared to be a lost cause so far as the United States was concerned, in spite of the fact that this country had a treaty of joint occupation with England. But in 1833 the picture began to change. A strange story drifted eastward from St. Louis that year, and it brought about a near-miracle; it brought America to Oregon.

The story went that four Indians—three Nez Percé and one Flathead—had traveled well over a thousand miles, from Oregon to St. Louis, to ask for the "White Man's Bible." The Indians were described as having heads which had been flattened from the eyebrows up in infancy, according to the custom of their people. The Indian trader who told this story—the authenticity of which is widely doubted today—stirred up a storm of zeal among missionary workers. The *Christian Advocate and Journal,* a Methodist publication, printed the tale. It caught on immediately, and from pulpits of every denomination came sermons pleading the cause of the unfortunate Indians. The Methodist Missionary Society sent out the Reverend Jason Lee the next spring, and his party arrived at Fort Vancouver in September, 1834. By then, winter was coming, and the mission group settled in the Willamette Valley, south of Dr. McLoughlin's hospitable stronghold. A thriving American agricultural community was soon under way, and Lee started a campaign for American emigration, including a petition to Congress to grant the settlers title to the lands under United States law. In addition to the Methodist Board of Missions, the American Board (Presbyterian) and the Catholic Church also took great interest in the natives of the Pacific Northwest. Their sympathy, incidentally, was not ill-founded. The Flathead and Nez Percé tribes had borne the brunt of the white men's struggle for control of the teeming beaver streams, so it was not surprising that they welcomed the appearance of the "black robes" brought into the Willamette Valley by French-Canadian settlers. But although Catholic missionaries, particularly the Jesuits under Father Pierre-Jean De Smet, were more successful than either Methodists or Presbyterians in securing Indian converts, it was a Presbyterian couple who eventually aroused the United States government to take the decisive step of creating the Oregon Territory in 1848.

The Presbyterians had entered the Northwest in 1835 with two missionaries, the Reverend Samuel Parker and the Reverend Marcus Whitman. Before they reached their destination, it became apparent that they were not well

enough equipped to make a successful start in the new
country, so Whitman turned back for the purpose of raising more funds in the East. In New York he was introduced to Miss Narcissa Prentiss, a blond, queenly young
woman who taught physics at Miss Willard's fashionable
academy. Miss Prentiss had been pressing the officials of
the Presbyterian Church to accept her as a missionary.

It was unthinkable that an unmarried female should be
permitted to set out into the wilderness and mingle with
the savages, especially a woman with Narcissa's attributes.
She had been blessed with great beauty and an exquisite
singing voice and had been brought up to wear lovely
clothes and move with ease in the élite social circles of the
day. And yet, at a time when women of breeding were
expected to occupy themselves with poetry, sewing, and
beaux, Narcissa taught science, and reveled in communion
—or conflict—with other vigorous intellects.

When Marcus Whitman met with authorities of the
American Board of Missions, he was asked to investigate
the extraordinary Miss Prentiss. The young physician, his
brown hair streaked with gray, tried earnestly to dissuade
the lady from her most unfeminine ambition. He failed in
this, but succeeded in persuading her to marry him.

Dressed in a gown of black bombazine, Narcissa Prentiss was married to Marcus Whitman in a little neighborhood church. She was twenty-seven; he was thirty-two. The
wedding was a social event; Narcissa was the daughter of
Judge Stephen Prentiss, and traced her ancestry back to
seventeenth-century New England, as did Dr. Whitman.

Once again Narcissa requested from the mission board
permission to go to Oregon. This time there were no ob-
jections. Now, his fund-raising errand accomplished, Whit-

man set out with his wife, another missionary couple, and two helpers, in the spring of 1836.

The newlyweds journeyed to Fort Loup, Missouri, by wagon, where they joined the American Fur Company caravan. Permission had been granted to travel with it on its yearly expedition to the Rocky Mountains. Whitman had qualms about subjecting his delicate-looking bride to a strenuous journey across the prairies, but Narcissa felt secure with her strong young husband. And, besides, they were accompanied by the other missionary couple (also Presbyterian), Henry and Eliza Spalding.

The American Fur Company was a vigorous community of about seventy men and four hundred horses and mules. When dawn broke on May 2, 1836, the mules began to fidget, and shouts of "Awake!" "On your toes!" interrupted the slumber of the encampment. Starting out across the plains, Narcissa rode horseback; occasionally she shifted to their Conestoga wagon, where she could relax atop the baggage. They spent the nights in a tent, wrapped in Indian blankets.

Timber was a rarity in this region, and they cooked over fires made from buffalo dung. Buffalo meat was virtually their only food. The cattle provided milk, and at times there was coffee of sorts to be had.

The party reached the Continental Divide on the Fourth

The Ordinance of 1785 provided for the rectangular survey of the public domain into six-mile-square townships as one feature of "the mode of disposing of lands in the Western territory." Shown is a portion of one of the first of these surveys, that of the "Seven Ranges" in central Ohio (a range being a north-and-south row of townships).

Courtesy of the New-York Historical Society, New York City

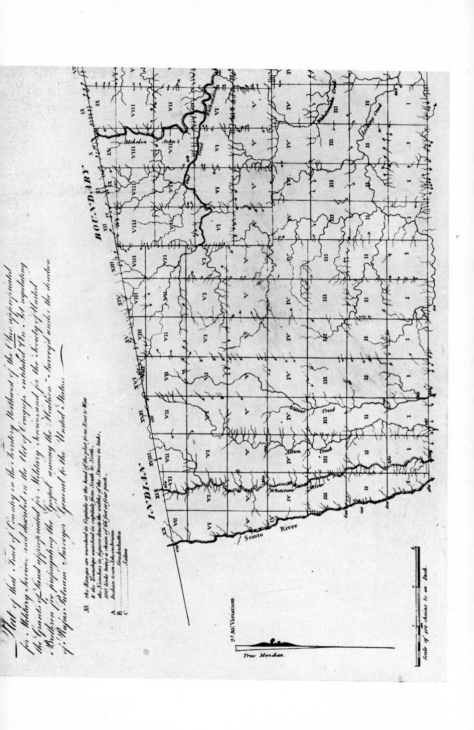

This caricature of Brother Jonathan (a nickname applied to Americans) winning a boxing match with John Bull refers to the capture of the British brig *Boxer* by the U. S. brig *Enterprise* off the Maine coast in 1813. The War of 1812 was ended by negotiation, but the United States gained new prestige abroad and stronger unity at home.

Courtesy of the New-York Historical

The completion of the Erie Canal in 1825 brought droves of pioneer farmers to the Northern Lake Plains, in one phase of America's first great migration westward. This aquatint by John Hill, dating from 1830, shows the junction of the Erie and Champlain Canals.

Courtesy of the New-York Historical Society, New York City

Between 1830 and 1840 some 60,000 Indians were moved from the East to the Great Plains, under the federal government's Indian Removal policy. Northern tribes were fairly tractable, but the Five Civilized Tribes of the South resisted bitterly. Shown here is Osceola, the leader of Florida's Seminoles in the Second Seminole War (1835-1842).

Courtesy Florida Park Service

Among the many casualties of early migrations to the Far West was the Donner Party, who set out for California from Illinois in 1846. After crossing the Wasatch Mountains and the desert south of the Great Salt Lake, they started the ascent of the Sierras just as winter was setting in. There they were trapped by a storm, and California rescue parties managed to save fewer than fifty of the original party of eighty-nine.

Fort Vancouver, western headquarters of the Hudson's Bay Company, was situated on the north bank of the Columbia River within the triangle of land whose possession was in dispute between Britain and the United States under the terms of their joint treaty of occupation. In 1845, just as war seemed imminent, the British company moved its headquarters to Victoria, and Britain agreed to a Canadian boundary at the 49th parallel.

Courtesy Oregon Historical Society

The annexation of Texas set off the Mexican War in May of 1846, which ended with Mexico's cession of all territory north of the Rio Grande and Gila Rivers. Shown is the storming of Chapultepec, a rocky hill crowned with heavy fortifications just southwest of Mexico City, which fell to American forces on September 13, 1847. Three days later Mexico City was taken.

The treaty with Mexico by which California was ceded to the United States was barely ratified when gold was discovered in this new American territory. Overnight, California was peopled with thousands of fortune-seekers, and soon became eligible for statehood. Here is "a scene from actual life at the mines."

Courtesy California Historical Society,

of July, having come into the Rockies by the South Pass. The entire company knelt in prayer. On the sixth they reached the trading rendezvous in the Rockies. This was in the neighborhood of the Green River, near what is currently Daniel, Wyoming.

The rendezvous had the appearance of a huge country fair. Indian and Spanish dialects mingled with the varied accents of American, Canadian, and English traders. Merchants of the fur companies east and west of the Rockies gathered here to barter for skins with the red-skinned trappers. Mountain men, clad in buckskin and sporting knives, corncob pipes, and tobacco pouches, galloped in with their squaws, whose papooses were tied to the saddle.

During trading periods, the white men and the tribes of unfriendly Indians effected a truce. The trappers and traders, along with their friendly Indians, drew up in ranks, forming three arcs of a giant ring. The hostile Indians, under their own protective guard, formed the fourth. Each tribe was represented by an elderly brave, who met the representatives of the fur companies in the center and offered his tribe's beaver skins.

The mountaineers, who had not glimpsed a white woman for years, made a great fuss over Narcissa and Eliza. But they took a dim view of the women's projected journey, and tried to persuade them to return home. They pointed out that the missionaries would no longer be enjoying the protection of the American Fur Company, which was scheduled to return to St. Louis, and from here to the Pacific Coast the mountain passes teemed with warlike Crow and Blackfoot braves.

These experts also warned Whitman that he would not be able to go much farther with his wagon. No one, they told him, had ever taken a wagon west of the Rockies. They urged him to sell it at Green River and continue over the mountains on horseback.

But their entreaties went unheeded. The doctor was determined to take the wagon through if there was any chance at all that he could do so. He knew that his experience would be of vital interest to families who wanted to travel out to Oregon, but who needed evidence that they could haul their possessions over the Rockies.

When the time for departure drew near, the vast encampment bristled with activity. Tents were folded, food packed, and thousands of horses and mules were spurred into marching lines. Farewells were taken as the caravans of the fur companies departed for their home stations and the Indians left for their far-flung villages.

Once more the Whitmans set out, accompanied by a small party of traders. They followed the southern route to the Pacific, more than five hundred miles away. Mountain travel was tedious, and Whitman was compelled to yield a point on his wagon. He took off one pair of wheels and their axle, turning the wagon into a two-wheeled cart. He succeeded in bringing it safely to Fort Boise, Idaho— the first time anything on wheels had gone that far west.

The travelers trudged forward through huge stretches of sagebrush and desert blistered by the sun. Goaded by gnats and sandflies, the cattle often refused to budge, and it took strenuous effort to coax them on. The most dangerous body of water to be negotiated was the Snake River in Idaho, which had to be crossed twice because of its tortuous windings.

Toward summer's end, the Whitmans left the sagebrush regions behind and reached the Blue Mountains. The unshod feet of the tired horses limped up the rocky mountain slopes. On August 29 the Whitmans had their first view of the Columbia River, and within a week they reached Fort Walla Walla, the Hudson's Bay Company's outpost.

After they had rested here for several days, the travelers sailed down the Columbia River to the headquarters of the Hudson's Bay Company, Fort Vancouver, the biggest community of whites in Oregon.

In early September the missionaries reached Fort Vancouver. To the weary foursome the modest little settlement seemed like the "New York of the Pacific," as Narcissa wrote in her journal. So came to an end the thousand-mile trip from Fort Loup, Missouri. Narcissa Whitman and Eliza Spalding were the first white females to cross the continent.

Oregon, at the arrival of the Whitmans, was a country reveling in the resources of nature. Aside from Dr. McLoughlin's Hudson's Bay post and a Methodist mission which had located in the Willamette Valley several years before the Whitmans' coming, Oregon was pretty much a wilderness, as remote from the dweller along the Atlantic seaboard as the Kingdom of Siam.

Narcissa remained at Fort Vancouver for several weeks while Marcus went on ahead to survey a location for their missionary work. After a thorough investigation, he resolved to settle among the Cayuse, who were allied to the Flatheads, along the Walla Walla River north of the Hudson's Bay Company post. The savages called this area *Waiilatpu*—"the region of the tall rye grass" (which grew to a height of almost six feet).

Upon reaching Waiilatpu, Narcissa was delighted to find that Marcus, with the help of Indians, had already begun construction of a shelter. The floor was laid, but no furniture, not even beds, was added during the first twelve months of their occupancy. The Whitmans slept on the floor in blankets.

Henry and Eliza Spalding had located a mission post ninety miles to the south of the Whitmans', and became their closest white neighbors. The only others in this vast wilderness were missionaries of the Methodist faith who had settled three hundred miles away. Occasionally trappers and representatives of the Hudson's Bay Company turned up in the region, but essentially the Whitmans lived in isolation.

To add to their loneliness, it was difficult to receive word from home. Mail from relatives in the East had to be carried in ships that went first to Hawaii around Cape Horn, then crossed the Pacific to the Columbia River, and at last sailed up to the Whitman mission.

The Cayuse, among whom they lived, were a community of about three hundred. They were proud and vengeful. It took a while for the doctor to gain their confidence in his medical treatments. At first they held him personally liable for his patients, and vowed to kill him if any died under his treatment.

In time, however, Whitman won their trust and Narcissa won their hearts with her charm and her singing. Transforming her kitchen into a schoolroom, Narcissa gave courses in English to the Cayuse children. She rang a handbell to begin classes. Textbooks were obtained from the Methodist mission in the Willamette Valley, which set aside its doctrinal rivalry with the Whitmans in a common effort to educate the Indians.

The Whitmans lived very frugally. Narcissa saved fruit

seeds and planted them. In the first few years of her stay there was a shortage of cattle, and the only meat available was horseflesh. Indeed, the first cow was not slaughtered for food until some years after the Whitmans' arrival, and she was an elderly animal who had outgrown her usefulness for milking.

Although the Cayuse in time became generally friendly toward the Whitmans, they remained difficult to deal with in many areas. Whitman tried to teach them the techniques of farm irrigation, but, too indolent to make their own trenches, they stole his water for their fields. When he protested, they wrecked his supply. In spite of this hostility, however, he managed to establish a successful farm operation, and designed a mill to supply flour for bread.

The missionaries' somber existence was brightened considerably by the birth of a girl before Narcissa's thirtieth birthday. She was christened Alice Clarissa, and was the first white child to be born in Oregon. But almost three years later, this light that had come into the Whitmans' life was tragically snuffed out. Little Alice had gone out to bring in water for their evening meal and did not return. Her body was found later, entangled in the roots of the stream's copse.

The loss of their child reinforced the Whitmans' resolution to stay in Oregon. Confronted with the antagonism of the Indians, their determination had wavered from time to time, and they had discussed the idea of returning East. But now that Alice lay buried in Waiilatpu soil, they felt bound forever to Oregon's destiny. Then, too, they had grown to love this burgeoning land, and to see the promise it held for other Americans. The adaptability of its rivers for commercial traffic convinced Marcus that the

Northwest was a region in which thousands of Mississippi Valley farmers, now impoverished by a fallen market, could begin a prosperous new life.

But this inviting territory was widely misunderstood in the East. Typical of one kind of misconception was an article which appeared in a contemporary Kentucky newspaper:

> Of all the countries on the face of this earth, Oregon is one of the last favored by heaven. . . . It is almost as barren as the desert of Africa, and quite as unhealthy as the Campania of Italy. . . . Russia has her Siberia, and England has her Botany Bay, and if the United States should ever need a country to which to banish its rogues and scoundrels, the utility of such a region as Oregon would be demonstrated.

This strongly negative feeling about the Pacific Coast was by no means universal. Oregon had many strong supporters who felt it imperative that this region be brought into the American fold. At this time, Oregon was still being jointly governed by Great Britain and the United States under the terms of a ten-year treaty executed in 1818 and subsequently extended.

An organization called the American Society for Encouraging the Settlement of the Oregon Territory had been founded in 1829 by Hall J. Kelley, but settlers did not begin to come in large numbers until Marcus Whitman opened the way six years later. In 1842 Whitman made a journey to the East, and the objective of this hazardous trip has given rise to a long-standing controversy.

Many earlier historians wrote that Whitman felt impelled to "save Oregon" for the United States, and met with President Tyler and Secretary of State Webster in a series of interviews. He had only one request: that American interests in Oregon not be abandoned to Great Britain until he had had an opportunity to lead a large number of settlers back with him so that they could learn for themselves the many advantages of the Pacific Northwest. Whitman, according to this side of the controversy, was directly responsible for overcoming strong opposition in Congress and securing passage of a bill extending United States law over the whole of the Oregon territory.

The other interpretation of his journey is that since the Presbyterian Board had decided to abolish the settlement at Waiilatpu and put Whitman in charge of another mission farther south, Whitman's trip to the East was undertaken to save his mission and not for any political reason. This version of the story is more popularly accepted today.

At any rate, Whitman's plan to visit the East took definite shape in the fall of 1842, when he learned of the Presbyterian Board's plan to abolish the post at Waiilatpu. He felt very strongly about the importance of the mission, and Narcissa's feelings were so much his own that she pressed him to go East and personally present his views to the Board even though this meant she would be left alone for at least twelve months.

Accompanied only by an American settler and an Indian guide, Marcus made his way eastward through a severe cold wave that descended upon the whole West that fall. It was a grim journey. Travel was made almost impossible by dense snowstorms. Months after he had started out, Whitman arrived at Bent's Fort on the Arkansas River. Four weeks later he came to St. Louis. Here, with friends, he recovered from his ordeal before going on to the East to confer with his colleagues.

The trip, whatever its motive, did produce two concrete results: Whitman argued the American Mission Board into continuing the strategic Waiilatpu settlement, and he assumed a vital role in leading the first emigration over the Rockies the following summer.

Hundreds of Americans, persuaded that Oregon was the land of the future, loaded their wives, children, and possessions into their Conestoga wagons in the winter of 1842-43, and converged at a spot nine miles west of Independence, Missouri. Although settlers had been infiltrating into the territory for a number of years, it was this expedition of 1843, consisting of more than nine hundred men, women, and children, and two thousand horses and cattle, that generated the epic migration into Oregon and began one of the most inspiring chapters in American history.

To an extraordinary degree, Whitman was the guiding spirit of the expedition. He trotted up and down the column of Conestoga wagons, exhorting the drivers, comforting the ailing.

When the party reached Fort Hall, Idaho, British officials issued the standard admonitions. The Conestoga wagon would never make it through the Rockies. To some extent this was propaganda intended to discourage American colonization; still, there was undoubtedly a high degree of truth in the warning. Scores of emigrants were convinced by the arguments. Some were on the verge of backing out of the Oregon trip altogether.

Marcus Whitman, who had been away on a reconnaissance trip, returned to find a very discordant company. Calling them together, he forcefully assured them that they could cross the Rockies with their wagons and possessions. He described how he had done this very thing seven years earlier.

This settled the matter. The column proceeded with its wagons and, as the missionary had guaranteed, succeeded in getting to the Willamette Valley.

As the company entered the Grande Ronde Valley, east of the Blue Mountains, Whitman received a letter from his friend Mrs. Spalding, begging him to hurry back to the mission to treat a seriously ill patient. He went on ahead of the rest, ordering an Indian convert to guide them the remainder of the trip. They were led over the Blue Mountains to Waiilatpu, where they rested before continuing on to the Willamette Valley.

With the completion of this overland migration, the future of Oregon was assured. Yankees now substantially outnumbered the British. The following year, a second group of emigrants, encouraged by the news that their predecessors had successfully hauled their wagons over the mountains, embarked from Independence, Missouri. To represent the settlers until the United States should officially take them under its wing, a temporary government was established in the Willamette Valley.

In the American settlement of the Northwest, the most optimistic dreams of the Whitmans were realized. But, at the same time, these successful migrations were the cause of a catastrophe. The neighboring Cayuse Indians grew angry over the increasing numbers of whites. Apprehensive of being robbed of their land, the elders of the tribe met in council and issued warnings of retaliation.

This talk of war among the savages engendered anxiety among the colonists. "Some of the settlers here want the Government to build fortifications," Whitman wrote in a letter to a friend in the East. The missioners' alarm increased when they heard that on the eve of the great overland trek of 1843, the Flathead Indians had dispatched an agent to brother tribes east of Fort Hall, exhorting them to massacre the whites on the trail. Nothing had come of this, but it clearly indicated that the Americans were indeed in danger.

Anxiety was further heightened by an occurrence in California. A chief of the Walla Walla tribe was killed in a fracas with an American. Indians up and down the Pacific Coast were incensed. Whitman called a meeting of the Cayuse and spoke to them frankly. He told them that he was their friend; that it was not true that the white men intended to rob them of their land. "But you are threatening our lives. I for one am ready to give up the mission and go home, if you wish me to do so. Tell me whether you want me to remain or not."

The Indians voted among themselves, and an overwhelming majority decided in favor of the Whitmans' staying at their mission. But the situation remained uneasy. In the fall of 1847, when the missionaries were celebrating the tenth anniversary of their arrival in Oregon, a shoeless, ill-clad half-breed named Joe Lewis appeared at the Whitman mission. With their usual kindness, the couple fed and clothed him and hired him as a laborer.

But the half-breed had not been with them long when Istickus, Whitman's Indian convert, came to him with troubling news. "Joe Lewis is no good. He is lying to my people that you are going to poison them, to take away their land for your white friends. I am afraid my people will rise in anger. You'd better leave Oregon."

The next day—November 29, 1847—an Indian died.

Marcus, who attended the burial ceremony, noticed with alarm that only a few braves were present. An ominous stillness had settled over the Indian village. When he returned home, Marcus discussed the grave situation with his wife. That evening after dinner, Marcus was told that two Indians were waiting in the kitchen to see him. When he entered the room, one of the savages drew him into conversation. The second slipped behind the missionary and in an instant pulled out a tomahawk from beneath his blanket and struck Whitman on the head. Then, as Whitman toppled to the floor, the two Indians fled.

Narcissa waited uneasily for a short while before coming to the kitchen. Then frantically she tried to revive her husband—but he died without recognizing her. As she rose to her feet, an Indian suddenly loomed up at the window and pulled the trigger of a rifle. Narcissa was killed almost instantly. In the ensuing carnage, eleven men and boys were murdered, and the mission buildings were burned to ashes.

News of the massacre stunned America. The missions were abandoned. Oregonians held a rally, and more than five hundred men volunteered to set out on an expedition to punish the Cayuse. So began the Cayuse War, the first of Oregon's Indian wars. Through bitter winters and through summers of indecisive engagements, the war dragged on until 1850, when five Indians surrendered themselves as murderers. The five were tried and hanged at Oregon City, and the war ended.

More than any other single event, the Whitman massacre awoke President Polk and the Congress to the need of providing the Oregon Territory with the safeguard of

an adequate government. As early as 1843, when the large-
scale migrations of Americans into Oregon began, the need
for a politically organized territory had been evident. In
that year a committee of nine settlers, chosen by their
neighbors, drafted a plan of government to be submitted
to the people, one that incorporated the Ordinance of 1787
with such revisions as local conditions made necessary.
Three years later, in 1846, the way for a definite territorial
organization was opened when the United States signed a
treaty with Great Britain that defined the northern boundaries of Oregon as the region lying south of the 49th
parallel. On August 14, 1848, Oregon was organized as a
territory. Its 292,000 square miles comprised the present
states of Oregon, Idaho, and Washington, 28,000 square
miles of Montana, and 13,000 square miles of Wyoming.
(In 1853 this area was reduced by the creation of the Territory of Washington.) On March 3, an administration was
launched by General Joseph Lane, the governor appointed
by President Polk.

The year 1848 is for many reasons an important one in
Oregon's history. News of the discovery of gold in California reached the new territory to the north, and an estimated two thirds of Oregon's able-bodied men rushed
down to the goldfields. Since, oddly enough, there were
those in Oregon who considered the region overpopu-
lated, this loss of settlers was not considered a disaster. In
fact, opportunists arose who took advantage of the influx
of gold to develop better farming and commercial facilities
than the territory had ever known, and a new prosperity
came to the Pacific Northwest.

Another crisis which arose in 1848 was related to Oregon's achievement of territorial status, with its implicit

promise of future statehood. President Polk, a Democrat, had appointed a Democratic governor for the territory, but Governor Lane lasted only until the Democrats were voted out of Washington and Zachary Taylor, a Whig, was elected President. Not only the governor, but other Democratic officials as well were replaced, at the will of Washington Whigs, by Whigs. At this juncture, the Democrats of Oregon mustered their forces in opposition to the new officials, and a bitter struggle began. Some saw their only alternatives as either statehood—which would do away with the odiousness of Washington-appointed officials—or complete independence from the United States. The resentment of Oregon's Democrats was a divisive factor in the territory until the election of a Democratic President, James Buchanan, in 1856. The would-be "secessionists" had actually had under way a plan for a Pacific Coast Republic to be comprised of the lands west of the Rockies: three states were to be formed from the state of California, three in Oregon Territory, two in Washington Territory, and two from western portions of Utah and New Mexico.

As for the alternative of statehood, the Democratic party —which commanded the strongest support in Oregon—was the party of the proslavery South. The provisional government set up in Oregon in 1843 had adopted the Northwest Ordinance's ban on slavery, and it was this clause which had delayed Congressional approval of her territorial status for two years. Unlikely as it seems, the issue of slavery could frustrate hopes of statehood even in the Pacific Northwest simply by being tied to the national policy of the party in control there.

In 1854, however, the picture was changed by the outbreak of civil war in Kansas. A flow of Whig emigrants headed for that troubled country, and many moved on farther west. The Whig cause was thus strengthened in Oregon, and in 1857 Oregonians voted for statehood by a majority—for the first time—of almost 6,000. When the constitution was submitted to the people, they were permitted to vote separately on the issues of slavery and the entrance of free Negroes into the state. The constitution was adopted by a decisive majority; slavery was voted down three to one, but the admission of free Negroes into the state was also voted down. This angered the abolitionists in Washington, and the statehood bill, though passed by the Senate in 1858 by a resounding majority, failed to pass the House of Representatives.

There was another political reason why statehood was not easily won. A Presidential election was at hand—the fateful election of 1860—and a state of Oregon (still preponderantly Democratic) might cast the decisive vote against the Republicans. At the last minute, however, fifteen Republicans in Washington bolted the party's stand and the bill passed the House on February 12. Two days later Buchanan signed it, and on February 14, 1859, Oregon became a state of the Union.

Ironically enough, far from being an obstacle to the Republicans in 1860, Oregon became a state just in time to help nominate Abraham Lincoln. At the Republican Convention Horace Greeley, editor of the New York *Tribune* (acting as proxy for Leander Holmes, one of the six delegates from Oregon), swung the tide toward the nomination of Lincoln on the third ballot. It was the five votes cast by Oregon delegates that gave the celebrated rail-splitter the Republican nomination.

The courage of Marcus and Narcissa Whitman and their colleagues is part of the legend of Oregon—and not only of Oregon, but of a family of Northwest states. Washington, which grew up in the area north of the Columbia River, was separated from Oregon when the latter was organized as a territory, but did not achieve statehood until thirty years later. One year later, in 1890, Idaho became the forty-third state. She had been organized as a territory in 1863, when her population boomed after gold was discovered in 1860. The western portions of Montana and Wyoming were also carved out of the original Oregon Territory.

The admission of Wyoming to statehood in 1890 was a new kind of milestone in the story of American statehood. For the first time, the United States of America had spanned the continent: From Oregon to Idaho to Wyoming to the Dakotas and Nebraska, through Iowa and Minnesota and through the Northwest Territory states of the early nineteenth century, to the British colonies of more than a century before, the nation stretched from coast to coast.

In 1883 the Northern Pacific Railway was opened between Ashland, Wisconsin, and Portland, Oregon. Silver and gold and cattle had already made the Pacific Northwest irresistible, but with the coming of the railroad the rest of the continent became accessible. The time was past when a crossing of the Rockies was a matter of life or death.

CHAPTER VI

Utah

THE SETTLEMENT OF UTAH is a unique chapter in the history of American expansion. It does not follow the main stream; its pioneers were not lured by gold, the desire to extend slavery, or the promise of free land. In fact, the motivation goes back to an earlier American pattern, one that had had currency three hundred years before. Utah was settled by a community in search of a place to live and worship as they chose, without interference from the unsympathetic.

Just as the Puritans erected a theocracy in Massachusetts, so did the Mormons establish one in Salt Lake City. And, again as in the case of Massachusetts, this hierarchical government was eventually modified by the inexorable impact of events. "Gentiles" who did not hold Mormon beliefs filtered into the community, and a new framework of tolerance had to be devised to deal fairly with them. The "Righteous" learned to live with the Heretic, the Dissenter, the Free-thinker.

New religions are born among restless folk. In the backwoods of America in the early nineteenth century, pioneers searching for the underlying meaning of the trials they were enduring poured the overflow of their feeling into a series of religious revivals. A rash of sects sprang up like exotic plants in the wilderness. Preachers of a variety of callings traveled around organizing camp meetings, exhorting men who worked and drank hard to pray even harder. These revivals were frequently scenes of unrestrained hysterics.

In the midst of this vigorous striving for emotional compensation, one sect sprang up in New England—a seedbed of Transcendentalism—that wove a scarlet thread through the pattern of American history. The origins of Mormonism go back to 1820, when a young New Englander named Joseph Smith announced that he had received in a vision a divine call to become the prophet of a new Gospel dispensation. Three years later, he declared that the angel Moroni had appeared to him and revealed the existence of a record containing the fullness of Christ's Gospel as it had first been given to the ancient inhabitants of America. This record, engraved on gold plates, was hidden in a hill near Palmyra, New York, where Joseph Smith's family now lived. In 1827, this *Book of Mormon,* as the angel Moroni had identified it, was delivered to Smith by an angel who also gave him a pair of stones, Urim and Thummim, for use in translating the record's "reformed Egyptian" hieroglyphics into English. Smith dictated the translation from behind a curtain, and returned the plates to the angel when he was finished. His father, two brothers, and several associates testified to having seen the plates.

The *Book of Mormon* was published at Palmyra early

in 1830, and the new religion quickly caught on. Smith was the prophet; under him were six elders.

Certain social aspects of the new religion were extremely progressive for the times. The Mormons deplored slavery, the exploitation of labor, and religious and racial bigotry. They preached the equality of man and equal privileges for women. The most controversial doctrine of Mormonism, however, was polygamy. Smith received the "revelation on the eternity of the marriage covenant, including the plurality of wives" in 1843; this was not officially announced until 1852, although polygamy began to be quietly practiced by the members. Long before this—in fact, from its very beginnings—the Mormon church had aroused ridicule and resentment for other reasons.

The persecutions of the Mormons involved them in a series of migrations which began in 1831, when their first colony—in Jackson, Missouri—fomented bitterness partly because of its strong abolitionist sentiments. Driven from Missouri, they migrated to Illinois in 1840, where they built the city of Nauvoo (The Beautiful). For about five years Nauvoo prospered under a charter which gave the Mormon settlement virtual self-rule, including the right to make its own laws—provided that none conflicted with the Illinois or the federal constitution. From about four thousand in 1830, the membership grew to twenty thousand by 1840. The town thrived so conspicuously, and attracted so many converts from abroad, that neighboring towns grew resentful of this powerful community possessing its own militia and courts.

This resentment flared into violence when Joseph Smith suppressed a newspaper set up by some Saints who had seceded from the church because of the Elders' secret practice of polygamy. Angry mobs began demonstrations in the city of Carthage, and the governor of Illinois had no alternative but to arrest Smith. He was brought to the jail in Carthage, along with his brother Hyrum and several followers, under a pledge of the state's protection. A mob of some two hundred men gathered outside the jail, and a rumor began to circulate that the Mormons were going to receive a pardon from the governor. On June 27, 1844, the mob made its way into the jail and shot to death Joseph and Hyrum Smith. The governor of Illinois now ordered the Mormons to leave the state "to preserve the peace of the community." The Elders appealed to President Polk for protection, but they received no answer.

Brigham Young, as the first of the apostles, became head of the church. He was forty-three years old at the time, with just eleven days of formal schooling but an extraordinary amount of self-assurance. His ability to inspire confidence would be needed in the hard years that lay ahead for his people.

There was no choice but to leave Nauvoo—which the Gentiles now called the "City of Venus." Calling the children of Israel together, Brigham Young told them the unhappy news. Only if they were to journey far west, out of reach of the United States government, could they prosper in peace. Perhaps they would go to California; perhaps they would find the Promised Land nearer home. He told them of a vision he had had of a broad and beautiful valley.

The fourth and last of the Mormon hegiras took place in the spring of 1846. This was an emigration not of a group of families, but of a whole people. The line of exiles, consisting of fifteen thousand persons with wagons and cattle, horses and sheep, stretched from the Mississippi River to the Missouri. Births and deaths took place in the covered wagons while fierce storms raged outside. Progress was slow, for those who went on ahead had to make provision for the people following. At strategic points the advance party stopped to build roads and bridges, and to plant crops which could be harvested by subsequent emigrants. There were those among them who were destined to achieve positions of wealth and eminence in the new country to which they were headed, but for the time being all were too hungry and ill-clothed to worry about anything but survival.

Brigham Young was everywhere—pouring out cups of hot tea for the shivering, sharing the night watch with the sentinels, encouraging the despondent.

The early days of the march were chaotic, and one of Young's children left this memorable picture:

> Such misery met our gaze as will never be forgotten. Dogs, chickens, cows, and children by the thousand ran hither and thither in the utmost confusion. Wagons were scattered about; babies screamed for their mothers. Women sat in open tents waving the flies away from their dead children. One child fell out of a wagon and was crushed under the wheels. Weeping sick ones lay here and there, while anxiety was in every heart.

Gradually Brigham Young instituted order. He organized a daily schedule for eating, sleeping, work, and recreation. The encampment rose at five o'clock in the morning at the sound of a bugle. Two hours later, with breakfast finished, the column was on its way. At noon it halted for lunch and siesta, resuming the march at two in the afternoon. At six it bivouacked for the night.

Where was the column headed? To this question not even Brigham Young had a definite answer. "But," he assured his followers, "I will know the place when I see it."

The first column, headed by Brigham Young and most of the apostles, reached the Missouri River, near the present Council Bluffs, Iowa, in June. After crossing into Nebraska, they decided to set up headquarters for the winter, a few miles south of what was later to become the city of Omaha. Not yet organized as a territory, Nebraska at this time had only a few dozen white inhabitants. It was still overwhelmingly Indian country.

During the winter Young studied maps and listened to reports of the country to the west. He was especially interested in the stories of Jim Bridger, the veteran scout who spoke glowingly of the valley of the Great Salt Lake, in the region of the Rocky Mountains.

An advance detachment consisting of 143 men, three women, and two children was assigned to hew out a trail to the new Zion. It started out in April, 1847. Since it had to pass through dangerous Indian country, it was organized into several military companies, each headed by an officer.

The chief objective was to cross the Rocky Mountains. The party moved westward, crossing the Missouri River and following the north bank of the Platte as far as Fort Laramie. From here they followed the Oregon Trail until, in July, they arrived at Fort Bridger, a fur-trading post in southwestern Wyoming. Orson Pratt, one of the apostles, described the Fort in his diary as consisting of "50 white men, squaws, and half-breed children living in two log houses with dirt roofs."

Several days later the pioneers said good-by to the Fort and to the Oregon Trail, which they had followed for seven hundred miles. Now they headed southwest into uncharted country, traversing gorges of the Uinta and Wasatch mountain ranges and sending ahead groups of tunnel diggers to prepare the way.

But as the party approached the Great Salt Lake, Brigham Young was stricken with mountain fever. For a spell, it seemed that he was destined to die before reaching the Promised Land. However, the crisis passed and Young lived. He lay in the rear convalescing while Pratt and another of the apostles, Erastus Snow, pushed ahead of the wagons. Ascending a western spur of the Wasatch, they saw stretched before them an immense valley to the rear of which the waters of the Great Salt Lake sparkled in the sunlight.

Overjoyed, they returned to camp with the news. Brigham Young's carriage hurried forward. On July 24, 1847, seventeen months after he led his people out of Illinois, he had found the ultimate haven for them. "This is the right place!"

Pratt called the company together for religious devotion. The Mormons prayed for rain to water the parched soil, but since it was one of their precepts that God helps those who help themselves, "two hours after our arrival" (Pratt wrote in his journal) "we began to plough and the same afternoon we built a dam to irrigate the soil."

The Mormons responded courageously to the challenge of this uniquely beautiful country. About them, on their great plateau, towered peaks of mountain ranges, colorful canyons, clay *mesas* carved into eccentric shapes by the elements. Nearby lay the Great Salt Lake, which had been in ancient times a vast inland sea. The mineral salts accumulated over thousands of years had grown so concentrated that, to their astonishment, the Saints found they were buoyed up like corks in the water.

They were to discover that this water was as useless as the desert. It could not be used in food. It was so salty that no species except brine shrimp could live in it. It could not be depended on for navigation, since it unpredictably receded from the piers, leaving them high and dry, or swept over them in waves four feet high. Attempts to remove the salts from the water were a failure. The Lake, its color changing capriciously from brilliant sapphire to heavy gray, acknowledged only the wind as its master.

According to legend, a tribe of giant Indians who traveled on elephants were supposed to live on the farther shore of the Lake. But in the years of struggle and deprivation that lay ahead, the Mormons did not encounter these fabulous natives. They had to make their peace instead with the flesh-and-blood Ute Indians to the south.

The Saints had a struggle on their hands to irrigate the land. They experienced frustrating periods when the crickets destroyed the crops. They had to share meager food rations; to provide housing for the hundreds of Saints who poured into the New Zion from places as far away as England and Denmark.

Upon arriving in Utah, Young lost no time in laying out a community. Staked off in 135 blocks of ten acres each, with three public squares and streets eight yards wide, Salt Lake City developed into one of the most charming settlements on the continent. Consulting with his apostles,

Young nominated a president, a high council, and a marshal. He himself remained at the head of the hierarchy. It was he who directed his people in how to care for the cattle, what fences to build, when to plant crops and cut timber. "Your present location is designed for a city of refuge, therefor see to it that ye pollute not your inheritance."

Brigham Young and the faithful built a community that was unique in nineteenth-century America. They undertook the country's first large-scale irrigation project. They launched cooperative business enterprises protecting the consumer's buying power. They gave the franchise to women, outlawed slavery, contributed funds toward the building of a Catholic church and a Jewish synagogue. They instituted a tithing system, apportioning one tenth of every man's wages for the support of the needy.

But Young had ambitions that extended beyond the frontiers of his little community. It was not enough to occupy a chain of valleys around the Great Salt Lake. He dreamt of an empire stretching from the Rocky Mountains to the Sierra Nevadas, and from the Oregon Territory to the country south of the Colorado. True, this land belonged to Mexico, but there were more than two thousand miles separating Salt Lake from the feeble Mexican government at Santa Ana, and the nearest settlement under the jurisdiction of the United States was over a thousand miles away. Unhampered by hostile Gentile neighbors, Young did not doubt that he could carve out an empire for the Mormon Church. But events were taking shape in a way that was to frustrate his ambition and eventually place the Kingdom of Zion under the American flag.

During the trek of the Mormons to Salt Lake City in the

spring of 1846, the army led by Zachary Taylor clashed with Mexican troops on the Rio Grande. On May 13 Congress declared war on Mexico. Needing volunteers from all quarters, Washington's attitude toward the Mormons changed from indifference to paternal interest. Until now, President Polk had ignored their pleas for protection from religious persecution. Now, deeming it wise to enlist their sympathies, he ordered General Stephen W. Kearny to enlist Mormon men in the Army of the West.

The invitation was presented by letter to Brigham Young, who considered it to be a stroke of good fortune for the Saints. "We must make a distinction between this action of the government and our former oppressions in Missouri and Illinois." Since the volunteers were to receive the regular pay granted to all recruits, and would be allowed to retain their arms and equipment after discharge, this would be a means of securing much-needed money for their Kingdom of God.

After being organized and equipped at Fort Leavenworth, the Mormon Battalion—consisting of about five hundred men—headed for Santa Fe to do battle with the Mexicans. The rigors of the march are described in a diary kept by one of the infantrymen:

> History may be searched in vain for an equal expedition. Half of it has been through a wilderness where nothing but savages and wild beasts are found or deserts where, for want of water, there is no living creature. Here, with almost hopeless labor we have dug deep wells which will save the lives of future travellers.

The war with Mexico ended suddenly with America's occupation of Santa Anna's capital before the Mormons arrived on the scene. The battalion was mustered out of service in Los Angeles, having made the longest U. S. Infantry march on record. Returning homeward, it sojourned at Sutter's Fort, five hundred miles to the north. The majority continued on, crossing the mountains into the Salt Lake Valley. A few remained at the fort and were there on January 24, 1848, when the gold was discovered.

Thanks to the peace treaty of Guadelupe Hidalgo, the Mormons who had trekked a thousand miles to be free of Washington's jurisdiction now found themselves once again under it.

Moreover, friction between the Mormons and the outside world mounted steadily. At first the Mormon Church had provided a practical framework for all political and social government. The edicts of Brigham Young served as the law. An ecclesiastical hierarchy of Bishops' Courts functioned as courts of justice, and the Church tithes served as state revenues.

However, as swarms of "Gentile" immigrants came into the territory, the Mormons deemed it advisable to set up a lay authority to provide equality before the law for Mormons and non-Mormons alike. A convention was summoned in 1849 at Salt Lake City to draft a constitution and form a government as a state to be admitted to the Union. The state was to be called "Deseret" (honey bee), and the Mormons claimed for it a tremendous area extending from the thirty-third parallel to the border of Oregon, and from the Rocky Mountains to the Sierra Nevada, together with territory now included in southern California and a strip of coastline between Lower California and 118° 30' west longitude. Delegates to Congress were elected, and Young was appointed governor.

Naturally, Congress boggled at this proposal. It rejected the aggrandized boundaries of the territory. Instead, it passed an act authorizing the territorial government's southern boundary at the thirty-seventh parallel, with California bounding it on the west, the Rocky Mountains on the east, and Oregon on the north. However, it softened its ruling by appointing Brigham Young governor of the new territory, to which the original name of "Utah"—after the tribe of Utes, or Yutas, who were the original inhabitants of the region—was restored.

This peaceful compromise between Washington and the Mormons lasted only briefly. It came to an end in 1852, when the Mormon Church issued a proclamation making polygamy a formal article of faith. Until then plural marriages had been sanctioned only quietly and unofficially. The clash that followed was inevitable. Polygamy was only one of its causes. Gentiles and federal officials living in Utah resented the continuing dominance of the Mormon hierarchy in the civil affairs of the territory. They were irritated at the church's claim that the Mormon prophets personified a higher authority than the Constitution of the United States.

When reports reached Washington that the Saints were in *de facto* rebellion against the government, President Buchanan in 1857 removed Young as governor. He assigned Alfred Cumming, formerly Superintendent of Indian Affairs on the upper Missouri, to take his place, and sent twelve hundred soldiers to Utah to assert United States authority. The government, however, neglected to notify Young formally that he had been replaced. Seizing upon this technicality, Young chose to regard the federal troops as "an unruly mob."

"Citizens of Utah," he addressed his people, "we are being invaded by a hostile force." Martial law was declared and the militia were instructed to harry the troops in any way short of bloodshed.

Moving slowly because of its extended supply trains, the army was harassed by bands of Mormon guerrillas. Troop movements were further hampered by heavy snows. When the troops finally converged at Fort Bridger, they found the post burned down by the Mormons.

Like Young, President Buchanan wished to avoid a full-scale conflict, and the "Utah War" fizzled to an indecisive end. However, the day of Utah's isolation from the rest of the nation was drawing to a close. Soon after the Civil War, in which the Mormons remained loyal to the Union, the community found itself in the environs of railroad tracks and mushrooming mining settlements.

As early as 1861, a telegraph line was completed to Salt Lake City, and Brigham Young had wired to Abraham Lincoln, "Utah has not seceded." Two years later, the first mine was discovered; six years later, on May 10, 1869, the Union Pacific Railroad, extended westward from Omaha, and the Central Pacific, stretched eastward from Sacramento, California, met at Promontory Point, Utah, to form the first transcontinental railroad; in 1870, the Utah Central was built to connect with this line. By now, whole communities of Catholics, Methodists, and Presbyterians had moved in with their clergy and churches.

Brigham Young, whose work had brought civilization to a desolate land, died in Salt Lake City on August 29, 1877. In his later years, his sanction of polygamy brought him legal harassment, and after his death polygamy continued to be the major source of friction between Washington and the territory. In their first national platform in 1856, the Republicans had coupled polygamy with slavery as "twin relics" of barbarism. Through one election campaign after another, Democrats also assailed the practice. In 1862 Congress passed the Morrill Act, which made polygamy an act of bigamy, punishable by fine and imprisonment. Twenty years later, the Edmunds Act disfranchised polygamists and prohibited them from holding public office. The Edmunds-Tucker Act of 1887 was the final blow. Under it, the Mormon church was dissolved as a corporation and its property was confiscated by the United States government.

There was no alternative for the Mormons but to surrender. Wilford Woodruff, the new head of the church, issued a proclamation on September 25, 1890, declaring that plural marriages would no longer be sanctioned. He counseled the people to obey the marriage laws of the land. President Benjamin Harrison, on behalf of the United States government, issued a pardon to all persons who renounced the practice of plural marriage, and Congress passed legislation permitting the people of the Utah Territory to frame a constitution and set themselves up as a state. The law decreed, however, that the new constitution must provide for religious toleration and free public school education for all.

In March, 1895, a convention met in Salt Lake City and framed a constitution to meet the requirements. It was ratified in November, and the territory which on six previous occasions had applied for statehood and been rejected was admitted—greatly pared down from its original size—into the family of states. The constitution of the state of Utah was among the first to give women equal rights with men in suffrage and in eligibility to public office.

The rift between the United States government and its new member state was formally and dramatically healed when President William Howard Taft visited Utah on a trip to the Pacific Coast, sixty-two years after Brigham Young had first set eyes on the Promised Land. From the tabernacle in which the elders had once preached rebellion, the President congratulated the Mormons on their establishment of a new Canaan.

The early years of hardship are commemorated in the seal adopted by the state. Against a background of two American flags, an eagle perches with wings outstretched. On a nearby shield, a beehive (the symbol of industriousness) is represented, together with sego lilies as a reminder of the time when the lily bulbs saved the Mormon pioneers from starvation.

America's most celebrated outcasts have contributed much to the nation from which they were so long estranged. The Mormons launched vast irrigation projects that have enabled the entire West to prosper in farming. They gave birth to a new industry—the raising of sugar beets—permitting America to lessen her dependence upon sugar imports. Moreover, they wrested from the mountains around the Great Salt Lake much of the coal and copper needed as fuel for the nation's industry.

The Mormons also played a dominant role in the development of several sister states. As far back as 1855, a party of Mormon migrants who believed they were in Utah settled down in what was later to be the state of Idaho. Non-Mormons were subsequently lured in by the discovery of gold in the Orofino region. The Mormons, however, remained a powerful minority in Idaho, so powerful in fact that the territorial legislature, angered by their practice of polygamy, could retaliate most effectively by taking away their right to vote. However, Idaho was admitted into the Union in July, 1890, and all Mormons who disavowed plural marriages were restored to complete citizenship.

The most curious offshoot of Mormonism occurred in Nevada. During the early days of its settlement, this area was controlled by the Mormons. In fact, it was included in the state of Deseret established by Brigham Young. Subsequently, however, silver was discovered in the Comstock Lode and adventurers poured in from the ends of the earth. By 1861 so many emigrants had moved into the mining camps that a new Territory of Nevada was formed out of western Utah.

"The Desert shall rejoice and blossom as the rose." Nevada, Idaho, Utah—these states fulfill the Biblical prophecy.

CHAPTER VII

Florida, Oklahoma, and Kansas

SINCE HER BEGINNINGS as a union of thirteen states, America had been able to assimilate white men of many diverse cultures and national origins as she expanded her geographical horizons. Two other races of man presented a constant reminder to the new nation that the amalgamation of her peoples was far from complete: the American Indian and the Negro.

The history of the relations between white man and Indian on the American continent is chiefly a succession of wars and of treaties "made to be broken." Considering that the Indians had originally held all the land, and that land was what the white man wanted above all else, war was inevitable—not that the white man introduced war to the Indian, for tribal warfare was an ever-present fact of Indian life. Under the earlier governments of Spain, France, and England, the Indian always had some protection of his person, at least, under the law. The United States government recognized his title to lands held by

Sectional differences on slavery were brought to a head by the Kansas-Nebraska bill of 1854, and Kansas became a battleground of pro- and antislavery factions. The territory rejected a proslavery constitution in 1858, and in January 1861 Kansas entered the Union as a free state. This sketch from *Harper's Weekly* shows President-elect Lincoln raising the new 34-star flag at Philadelphia on February 22, 1861.

The government's policy of making treaties for exchange of desirable tribal lands for out-of-the-way reservations led to the Indian Wars which raged in the Great Plains during most of the second half of the nineteenth century. This sketch from an 1877 issue of Leslie's *Illustrated Magazine* shows one of the methods used by General George Crook to conquer the Apaches of the Southwest and the Sioux of the North: pay "trailers" of their own people to scout for the Army.

The Golden Spike Celebration at Promontory, Utah, marked the joining of the rails of the Union Pacific and Central Pacific Railroads on May 10, 1869, to complete the first transcontinental railroad.

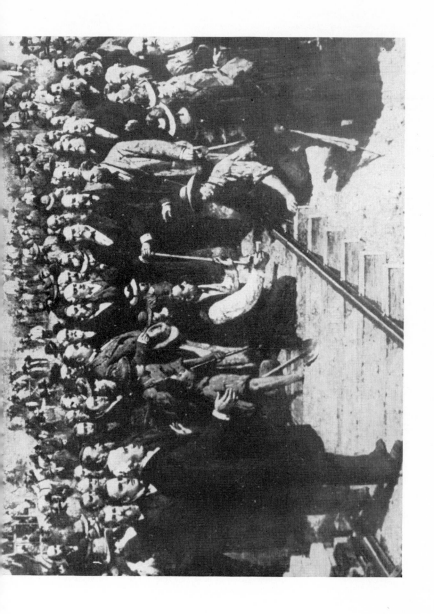

Among the existing records of life in the little-known Northern Plains region in the 1870's is a group of paintings by H. Stieffel of the Fifth U. S. Infantry. Reproduced here is "The Yellowstone River near Fort Keogh, Montana." Courtesy of the New-York Historical Society, New York City

The Homestead Act of 1862 enabled settlers to acquire quarter-sections of public land free, encouraging settlement of the Plains. The Indian Territory, then part of Oklahoma, was opened to Homesteaders at noon on April 22, 1889; when the bugle sounded, an estimated 100,000 persons rushed over the borders to stake their claims.

The aridity which characterizes the Great Plains was long a deterrent to settlement. The Reclamation Act of 1902 provided that proceeds from the sale of public lands be set aside for irrigation projects; construction costs were to be repaid by settlers, making for a revolving fund. Arizona's Roosevelt Dam, completed in 1911, recovered 200,000 acres of desert land for agriculture and to supply water for Phoenix.

At Anchorage, Alaska, the achievement of statehood on January 3, 1959, brought the largest crowd ever assembled in Alaska—30,000 persons—to a ceremony at which the old Organic Act was burned. The pyre consisted of a ton of wood for each of the forty-nine states, and one for Hawaii (then seeking statehood).

Mac's Foto, Anchorage

treaty. The laws were flaunted in many ways, however, and even under the law itself the Indian was often subjected to great hardship.

The mass transplantation of Indian tribes, as the white man expanded his territorial claims, is one instance of such hardship, and in Florida it was well exemplified.

The first white man to set foot in Florida was the Spaniard Ponce de León, who landed on the coast at Eastertime in 1513 and named the land for Easter, which in Spanish is *Pascua florida*. In 1763, at the end of the French and Indian War, Spain ceded the region to England, which had seized it in the course of the war. George III divided the cession into East Florida (the present state) and West Florida, which included those parts of the present states of Alabama and Mississippi south of the thirty-first parallel, and that part of Louisiana lying east of the Mississippi. Then, in 1779, Spain declared war against Great Britain and seized West Florida while the British were trying to stop the revolt of their American colonies. In 1783, Spain formally received from Great Britain both East and West Florida, but their northern boundary was left undefined and England kept her agents active in East Florida. As time went on, matters were further complicated by the growing interest of the United States, which in 1803 acquired Louisiana, in the land which now made up her

On March 12, 1959, the bill was passed which granted statehood to Hawaii. Sixty years earlier, on August 12, 1898, the American flag was first raised over Iolani Palace when the one-time Kingdom, then Republic, of Hawaii was "annexed as a part of the territory of the United States."

Courtesy Archives of Hawaii

southeastern extremity. Florida became a hotbed of rivalries; spies and soldiers of fortune rubbed shoulders with runaway slaves, and smugglers enlisted under the pirate's traditional skull and crossbones.

Spain was by no means willing to relinquish her "right by conquest" to the Floridas, and even claimed the land between the Alleghenies and the Mississippi River which Great Britain had ceded to the United States. What she herself didn't own, said Spain, the Indians owned; the United States had no claim. She built a fort at Vicksburg and one just below the mouth of the Ohio on the west side of the Mississippi River, and made American vessels declare their cargoes.

Toward the end of December in 1806, a Spanish military force moved westward across the Mississippi and set up quarters on the Red River, in territory acquired by the United States through the Louisiana Purchase. The Territories of Orleans and Mississippi raised a five-hundred-man volunteer cavalry to oppose this quiet invasion, but no clash of forces occurred. In 1810, the American settlers, irked by the high taxes levied on their commerce by the Spanish, revolted and organized the Republic of West Florida. President Madison then issued a proclamation formally claiming, by virtue of the terms of the Louisiana Purchase, the territory of West Florida from the Mississippi eastward to the Perdido River. Governor Claiborne of the Territory of Orleans took possession of the region held by the Republic of West Florida, but did not extend his authority beyond the Pearl River; this area was later incorporated into the Territory of Orleans, and eventually became part of the state of Louisiana.

Despite the moves made by both Spain and the United

States, there was still no clash of arms between them. The War of 1812 changed the picture. Spain violated her neutrality by permitting British troops to occupy her forts and use her harbors in Florida, and by countenancing the Seminoles' acts of hostility against American settlers along the Georgia border.

In 1818, Andrew Jackson, now a major general in the regular army and fresh from his victory in New Orleans, invaded Florida with his frontier troops and drove the Spanish garrison out of St. Marks and the Spanish governor from Pensacola—with no loss of life in either case—in what is called the First Seminole War. Jackson then established a provisional government over West Florida. The United States had long been trying to negotiate with Spain for Florida, and there were many Americans who felt that Jackson's invasion could not be justified. Spain, after protesting the action, faced the obvious fact that she would not be able to hold the land forever. On February 22, 1819, therefore, she signed the Adams-Onís treaty ceding to the United States all her lands east of the Mississippi and her ancient rights to the Oregon country for five million dollars. The boundary between Mexico and the United States was also determined, with Texas on the Mexican side of the line.

The treaty was not ratified for two years, and in the meantime Spain's authority was reinstated and the provisional government withdrawn. In 1821 the United States officially occupied Florida, with Andrew Jackson as its governor. In 1822 the Territory of Florida was organized with the present state boundaries. The portion which had been West Florida had been apportioned by Congress ten years earlier as follows: The state of Louisiana received an extension of her area eastward to the Pearl River. The area between the Pearl and the Perdido Rivers, north to the West Florida boundary line (31°), and south to the Gulf of Mexico was annexed to the Mississippi Territory, which was divided into an eastern and a western portion in 1817. The western portion became the state of Mississippi that year, and the Territory of Alabama was organized in the eastern part. Two years later, Alabama entered the Union as the twenty-second state.

By 1819, then, all Florida was under the American flag. Bitterness had long existed between American settlers and the new state's Creeks and Seminoles, and this problem—now that the Spanish were officially out of the picture—became one that had to be dealt with by the federal government.

Under Spanish rule, the Florida Indians had had almost complete freedom of action and the run of the land, because the Spanish were not settlers and had hardly ventured inland at all. Americans were intrepid settlers, and the Deep South's economy was based widely on the plantation system. The citizens of Georgia had had many clashes with the Seminoles, who received runaway slaves into their tribes and refused to surrender them to the whites. As soon as the peninsula was ceded to the United States, Georgians were eager to move into this red man's domain and take it over.

The federal government was now prevailed upon to move all the Seminoles west of the Mississippi, and in 1832, by the treaty of Payne's Landing, a three-year time limit was given the Indians to complete this migration. But the Indians—several thousand braves strong—refused to go. One red man in particular personified the defiant attitude of his race: Osceola, whose name meant "Black Drink."

Osceola was born near the Chattahoochee River in Georgia in about 1804. In 1808, his mother brought him to Florida. He first came to the attention of the American authorities when he accompanied old Micanopy, the head chief of the Seminoles, to a series of negotiations as his interpreter and adviser. His linguistic abilities—he knew Spanish and English—were unusual for an Indian.

Although by reason of his youth and subordinate position he ordinarily sat silently by Micanopy's side, during one meeting with the whites the defiance blazed through his stoic reserve in a manner to warn the Americans of the man they would one day have to contend with. The negotiators had met to discuss once again the signing of a treaty that would remove the Indians from Florida. One treaty had been signed by some of the Seminole leaders, but most of the tribe refused to recognize it. In the midst of the parrying and bickering, Osceola lost his patience. He rushed to the table where the leaders were sitting and plunged his knife through a document. "The only treaty we will execute is with this!"

Goaded by Osceola, in 1835 the Indians did make war. They struck like lightning one dawn and ambushed a company of militia who were transferring supplies from Tampa Bay to Fort King. So sudden was the attack that the first round of Indian fire all but wiped out the company. The regulars fought courageously until their ammunition gave out. By playing dead, two soldiers managed to escape alive.

Intoxicated by this triumph, Osceola made an ominous

vow. "I will dye the land the Great Spirit has given us with the blood of the white man until it is red like the sunset sky."

Osceola took complete charge of military operations, and the cunning with which he pitted his few thousand braves against five times the number of whites is unequaled in the annals of Indian warfare. To offset his inferiority in numbers, he dealt in hit-and-run tactics. He ambushed troops with lightning-like forays, and plunged into the protection of the mysterious swamps where the fresh reserves who came up to support their comrades could not follow.

Unable to pin down this galloping ghost, the soldiers suffered increasing frustration. One general was replaced by another. Each was outwitted by Osceola's techniques of guerrilla warfare. By 1836, the whole southern portion of the Peninsula came under the control of the Seminole chief. Dogs were brought down to track the Indians to their hiding places, but without success. Trained to follow the scent of Negroes, the animals were simply not interested in Indians.

Nevertheless, the Indians fought against mounting odds. The whites threw fresh troops into the struggle and gradually forged a noose around the red men. Hidden away in the jungle, the wives and old men of the tribe toiled for their braves. They denied themselves food so that even their meager portions might be given to the fighters.

On one occasion, when Osceola was away on business, old Micanopy couldn't stand their privations any longer, and with several other old chiefs appeared at the American commander's camp to surrender the nation. However, that night an Indian crept into the camp and made his way unnoticed to where the chiefs were bivouacked. It was Osceola. On his return to the swamps he had learned of the desertion of his colleagues. The magic of his presence inspired new hope. By daylight, the Indian camp was deserted; the warriors had retired to the jungle to continue the fight.

Two more years of semi-starvation under the relentless siege and even Osceola came to realize that further resistance was hopeless. At the urging of his colleagues, he visited the white men under a flag of truce. He was arrested by the Americans and thrown into Fort Moultrie, near Charleston. Utterly crushed, he refused all food. He would not see visitors or talk to anyone. He died on January 30, 1838, at the age of about thirty-three.

Even in death, Osceola continued to dominate his Indians. Indignant over his arrest, they dragged on the war incredibly for another five years, until in 1842 it came to an end. This bloody conflict—the Second Seminole War— was not only a humiliating military experience for the United States. It sapped the treasury of twenty million dollars, and it wasted the flower of the nation's youth. Three American soldiers were killed for every Indian who died under Osceola's command.

With the cessation of hostilities, the majority of Seminoles who survived were moved by the United States government to Indian territory west of the Mississippi. However, a few hid in the Florida swamps and remained there; those are the ancestors of the present-day Florida Indians. These Seminoles did not sign a peace treaty with the United States government until 1934, thereby formally ending what is undoubtedly the longest war in American history.

The actual hostilities, of course, were over in 1842, and not until then was Florida in a condition to be considered for statehood. But for three years the admission was held up by the usual struggle between the slavery and anti-slavery interests in Congress. Then, on March 3, 1845, in accordance with the policy of admitting northern and southern states together to maintain a balance of power, Florida was admitted into the Union together with Iowa (which entered the Union on December 28, 1846) by concurrent acts of Congress. William D. Mosely became the first governor chosen under the new constitution, and Tallahassee, which had been the territorial capital, became the capital of the new state.

Under a supplemental act of Congress, the sixteenth section in every township was set aside for the support of public schools, and five percent of the net proceeds from the sale of public lands was to be set aside for purposes of education.

The Seminoles of Florida, together with the Creeks of Alabama and Georgia, the Chickasaws of northern Mississippi, and the Choctaws of southern Mississippi and parts of Alabama and Georgia, were moved west of the Mississippi to what was designated the Indian Territory. These "Five Civilized Tribes," according to the treaty of 1832, were to have this vast expanse of land "for as long as grass shall grow and rivers run."

It was not until 1823 that the Supreme Court gave a ruling on the Indian's title to land. Chief Justice Marshall delivered the opinion of the court (in the case of Johnson v. McIntosh) that discovery gave title to the country by whose subjects or by whose authority it was made, as against all persons but the Indians as occupants. The Indians had the right of occupancy, not of ownership, and the exclusive power to extinguish that right was vested in that government which might constitutionally exercise it. The land, in other words, could not have two owners; either the Indians or the American government must own it, and ever since the treaty of peace which ended the American Revolution the United States had come unreservedly to possess the land formerly possessed by the monarchs of Europe.

Once this principle was established, the Indian tribes east of the Mississippi were given to understand that the land they presently occupied must be ceded to the United States, and they themselves must move to reservations in the unorganized territory west of Missouri and the Territories of Arkansas and Iowa. Here, under the protection of the federal government, the Five Tribes set up a remarkably advanced government modeled on that of the white man. Each tribe formed a "nation," and established a capital, a written constitution, a legislature, courts of law, schools, and churches.

These red men assimilated other of the white man's ways. Some communities had their own newspaper. Many Indians became prosperous farmers and ranch owners, bringing in white teachers to educate their children. Others became wealthy slaveholders.

The extent of the Indian Territory was greatly reduced in 1854 by the creation of the Kansas and Nebraska Territories, and in the aftermath of the Civil War it shrank to the eastern part of the present state of Oklahoma. Each reduction of Indian lands required that room for the displaced tribes be found within the narrowing boundaries of the Indian Territory; this was done by treaty with tribes already in possession of large tracts of land. The great reduction in Indian lands after the Civil War was brought about by the abrogation of old treaties between the tribes and the United States government. In the southern portion of the original Indian Territory, the natives had allied themselves with the Confederate side, largely because they were within the geographic purview of the South and were convinced that the Confederates would win. It was on the basis of this "defection" that the federal government broke the treaties at the war's end.

After the war there was a long period of Indian warfare which racked the Plains from north to south. There were many causes: the white men were pushing westward in greater and greater numbers, and "boomers," as would-be settlers of Indian lands were called, vied with cattlemen to acquire tracts of these lands which were barred by law from white settlement; government agents responsible for providing supplies to the Indians on reservations were in many cases cheating them; the railroad-builders were making their way across the continent, and the Indians saw the "handwriting on the wall" foretelling of further and further encroachment on their land.

While the Indian had good cause for dissatisfaction, he was by no means guiltless of much wanton bloodshed. His atrocities against the whites—male and female, old and young—aroused hatred in the West that could scarcely be imagined in the civilized eastern cities. As the buffalo became scarce, however, the Indian became less and less well able to sustain himself, and the last days of 1890 saw the last of America's Indian wars.

Two years earlier a delegation of Creek Indians had come to Washington to offer to relinquish to the United

States government their territorial claims. For two and a quarter million dollars, they gave up their entire cession, and these negotiations had scarcely been completed when two Seminole delegates came to ask for the same type of agreement worked out with the Creeks. For close to two million dollars this was accomplished, and Congress immediately authorized the President to open these Oklahoma lands to settlement. On March 23, 1889, President Benjamin Harrison proclaimed "Opening Day" to be April 22, with settlement to be under the terms of the Homestead Law. No territory was ever settled so quickly. Fifty thousand pioneers poured into Oklahoma within twenty-four hours.

For the next two decades the white and red races of Oklahoma and the Indian Territory lived side by side as separate entities, the Indians under their tribal aegis, the Americans under a territorial government organized by Congress in 1890. In 1898 Congress abolished tribal courts in the Indian Territory, transferring all legal cases to the United States courts, and the various tribal school systems were taken over by a federal school administration which instituted a uniform system for all. In 1893 Congress created the Dawes Commission to begin negotiations to extinguish the remaining territorial claims of the Indians with a view to eventual statehood for the Indian Territory. By mid-February of 1899 all five tribes had concluded agreements with the United States government—ratified by tribal vote—to take their lands in severalty (that is, on the basis of individual rather than tribal holdings), to abolish their tribal governments, and to allow themselves to be brought under state and federal laws. The work of the Dawes Commission applied only to the Five Civilized

Tribes. In 1887 the Dawes Act had achieved the same end with all tribes except these five: in exchange for dissolving tribal government and tenure, each head of a family was to receive a quarter-section, with lesser grants to individuals, and conveyance of the land was prohibited for twenty-five years to prevent speculators from acquiring it; the Indian in severalty received American citizenship. By this means it was hoped that the red man would cease to be a ward of the nation and would become a self-sufficient citizen.

An act of March 3, 1901, declared that all the Indians in the Indian Territory were citizens of the United States, and in 1906 Congress passed an act enabling Indians and whites to form a constitution for a state comprised of Oklahoma and the Indian Territory. The following year, on November 16, 1907, the state of Oklahoma (a Choctaw word meaning "home of the red man") was admitted to the Union. One hundred thousand Indians, in a total population of one and a half million persons, were guaranteed all the rights of the majority.

The state constitution was typically Far-western in its philosophy. It provided for initiative and referendum, and added a unique feature—the regulation of public utilities by legislative enactment and a corporation commission.

As a result of their original territorial status, the Indians in Oklahoma today enjoy unique privileges. Unlike the five states in which they may not vote (Utah, New Mexico, Arizona, Colorado, and Washington), the Indians in Oklahoma not only vote but are full citizens in every respect. There is, moreover, no "color line" perceivable. Two of Oklahoma's governors have married women who were part Indian. Will Rogers, America's celebrated humorist, had

Cherokee blood from both sides of his family, and Charles Curtis, Vice President in the Hoover administration, was part Kaw. The state's Indians are prominent in business and on the bench.

Oklahoma today ranks second to Arizona in Indian population, with approximately one eighth of the nation's total. The Osages are the wealthiest of the American tribes. Years ago they were allotted the least desirable land in the north, but under their rocky soil was found the mid-continent oil field. Today combined Indian income from oil, gas, and other minerals approaches sixty million dollars, though some of America's two-hundred-odd tribal groups profit heavily and some not at all. Only in the past decade have steps been taken by Congress to remove some of the Indian lands from federal trusteeship under management of the Bureau of Indian Affairs.

Just as there is not a state in the Union without its Indian traces, so the story of the American Negro belongs to both North and South. Missouri, Kansas, and West Virginia typify the states in which the Negro's struggle for freedom took place. The divisive power of the slavery issue had been keenly felt in Missouri in 1819, but the Compromise of 1820 had left the matter in a state of uneasy rest for thirty years. The Compromise of 1850 did little more than bridge temporarily the ever-widening gap between North and South. Within four years, this breach had widened beyond hope of further compromise.

Until 1821, when Missouri achieved statehood, Kansas had been part of the Missouri Territory, and for another thirty years Kansas remained an unorganized territory. Then, with the first permanent settlement at Fort Leavenworth, the white population burgeoned, and in 1854 Congress organized the Kansas Territory. At the same time, Nebraska, immediately to the north, was granted territorial status. The Nebraska Territory extended to the Canadian border, the northern limit of the Louisiana Purchase; in all, it comprised over 350,000 square miles.

All this was ratified by the Kansas-Nebraska bill put forward by Stephen A. Douglas, which, to the consternation of Northerners, abrogated the provision of the Missouri Compromise banning slavery north of 36° 30'. The new bill provided that the settlers themselves should decide whether either or both territories were to be slave or free.

A fierce struggle ensued which was centered in Kansas. Proslavery men from Missouri moved in in such numbers that the first elections for a territorial legislature, in 1855, resulted in a victory for them. The Free-staters, who challenged the legality of the votes, retaliated by calling a convention at Topeka, setting up a rival government—the Topeka Free State—and drafting a constitution. The United States government refused to recognize the constitution of the Free-staters, and the struggle went on.

There now came upon the scene one of those baffling individuals who are destined to become controversial figures of legend—a man who is labeled by his detractors a madman, and by his admirers a saint.

John Brown, an itinerant farmer, was a fervent abolitionist who, before coming to Kansas, had conducted a station on the "Underground Railroad" at Richmond, Pennsylvania. After five of his sons had gone into the Kansas conflict, he himself, in 1855, laid down his plough and followed them with a wagonload of weapons.

Brown was aroused over the killing of five Free-soil men at Lawrence by the Southerners. Asserting that he was an instrument in the hands of God, he avenged their deaths by slaying an equal number of proslavery men at Osawatomie. Out of this retaliatory bloodletting he envisioned the establishment of a "social Utopia" in America.

When the Free-soil settlers proclaimed an antislavery government in Kansas, two governments, each with an army, locked horns in the territory. John Brown became the leader of the Northern cause. "Old Brown of Osawatomie," as he was called, soon became a terror to the South and a heroic legend in abolitionist circles for his nimble exploits. Assisted by nine men, he routed a troop of thirty at the "Battle of Black Jack," and vanished before the militia could be dispatched to find him. Many times this guerrilla fighter, nearing sixty, was reported captured or dead; but again he would spring up out of the prairie grass, and, after striking a quick and vengeful blow, disappear once more. John Brown now conceived another and even more ambitious plan. Goaded by the Supreme Court's Dred Scott decision of 1857, in which the Court ruled that a Negro was not a citizen and therefore had no redress in a federal court of law, and, further, that Congress had no constitutional right to prohibit slavery in the territories, Brown dreamt of nothing less than a nationwide repudiation of slavery, toward which end the first step would be a revolt of the slaves. He felt himself ordained to lead this revolt.

Brown's audacious, though often childish, efforts on behalf of freedom for the Negro had earned many friends for him in the North. Such men as Whittier and Lowell and Emerson and Thoreau were sympathetic to his schemes, although they realized their impracticability. When they learned of this latest plan, they considered it madness. Such an effort, they felt, could only end in failure.

At Harper's Ferry, Virginia, on the night of October 16, 1859, the legend of John Brown was ineradicably established. Marching at the head of twenty-one followers, he descended upon the peaceful town and occupied the arsenal. His intention was to collect the slaves, lead them off into the hills, and organize them into an army.

Ironically, the first man to be killed in this endeavor to emancipate the Negroes was a Negro—Shepherd Heyward, baggage master at the station. As Brown's raiders approached the arsenal under cover of dark, one of them cried, "Halt!" But Heyward, not understanding what it was all about, continued to move forward. He was shot down.

The sleeping town of Harper's Ferry was taken by surprise. But when daylight broke, wild rumors reached the people. A whole battalion of Northern troops had captured the arsenal, it was reported, and was going to invade the South. The alarm was spread, and as the church bells rang in all the neighboring towns the frightened inhabitants gathered to fend off the attack.

The entire state militia was called out, and late in the evening the United States Marines arrived, under the command of Colonel Robert E. Lee. By this time, only four of Brown's original company were still alive; two of his sons were among the dead. Still he refused to surrender.

On October 18, the inevitable occurred: The Marines forced in the door, and Brown was captured. He was taken to prison, and on October 27 went on trial for treason.

When asked who had sent him to Harper's Ferry, he replied, "No one sent me here. It was my own prompting and the will of God."

On October 31 he was found guilty of conspiring with Negroes toward insurrection, of treason against the Commonwealth of Virginia, and of murder. His sentence was death.

John Brown, a fanatic to the end, never doubted that his deed at Harper's Ferry was justified. Just before his execution on the scaffold on December 2, 1859, he wrote: "I am now quite certain that the crimes of this guilty land will never be purged away but with blood."

The martyrdom of John Brown epitomized the sorest point of the grievances which had for a period of many years been growing between North and South. Sectional interests differed in such national matters as the protective tariff, which benefited the North more than the South, the heavy federal subsidization of northern railroads, and the Northerners' persistent demands for free land—which would promote settlement of the vast northern territories. The issue of slavery, however, was inextricable from any and every sectional problem, and John Brown represented the antislavery North in what were, to the South, its most belligerent activities: abolitionism, the underground railroad, and above all, the wide publication of the conviction that slavery was a moral evil.

New compromises were offered during the winter of 1860-61, but Lincoln and his Republican party would hear of no extension of slavery into any federal territory. The Crittenden Compromise and the Virginia Peace Convention, which would have permitted such extension, were therefore rejected by Congress. The election of Lincoln was the "signal" for South Carolina to take action. On December 20, 1860, she repealed her 1788 ratification of the Federal Constitution. By February 1, 1861, the states of Mississippi, Florida, Alabama, Georgia, Louisiana, and Texas joined her in secession, and on February 4, delegates from these seven states met at Montgomery, Alabama, to draw up a provisional constitution. On February 8, the Confederate States of America was formed, and the next day the congress elected Jefferson Davis provisional President and A. H. Stephens Vice President. After the bombardment of Fort Sumter on April 12–13, four more states joined the Confederacy: Virginia (except the western part), Arkansas, Tennessee, and North Carolina. The border slave states of Delaware, Maryland, Missouri, and Kentucky did not secede.

The story of the Civil War has been told a thousand times and from many viewpoints. Its bearing on the concept of statehood, which concerns us here, is not only that slavery was forever abolished and the plantation system destroyed, but that the relationship between state and federal government was permanently changed.

The act of secession alone raised a constitutional question: Did a state have the reserved right to secede from the Union? This question was by no means a new one. As early as 1810, the Supreme Court was accused of encroaching on the rights of the individual states when it held to a policy which subordinated their rights to those of the national government. Threats of secession had been heard from both North and South since the 1790's, in matters of national policy ranging from tariffs to fugitive slaves. The Kansas-Nebraska bill of 1854 was an attempt to nullify the acts of Congress legislating on slavery within the territories, by recognizing "squatter sovereignty"—that is, the right of the citizens of a state to decide the matter for themselves by majority vote. The result had been chaos and the birth of the militantly antislavery Republican party. The ascendancy of this party to power in 1860, on the basis of its hostility to the Dred Scott decision, was the catalyst which brought the South's thoughts and threats of secession to the state of concerted action.

Lincoln's view of the "reserved right" of the states to secede was plain: "The states have their status in the Union, and they have no other legal status." The very existence of state governments under the Confederate flag was therefore ignored by the President when he issued his Emancipation Proclamation, when he proclaimed a blockade of the ports of the cotton states, when he called for volunteers from all the states of the Union. The Confederate government was not recognized as a belligerent nation; it was not even recognized as a government. All state ordinances of secession were thus looked upon by the United States government as nullities, and the President viewed the states in rebellion as governments which had temporarily fallen into disloyal hands and must be properly reconstructed as soon as possible. To this end, as early as 1862 he appointed provisional military governors in Tennessee, Louisiana, and North Carolina. Their job was to reestablish loyal governments and restore federal authority. In December of 1863, Lincoln issued his Proclamation of Amnesty and Reconstruction, which permitted individuals to receive full pardon and the return of all confiscated property (except slaves) on taking an oath to "support, protect, and defend the Constitution of the United States" and to abide by the acts of Congress and

Presidential proclamations in regard to slavery. As soon as ten percent of the voting population of a seceded state had taken the oath and had duly reestablished a republican state government, this government would be recognized by the President as the "true government of the state" and could once again take its normal place in the Union. By 1864, Louisiana and Arkansas had reconstructed according to this plan—but Congress refused to recognize their restored status or to admit their representatives.

Here was the crux of the problem of reconstruction, which was soon to be so badly solved. There were many Unionists of both parties who felt that Lincoln was being far too liberal, and that, moreover, the determination of the status of the rebellious states was the business of Congress, not of the executive. Many saw the seceded states as having in fact withdrawn from the Union, thereby losing all identity as duly constituted states. After Lincoln's death, Andrew Johnson tried to follow his predecessor's benign policy toward the defeated South. During the summer of 1865, when Congress was not in session, Johnson continued the policy of amnesty toward all qualified persons who took the prescribed oath, and appointed "provisional governors" for North Carolina, Georgia, Mississippi, Alabama, South Carolina, and Florida. These governors called conventions to amend the state constitutions, and by the end of the year all the states except Texas had held conventions; they had abolished slavery, amended their constitutions as necessary, and held Congressional elections. All but Mississippi and Florida had ratified the Thirteenth Amendment to the Federal Constitution.

When Congress reconvened in December of 1865, it refused to support this program instituted by Lincoln and carried on by Johnson. It refused to seat the South's elected representatives. The state governments were declared to be provisional only; the South was divided into five districts under United States military jurisdiction; new constitutional conventions were called, at the elections of which the newly-enfranchised Negroes voted while many whites were disqualified. Not until 1870 was the last of the new state constitutions ratified. At this point state government was at last restored throughout the South and federal supervision withdrawn. By this time the Fourtenth and Fifteenth Amendments had been added to the Federal Constitution, by which the Negro won a guarantee of his civil rights against any state legislation to the contrary, and the right to vote.

The abuses which followed on the reconstruction program of Congress may be followed in greater detail in a number of works on the subject. Briefly, the Southern states' governments went through a trying period in which four million emancipated, but uneducated, slaves won a voice in politics which they had neither the experience nor the ability to use wisely at the time. "Carpet baggers" from the North seduced their vote, while the Negroes themselves won little in the way of benefit by act of Congress. Emancipated, they were free from servitude on the plantation, but had no place else to go. Many stayed with their former masters on a tenant-farmer basis, but thousands of the illiterate, footloose, and unwise found themselves in a far worse condition, physically at least, than before. The Ku Klux Klan, reputed to have originated in Tennessee in 1866, was the disfranchised white men's retaliation against the new power of the former slaves who now held the reins of government under the guidance of Northern Republicans.

In short, the reconstruction policies of Congress disrupted the state governments of the South for a decade and more, chiefly because the spirit of sectionalism—one cause of the Civil War—was not satisfied by mere military victory.

The decade during which the Civil War was fought saw the admission of four new states. Kansas came in on January 29, 1861, just before the war started, and Nebraska, on March 1, 1867, was the first state admitted after it ended. The Territories of Colorado and Dakota, constituted in 1861, and of Idaho in 1863, had been carved, wholly or partly, from the Nebraska Territory of 1854, so that by 1867 Nebraska had been reduced to its present area.

West Virginia entered the Union during the most critical part of the war, two weeks before the battles of Gettysburg and Vicksburg. For more than fifty years the western part of the state of Virginia had had grievances against the more powerful eastern section, chiefly on the matter of equal representation in the General Assembly and, after the Revolution, in the state legislature. When Virginia voted to secede from the Union on April 17, 1861, forty counties in the western part of the state opposed the move, and on June 11 held an election which gave Virginia two governors—one with allegiance to the United States and the other a Confederate.

Determined to become a separate state, the western counties held a constitutional convention in Wheeling, which met on November 26. The constitution was adopted by a vote of 18,061 to 514, and was approved by Congress the following year—but only after it had been amended to provide for the gradual emancipation of the slaves. On June 20, 1863, by proclamation of President Lincoln, West Virginia became the thirty-fifth state.

Nevada followed in 1864, entering in a highly unorthodox way. President Lincoln issued his Emancipation Proclamation in 1863, but in order to win the constitutional amendment necessary to make the emancipation of slaves enforceable he needed another antislavery state represented in Congress. Although Nevada had less than one sixth the number of inhabitants normally required for statehood, the President and Congress admitted the territory under emergency provisions. To facilitate approval of the state constitution, Lincoln asked that it be telegraphed to Washington. On October 31, 1864, Nevada was admitted as the thirty-sixth state.

Thus, at the end of the war, there were thirty-six states in the Union—all those east of the Mississippi (Minnesota in 1858 and West Virginia in 1863 were the last of these), and Texas, Kansas, California, Oregon, and Nevada. The country which remained was the dry, the mountainous, the all but inaccessible. Between 1867 and 1907 ten states were carved from the Plains and the Rockies, made penetrable by railroads, cultivable by laborious irrigation projects, and attractive to settlers by the Homestead Law. By 1907, forty-six states spanned the continent; not until 1912 were there forty-eight.

CHAPTER VIII

Arizona and New Mexico

In ARIZONA and New Mexico, there are people still alive who remember the days of Geronimo, the outlaw Apache chief. For a few, Indian scalpings are not merely a matter for the history books, but a living memory. The first white child born in Tucson died fairly recently. These two southwestern states entered the Union within a month of each other in 1912—the last to be admitted before Alaska and Hawaii in 1959.

The formal admission of the Southwest into the United States was a result of the war with Mexico which erupted in 1846 because of a boundary dispute over Texas. General Stephen W. Kearny was assigned command of the Army of the West to invade New Mexico. By the time he reached Santa Fe, opposition had crumbled. He entered the town in August, 1846, raised the flag over the *palacio* of the Spanish governor, and a month later inaugurated a civil government. Final transfer was made by the treaty of Guadelupe Hidalgo in 1848. (In 1853, the United States

bought an additional strip of land from Mexico—the Gadsden Purchase—which today comprises the southern edge
of Arizona and the southwestern corner of New Mexico.)

It soon became apparent to Congress that Nuevo Mexico
was too large for efficient administration, and that a division should be made. Tucson, the biggest city, was 250
miles from the county seat at Mesial and more than five
hundred miles by stage from Santa Fe, the territorial capital. Accordingly, in 1863 the United States government
set up the separate territory of Arizona (derived from the
Pima Indian word meaning "little spring"). This reduced
New Mexico by almost half, and the territory was reduced
further when Congress, in 1867, attached all her lands
north of the thirty-seventh parallel to Colorado, leaving
New Mexico with her present limits.

Some strange social communities mushroomed in the
Arizona territory. One of them outdid the New England
Transcendentalists with their Stony Brook Farm and Fruit-
lands. The village of Tubac, two hundred miles north of
Tucson (population 800), had, in the words of one contemporary, "no law but love; no government, no taxes, no
public debt; no politics. It was a community in a perfect
state of nature."

In this "Utopia," local paper money known as *boletas,*
redeemable in silver, was the medium of exchange. As few
of the Mexicans could read, the different denominations
of currency were indicated by the pictures of animals. A
pig denoted "one bit" (twelve and a half cents); a calf,
twenty-five cents; a rooster, fifty cents; a horse, seventy-five
cents.

One of the glories of pioneer Arizona settlements was

their newspapers. The printing press was brought in with the first pick and shovel, but there were numerous obstacles to doing business. The Arizona *Tri-Weekly Star,* whose name was later changed to the *Daily Star,* and whose editor, L. C. Hughes, eventually became governor of the state, had a news wire which was strung on giant cactus and mesquite trees. Hughes could never be sure that a message would get through, since teamsters frequently cut down the wires and used them to repair their wagons.

Editors in those days had their own notions about the value of news. A new shipment of groceries that came in safely for the general store was a banner event. But since violence occurred daily, it was reported casually or even ignored. An amusing illustration is provided by the *Prescott Miner:*

> Charlie Genung is in from Peeples Valley to buy some bacon. The weather is cold in his locality and there is little news. He says that he and his neighbors were annoyed last week by a bunch of Yavapais who came into the valley and ran off with a couple of mules. Genung and several other ranchers pursued and killed the redskins. George Brown got a bad arrow wound in the shoulder.

New as its political orientation is, the Southwest, according to archeological findings, is the oldest continuously inhabited section of the United States. Santa Fe, the capital of New Mexico, was a thriving Spanish community more than a century before the United States was born. Here is the country of the prehistoric cliff-dweller, the mesa, and the Indian pueblo immortalized by artists. Here is the country of the Spanish conquistadors, the Santa Fe trail, and Billy the Kid. And here nature's genius for improvisation ran riot, splitting the earth into the Grand Canyon, splashing the desert with upjuttings of sandstone, freezing trees into a petrified forest.

The territory is dominated by three races—American, Spanish, and Indian. New Mexico is the only bilingual state in the Union. Its constitution was ratified in both English and Spanish, and until recently interpreters were needed by the legislature to carry on its business. To this day legal notices are published in both tongues, although the study of English is mandatory in the schools.

The first white man to venture into what is now New Mexico and Arizona proper was Francisco Vasquez de Coronado, who in 1540 led an army north from Mexico City in search of the legendary "Seven Cities of Çibola." Although the route he followed is not certain, Coronado is believed to have followed the San Pedro River to the Gila, then north to the sources of the Little Colorado. After a vigorous fight with the Indians, he entered one of the "seven cities"—actually a Pueblo village—calling it "Granada." For two years he searched for the gold which legend reported abounded in the region, but he found nothing but starvation and disease. He returned to Mexico City with the ruins of a once formidable army.

In the sixteenth century, Franciscan missionaries initiated missionary work among the Indians along the Rio Grande. These pueblo-dwelling red men of the early Southwest, including the Zuñi and Hopi tribes, and their wild, nomadic neighbors—the Navahos, Apaches, and Comanches—have provided a field day for sociologists. The savages believed that animals had the gift of speech; that the coyote first brought man fire; that the hibernating bear communed with the spirits of the dead and imparted this wisdom to the tribal medicine men. The Indian asked forgiveness of the animal he was about to kill, assuring the victim that hunger alone made the act necessary, and promising it that a happy future awaited it in the life to come.

Relations between the Spaniards and the Indians had started off smoothly enough with the arrival of Coronado in 1540, but the incredible harshness of the conquistadors toward the natives undid all the missionary priests' efforts to promote Christianization. Missions were founded, and in many cases the Indians had very amicable relations with their neighboring *padres,* but by and large the natives became Christians in name only while continuing to observe their tribal religions.

When Mexico won its independence from Spain in 1821, the people of the Southwest rejoiced; and when the Republic of Mexico was set up in 1824 they rejoiced again. (By now, Spaniards so far outnumbered Indians in the region that the natives posed less of a problem than revolutionists and invaders.) The Republic included the present states of Arizona and New Mexico, as well as a vast amount of surrounding territory in the Far West. It was to be only a matter of time before another change would be made in the administration of the Southwest, partly because many Americans—chiefly those who had moved into Texas—began to push on to the Southwest as reports of its rich resources reached them. The value of merchandise sent by New England merchants over the trail between Independence, Missouri, and Santa Fe increased from $15,000 in 1822 to $450,000 in 1844.

Texas won her independence from Mexico in 1836, and in 1848, at the conclusion of the Mexican War, the United

States received the more than 850,000 square miles of her present territory that includes the present Southwest. This area added to the national domain became at last a "legitimate" new frontier.

In the 1850's, eastern political leaders, supported by such thinkers as Horace Greeley, editor of the New York *Tribune,* lobbied vigorously for Congress to provide land to settlers free of charge. Indeed, the platform of the newly organized Republican Party, upon which Abraham Lincoln ran, featured a promise of free homesteads for bona-fide settlers of the West. The Homestead Act was finally passed by Congress in 1862. It offered to any citizen or applicant for citizenship who was the head of a family or over twenty-one years of age, a maximum of 160 acres of unappropriated public land title free after five years of continuous residence and payment of a small registration fee.

Moreover, this land was to be exempt from attachment for any debt contracted prior to the patent date. A purchaser had the alternative of buying the land after six months' residence for $1.25 an acre. In 1864, more Americans were brought into the picture when a Homestead bonus was handed out to soldiers with two years' service in the Union Army, subject to a year's residence on the land.

It was this legislation which brought a rush of settlers into the Far West and Southwest after the Civil War. By the turn of the century, 147,000,000 acres had been disposed of in this way. (Beginning in 1910, Congress began withdrawing public lands, and in 1935 President Roosevelt closed the areas still remaining within the forty-eight states for conservation purposes. The Homestead Law is still in effect in Alaska, however.)

While the Homestead Law brought thousands of prospective landowners across the hundredth meridian, a new kind of legislation was needed for the "high and dry" half of the country, which extends to the Rockies from the center of the Dakotas, Nebraska, Kansas, Oklahoma, and Texas, and includes the arid lands of New Mexico.

The farmer east of the hundredth meridian had, generally speaking, only the problem of clearing his land of rocks and trees. West of the meridian, however, his problem was more serious: the soil was excellent, but too dry for profitable cultivation. In the Southwest, no forests stood in the farmer's way because there wasn't water enough to sustain them.

In 1877, therefore, Congress passed the Desert Land Act, which differed from the Homestead Act in that it did not require residence on the land, it permitted a maximum of 640 acres to be entered, and it required that the land be reclaimed (irrigated) by the entryman by the end of three years. Bringing water into desert lands is a difficult and expensive undertaking, but Congress was unwilling to surrender public tracts large enough to attract corporations or individual investors.

In order to determine the real extent of the irrigation problem, a United States Geological Survey was undertaken in 1879. The director of this project was Major John Wesley Powell, who ten years before had performed the all-but-unbelievable feat of "shooting the rapids" of the Grand Canyon.

Powell was a veteran of the Civil War who had lost his right arm at the battle of Shiloh, but even with this handicap he undertook stunts that the fittest of men would have blanched at. He had no college degree, yet he became a curator of the museum at Illinois Wesleyan University, so well known were his talents for scientific research.

It was during one of his specimen-collecting expeditions that Powell first saw the immense canyons of the Colorado River. Immediately he devised a bold plan. He would explore the river for the Smithsonian Institution. In those days, little was known about the Colorado River from its source to where it enters into the valley of the Grand Wash, except what could be seen from the few places where descents had been made to the shore. Major Powell hoped to solve the mystery by traveling down the river himself. If the trip were successful, he would have answered a major geographical question. The expedition he had in mind would carry him through the depths of the Grand Canyon of Arizona, into whose abyss only a handful of white herders and trappers had ever looked. Only one party of explorers had ever tried to penetrate the canyons of the Colorado, and the whole group had perished in the rapids several miles from their point of embarkation. The Indians spoke of underground passages, and of evil spirits that dwelled in the winding depths.

In spite of these tales, Powell set about preparing for the exploration. He obtained four lightweight rowboats with waterproof compartments, and recruited a crew of nine men. The costs of the trip were paid by the Smithsonian Institution. When it became generally known that this one-armed scientist had determined to navigate a thousand-mile stretch of the Colorado, shooting over uncharted rapids in a rowboat, he was considered mad.

The party stored up enough rations to last for a ten-month voyage. In December, 1868, they bivouacked for the winter in Utah, in the area where the Union Pacific Railroad crossed the Green River. Here they awaited the melting of the mountain snows. On the morning of May 24, 1869, they embarked on their journey. Their plan was to row from daybreak until sundown, camping on the shore at night.

At the very outset they encountered fierce rapids that capsized their boats and threatened to drown them all. Near encounters with death became almost daily experiences.

As they continued mile after mile through unmapped gorges and over formidable rapids and difficult portage paths, they passed from Colorado into Wyoming and headed toward Arizona's Grand Canyon. Here the scenery was breathtaking. The walls of rock shone like marble, sparkling with many colors and rising to overpowering heights. A series of caves hollowed into the sides of the canyon had been used as fortresses by ancient tribes of Indians.

The weeks turned into months as the crew persisted down the labyrinthine Colorado, past shores so sparse it took the navigators hours to find wood enough to make a fire for cooking.

By examining the quality of rocks, Powell was able to calculate whether a stretch of river ahead would prove perilous. Soft strata meant that the water would be calm. Hard strata warned of dangerous currents.

During the second week in August, the party reached the mouth of the Grand Canyon in Arizona, so named by Powell himself. Where the river entered the canyon, it cascaded almost a mile between mammoth walls of granite, and from there on the current was swifter and the river narrower than before. It turned so precipitously that often the explorers could not see more than a hundred yards ahead.

Secured by a strap extended between the gunwales, Powell posted himself on deck as his boat bucked like a bronco. Ceaselessly and strenuously he fended with his oar to prevent the boat from being dashed against the rocks. Fickle weather added considerably to the wretchedness of the trip. Torrential showers were followed by sunshine that heated the atmosphere to 115 degrees; then suddenly the sky might darken and the air turn frigid. The crew could find no comfort; they were hatless and their blankets had been lost.

On August 29, at noon, ninety days and over a thousand miles after their embarkation from the Green River, Powell and his party emerged from the Grand Canyon. They were the first human beings to shoot its depths and survive.

While the explorations of scientists brought to Americans a better understanding of the Southwest, the lure that succeeded in bringing settlers into the territory in great numbers was of a more mundane nature. It was the same magnet that had tempted Coronado three centuries earlier: gold.

A cluster of legends has developed around the Arizona miner. An entire folk literature has also grown up around the burro, the stubborn little animal known more familiarly as the jackass. Brought originally to the Southwest by the conquistadors because of his sure-footedness and ability to do without food and rest for long periods on the trail, the burro, according to old-time Arizonans, was responsible for the discovery of a number of important gold fields. In foraging for food, he frequently assumed the role of a prospector, stumbling across precious mineral deposits.

A burro belonging to one Henry Wickenburg is said to have been responsible for the greatest gold discovery in Arizona history. One morning, the animal wandered from camp, and when Wickenburg looked for it in the surrounding hills, it tried to elude him. The miner, angered, threw stones. They were heavy and fell short of the mark. Examining them more closely, Wickenburg discovered that what he had thrown were not stones at all, but nuggets of gold. In this accidental fashion, so the story goes, the lucrative Vulture Mine was discovered.

Other types of adventurers, more greedy and less scrupulous even than the gold miners, were attracted to the Southwest. The theme of human greed has motivated a galaxy of novels and plays. Stranger than fiction, however, was the audacity of an Arizonan who, in the summer of 1883, threatened to reshape the map of the Southwest, wipe out the property of thousands of settlers, and bring the entire region under his dictatorship.

One morning the people of Phoenix gathered in front of the posters that had been nailed up overnight throughout the city:

Aviso. Hearken ye, all men. That person or persons now situated on La Baronía de Arisonac, known also as the Peralta Grant, will be subject to removal unless proper arrangements are made and set forth as a matter of record. By order of the Baron, Don James Addison de Peralta-Reavis.

The crowds that gathered to read the placards were bewildered and angry. But above all they were curious. Later in the day the Phoenix press carried the entire story, and it was one of the most amazing tales ever to appear in an American newspaper. The person responsible for the posters was Don James Addison, a mysterious figure known as the Baron de Arisonac. He declared that he possessed title not only to the entire city of Phoenix, but to nearly twenty thousand square miles of territory in Arizona and New Mexico.

If the Baron's claim could be proved, everybody living in that area would find himself dispossessed. This acreage with its farms, buildings, railways, and mines would become a kingdom within the borders of the United States, and Phoenix would be a city within that kingdom. Every inhabitant would be subservient to the Baron. All would be required to pay him tribute in the form of rent.

The incensed population gathered in a mass meeting. They established a committee to investigate Don James and see what they could do to safeguard their rights. But thorough examination showed that there was little they could do; the Baron's claim appeared to be beyond dispute.

The grant, he said, was a gift from King Ferdinand to his soldier kinsman, Miguel de Peralta, on December 20, 1748. He could produce copies of all the records, and could lead any skeptic to the archives where the originals were kept.

Before such documentary evidence, the members of the committee—confronted with the total loss of their property and their independence—were stunned. Was he a lunatic, or an honest man with a just claim?

When all the evidence was in, after the documents had

been checked and rechecked, there seemed to be no question as to the validity of the Peralta claim. He had even produced an affirming letter from Santa Anna, the President of Mexico.

In spite of the evidence, however, there were a few who continued doggedly to argue this Peralta Grant. They engaged lawyers, scholars, handwriting experts, and investigators to track down Don James' story, step by step, document by document. The dusty shelves of archives were searched, the parchments were scrutinized with microscopic closeness, the most exhaustive research was conducted.

But in the end there was a single decision: "The right of the Baron de Arisonac to the Peralta Grant is beyond dispute."

One by one the fighters abandoned the struggle. Skepticism gave way to belief. The Southern Pacific Railroad purchased its independence for fifty thousand dollars. The Silver King Mine paid Don James a first installment of twenty-five thousand dollars toward the price of their freedom. Landowners on his "domain" submitted to his demands and bought him off. Before long Don James Addison was the richest as well as the most powerful man in the West. And he lived extragavantly, as befitted a king. He invested his money in lucrative mining, lumber, and real estate ventures; he purchased palatial homes in St. Louis, Washington, and Mexico City; his carriages were drawn by horses with harnesses of silver and gold.

Still, there were a few die-hard skeptics who continued to believe that he was a fraud. Then, one investigator who went to Mexico City to examine a Peralta document turned up a clue. The document consisted of several sheets of old parchment, dated September 3, 1759. In scrutinizing one of the sheets, the examiner inadvertently raised it to the light. Then his eyes widened. The sheet carried the watermark of a paper mill in Wisconsin. This mill, he knew, had been built just recently—almost a century after the date on the record. Impatiently he held up the other sheets to the light. They had no watermark.

It was clear now what had happened. The sheet with the watermark was a forgery. It had obviously been substituted for another sheet that had been taken out of the document. And here was the telling point: All the details relating to the Peralta Grant were to be found on the new sheet. The other sheets—which were authentic—did not make a single reference to the "grant."

With this clue, the entire story of the Peralta Grant could now be retraced. From beginning to end, it proved to be a hoax.

At his trial, James Addison Reavis was revealed as an American born in Missouri, with no Spanish ancestry whatever. He had discovered his talent for forgery when, as a Confederate soldier in the Civil War, he had signed his captain's name on a pass and secured with it a leave of absence. After the war he perfected his skill and before long found himself in the border city of Santa Fe, a gathering place for the scoundrels of the day. Since the ownership of much of the land in New Mexico was under dispute as a result of the treaty of Guadelupe Hidalgo, the territory offered rich opportunities for the unscrupulous—particularly as the treaty contained an article providing for the settlement of the ancient land grants made by the Spanish kings to various individuals before Mexico's emergence as an independent state.

One of the results of the treaty was the many claims—fraudulent as well as valid—to these ancient land grants. To sift out the true claims from the false, the American government had set up a bureau of investigation at Santa Fe. James Addison Reavis had got himself a job at this bureau, and here was born the plot for the historical fantasy that he almost turned into reality.

Reavis was sentenced to imprisonment in the Santa Fe penitentiary. When he emerged six years later, a poor and lonely man, the former King of the Golden West could only recapture the days of his glory in the old newspaper files that were now a part of this fabulous legend.

The Southwest's first twenty-five years as United States territory were hard and disappointing. By the treaty of Guadelupe Hidalgo, New Mexicans who "shall not retain the character of citizens of the Mexican Republic" were to be incorporated into the union of American states, and "admitted in opportune time (at the discretion of the Congress of the United States) to the enjoyment of all the rights of citizens of the United States, in accordance with the principles of the Constitution. . . ." In the meantime, their liberty, property, and the exercise of their religion were guaranteed. From 1850 until 1911, however, their petitions for statehood were fruitless.

New Mexico's first application for statehood, in 1850, had submitted a constitution which contained—among other liberal provisions—a clause prohibiting slavery. At that time, though everything necessary had been done and a duly elected senator was sent to Washington to present the constitution and ask for admission to the Union, Congress had just passed on the Compromise of 1850, which gave territorial status to New Mexico. The elected senator returned home, and Congress appointed a territorial governor.

The Gadsden Purchase of 1853 enlarged the Territory of New Mexico, and ten years later Congress set off Arizona as a separate territory. By now the Civil War was under way, and both Arizona and New Mexico became battlegrounds for Union and Confederate troops; since most of the American settlers in the area were Southerners, the sentiments of this region were strongly proslavery. Arizona had delegates in the Confederate Congress.

Not until 1912 did New Mexico and Arizona win their long struggle for statehood. New Mexico nearly made it in 1875, but the bill failed on a technicality after both houses had approved it. The same thing happened in 1888. In 1906 the Joint Statehood Act united the Indian Territory with Oklahoma and offered the same type of union to the Territories of New Mexico and Arizona, for a state to be called Arizona. A vote on the question was to be taken in each of the territories, and, strangely enough, it was Arizona which rejected the proposal. Several more attempts were made toward obtaining joint statehood, but all failed. A separate attempt by Arizona failed in 1908, but on January 20, 1910, Congress passed an act enabling the governor of Arizona to proclaim an election for delegates to a constitutional convention. The constitution which resulted was considered highly radical—but Oklahoma had already paved the way with its own constitution in 1907. President Taft insisted that Congress adopt an enabling act for New Mexico in June, and on January 21, 1911, another highly "radical" constitution was overwhelmingly approved by the voting citizens of the territory.

Sixty-two years had passed since the admission of California, and sixty-six years since that of Texas, yet they, too, had been part of Mexico until the 1840's. Nevada and Utah, from the same "cut of cloth," had become states in 1864 and 1896 respectively. The Southwest had lagged behind not only because of its aridity, but also because it existed in isolation.

There were no roads connecting Arizona with East or West. Twenty thousand miles of railroad track were laid in the 1850's, but chiefly in the North and East. In the next decade, another twenty thousand miles were laid, chiefly in the West. On May 10, 1869, the Union Pacific, built westward from Council Bluffs, Iowa, and the Central Pacific, extended eastward from San Francisco, were joined at Promontory Point, Utah, to form the first transcontinental railroad. But Arizona was far from the iron roads until 1877, when the Southern Pacific line from California reached Yuma. In 1880 the tracks finally reached Tucson.

When the first locomotive steamed into Tucson in 1880 amid the thunder of cannons, the citizens of the pueblo sent telegrams to the President of the United States, the governor of the territory, and other dignitaries. One message, according to local annals, was addressed to the Pope:

The Mayor of Tucson begs the honor of reminding Your Holiness that this ancient and honorable pueblo was founded by the Spaniards under the sanction of the Church more than three centuries ago, and to inform Your Holiness that a railroad from San Francisco, California, now connects us with the Christian World.

Three jokesters hunted up the telegraph operator and persuaded him to join in a little prank. The telegram was not sent to Rome, but that evening, during a banquet, a "manufactured" reply was delivered and read aloud:

> His Holiness the Pope acknowledges with appreciation receipt of your telegram informing him that the ancient city of Tucson has at last been connected by rail with the outside world and sends his benediction, but asks for his own satisfaction where in the Lord's name is Tucson?

In 1881 the Southern Pacific track joined that of the Atchison, Topeka, and Santa Fe at Deming, New Mexico. Within the next four years, more than a thousand miles of railway were constructed in New Mexico. At last the Southwest had access to the nation's commerce, and to Arizona and New Mexico this meant progress and a new life.

New Mexico's constitution was subjected to Congressional haggling from March until August of 1911, when President Taft at last received from Congress a resolution approving the constitutions of both New Mexico and Arizona. The President warmly approved New Mexico's constitution, but, as an ex-judge, he boggled at Arizona's, which contained a clause providing for the popular recall of judges—that is, the people's right to remove them by vote at a general election. Since the two constitutions had been submitted under a single resolution, both were rejected when the President refused to sign it. (Ex-President Theodore Roosevelt was strongly in favor of the controversial clause.)

The framers of Arizona's constitution obligingly deleted the clause, and on August 21 Taft signed the resolution which brought New Mexico in as the forty-seventh state and Arizona as the forty-eighth. (New Mexico was formally admitted on January 6, 1912, and Arizona on February 14.)

Now safely within the fold, the Arizonans crossed up President Taft at their first state election by voting an amendment to their constitution providing for popular recall of judges.

It is in a way ironic that a region which America had "left behind" for so long entered statehood with constitutions so broadly social. Arizona's constitution provided that "an employers' liability law shall be passed" making employers liable for the death or injury of an employee in any case where the employee did not bring the misfortune on himself through negligence. In the area of child labor, Arizona prohibited the employment of any child under the age of fourteen in any gainful occupation during the school year; private industry was given a number of investment incentives to expand and prosper.

Over a century ago Daniel Webster, decrying America's expansionist policies westward, thundered: "Arizona is a barren waste of prairie dogs, cactus, and shifting sands, incapable of producing anything and therefore not worth retaining."

Today the "barren waste" of Arizona is a grassland for one of the nation's most lucrative beef cattle and sheep growing industries; the "shifting sands," irrigated by some of the world's hugest dams, yield an abundance of fruits rivaling those of Florida and California; and Arizona ranks first in the nation in copper production.

Daniel Webster was a poor prophet, indeed!

CHAPTER IX

The Plains States

THE SETTLEMENT of the United States followed a pattern that would seem strange to anyone unfamiliar with North American geography. The westward movement of the earliest pioneers had been briefly discouraged by the Appalachian Range, but only until it was learned that smooth, fertile lands lay beyond the mountains. The Northwest Territory had had its "barrier" of Indian tribes, but the land was good and the American frontiersman lost little time in wresting it from the natives. The fertile lands of east Texas attracted American settlers when the land still belonged to Mexico. The Mississippi was not considered a hurdle to cross; its fertile valley drew westward many farmers who found the eastern shores getting "crowded" by 1820.

Suddenly, however, the tide of westward expansion— which typically appropriated the land it crossed—stopped short. It had come to another barrier: the Great Plains. Now the pattern changed. The objective of the westward push became the Far West, well over a thousand miles away. To get there it was necessary to cross the Plains, but this was done as quickly as possible. There was no stopping along the way—at least, no voluntary stopping.

The American pioneer was venturous, willing to take great risks when the goal was worthwhile, but he was no more willing to take senseless punishment than the Spaniards had been. They, too, had avoided the Great Plains; from Coronado in 1528 to the end of the Spanish-Mexican regime in 1848, the Spanish made no attempt to settle on the Plains. There were two obvious reasons for this. One was that the Plains had nothing to offer the Spaniards in the way of mineral wealth, and the other was that the Plains Indians could not only not be subjugated and converted, like the Pueblo Indians of Mexico, but were formidable warriors well able to drive back any attempt of the white man to invade their territory. Thus, until 1848, when Spanish-Mexican "rule" ended, that part of the Plains region which had been nominally theirs was still in actual possession of the Indian, the buffalo, and the smaller animals which thrived on the vast expanse of grasses.

Until the time of the Civil War, this was the state of the entire Plains region—the heart of the Louisiana Purchase. From North to South, from the present Montana and the western Dakotas to the upper Rio Grande, tribes of Sioux, Blackfoot, and Crow, Ute, Cheyenne, and Kiowa, Comanche and Apache, roamed the grasslands with little interference from white men. Mounted on the horses they had first acquired from the Spanish in the early sixteenth century, they hunted the buffalo on which their lives depended—for food, clothing, and shelter—and trained themselves to perfection in the skills of warfare.

The reasons why westward-bound Americans limited themselves to a few well-worn trails across the Plains were not the same reasons the Spanish had had. To the Spanish, the lack of water and timber which characterize the Plains region were not discouraging; Spain is much like the West in these respects. As for the Indian menace, the American pioneer had a history of coping with it ruthlessly enough in the East, and was to do battle with the natives of the West as soon as their treeless, arid land became valuable in his eyes. To the American settler, land had value only insofar as it could be made productive. The legend of the "sandy waste," the "Great American Desert," which had been in circulation since Major Stephen H. Long's exploration of the upper Arkansas, Canadian, and Red River valleys in 1819-20, deterred American interest in Plains settlement for decades.

The line at which the broad, steady sweep of westward migration stopped short, except for some heroic treks to the Far West, was the 98th meridian. Once the westward-bound pioneer crossed this line, he found himself in a dry and treeless land totally unlike the humid, forested East which he had conquered with comparative ease. No wood was at hand to build houses and fences with. The rivers were too shallow for navigation—some dried up completely in dry seasons—and their waters had an offensive taste. Springs and streams were rarities. No natural markers existed for miles and miles on end to give the traveler a sense of location; as far as he could see in any direction the land was flat, unbroken, like a smooth sea of grass. The north and south winds blew strongly and incessantly.

One point which the Spaniard and the American did have in common was an avid interest in exploitable mineral wealth; furs, too, held an irresistible attraction for the adventurous and the avaricious. Though they were interested only in locating mines and securing pelts for trade, the Americans who began to venture across the Plains to reap these riches of the Far West in the early nineteenth century contributed to the world a greater wealth of information about the American West than did most of the government's explorers. Following on the heels of Lewis and Clark, the trappers preceded every subsequent official exploration party, the most notable of which were that of Zebulon M. Pike across the middle Plains in 1806-07 and the Stephen H. Long Expedition. The objectives of the official expeditions were, like those of the trappers and miners, the Rockies and the West Coast; it was along the trails marked by these first pioneers that trade and migration between East and West were to be carried on for a period of more than a half-century.

Fur trappers learned the northern Rockies by heart before the trail of Lewis and Clark had turned cold; the Santa Fe trail was blazed by traders who found the door to New Mexico's capital open to them after Mexico won her independence from Spain in 1821. The Oregon trail, later the route of numberless migrations, was opened in the mid-1820's by Jedediah Strong Smith's party of trappers in search of beaver streams to the west of the Rockies. Though the beaver supply ran out by the mid-1840's, bringing the Mountain Men's regime to an end, the knowledge of the Far West that the trappers had gleaned was to bring hordes of settlers across the Plains a decade and more later.

The pause at the 98th meridian lasted from about 1840 until the late 1880's, when the coming of the farmers was to close at last this "last frontier." Within this time-span, the legendary "wild West" of the Indian, the buffalo, the cowboy and the cattle drive, was to reach its full development and then give way to extensive agriculture and the intersecting boundary lines of statehood. Within this period, too, the Civil War would be fought, and the Union's victory would eliminate forever the old, nagging question as to whether the new states should be slave or free. In the West the question would have been an academic one—the Plains could never have supported a plantation economy—but it would certainly have arisen for political reasons.

Probably the first step toward the conquest of the Great Plains by white men was taken by the Texas Rangers, who were organized to defend the settlements of the young Texas Republic from the incursions of southern Plains Indians and marauding Mexicans. The Rangers were mounted (they had to be, because their enemies were), but no matter how expert they became as horsemen, they remained at a disadvantage in combat with the Indians until they acquired Samuel Colt's invention, the six-shooter. Until the white man replaced his pistol or rifle with this revolver, he stood little chance against a breed of Indian able to discharge volleys of accurately aimed arrows while riding horseback at full speed. Eventually, of course, the Indian got hold of the revolver, too, but it was some years before this happened, and in the meantime the white men had gained the upper hand in the West.

During the existence of the Texas Republic, from 1836 to 1845, many Mexicans were expelled from within its borders; Mexican ranchers who left in a hurry often left livestock on their ranges. The untended animals wandering about were declared public property by the Republic, and a number of enterprising Texans began to round up herds and brand them. Despite the wholesale appropriation of cattle by private Texans, unclaimed strays continued to roam and to multiply, lowering the value of beef in Texas until no market existed for it there.

This was not the case in other areas of the country. The obvious thing to do, then, was to take the cattle to where they were wanted and would bring a good price. The job of moving the animals fell to the "cowboy," and the nature of the work and of the country he traveled over gave him a distinct character and appearance. Like the Rangers, he was an expert horseman and relied on his six-shooter as much as on his horse. The rope, the gun, and the horse were absolute necessities in rounding up and driving a herd of longhorns, a dangerous breed of cattle once it had lost its fear of man. The cattle were not the only threat to the cowboy's life in the early days. There were still the Plains Indians to the north, and even these were less formidable than the outlaws who lay in wait along the eastern trail to stampede the herds and later round up the animals themselves. No law existed that could protect the cowboy and his herd; he had to do this himself, which meant that he needed courage as well as physical strength and sound judgment. The vast, shadeless prairies and plains afforded him a sense of almost limitless freedom, but his responsibility was great. As the valuable northern markets developed, the "cattle baron" who employed the cowboy might easily have an investment of a hundred thousand dollars or more at stake on a single drive, a drive that would take several thousand cattle more than a thousand miles across the Plains.

The first drives, in the late 1830's, numbered up to a thousand head, and moved chiefly from the river valleys of Texas to the interior. In the early 1840's drives to New Orleans began, and the year 1846 recorded the first northern drive—from Texas to Ohio. During the fifties, the drives reached such far-flung places as California and Chicago. Shipment of the animals by boat was another means of reaching coastal markets, such as New Orleans, but it was the overland drives which, in their short lifetime, changed the character of the West.

It was just after the Civil War that the rapidly growing northern markets beckoned to the cattlemen. The war had curtailed the drives, but the animals continued to breed in their Texas homeland. When, after the war, the markets of Chicago and Kansas City were paying up to forty dollars a head for beeves which would bring four dollars in Texas, cattlemen began rounding up herds again and sending them up to Sedalia, Missouri, where the Missouri Pacific Railroad then had its western terminus. A better terminus was located in 1867, when J. G. McCoy, a livestock shipper from Illinois, established Abilene, Kansas, as the West's first "cow town." Here, unmolested by Missouri outlaws, seller could meet buyer and come to terms, and the cattle could be put aboard trains bound for Chicago and other eastern markets.

The Great Plains proved to be a natural habitat for cattle. As soon as the cattlemen recognized this fact, as well as the fact that thousands of square miles of free grass were lying about, they spread their enormous operation (with the establishment of Abilene, cattle-raising had become a very businesslike operation) to the far edges of the Plains. By the year 1880, the ranges of the cattle kingdom extended from western Texas to the Canadian border, and from the Mississippi Valley to the Rockies.

This extension of an "empire" was not as simple as it sounds. It was not until 1876 that the northern Plains saw the last of the free-roaming buffalo and his dependent, the Indian. Both had survived very well, on the whole, such narrow incursions into their land as had been made by passing explorers, fur-trappers, westward-bound missionaries, and Forty-niners. Neither the Butterfield Overland Mail, which began its stagecoach transport service from Tipton, Missouri, to San Francisco in 1858, nor the Pony Express (which began to compete with Butterfield via the Central Route in 1860 and quickly failed), nor Wells Fargo & Company (which acquired Butterfield in 1866), nor any other trailbound vehicle, had posed any serious threat to the Indian as they sped across the Plains in their effort to bring the East and West closer together—in time, at least. Indian attacks were always a danger, of course, but as in the case of the Southern cowboy, more was to be feared from American outlaws than from the natives.

Until 1851, trouble with the Indian of the Plains was sporadic, and almost always resulted from a specific, and more or less local, cause. In that year, however, the federal government was still contemplating the problem of communication and transportation between its two nearest settled regions—the Mississippi Valley and the Far West—and entered on a policy of assigning certain hunting grounds to the Indians. The purpose of the treaties made to this effect was to move the warlike tribes out of areas earmarked for regular overland travel. By 1861, several tribes had been cleared out of Nebraska and Kansas and moved north or south, with no great show of bad feeling.

(The buffalo was still in plentiful supply at this time.)

A serious degree of ill feeling was aroused that year, however, when the government demanded the surrender of the tribal lands of the Cheyenne and Arapaho in eastern Colorado, and relegated the Indians to a barren reservation on Sand Creek, a tributary of the Arkansas River. After three years of wanton retaliation on the white men's stagecoaches and scattered settlements, the Indians made peace and returned to their reservation on Sand Creek. In November of 1864, Colonel J. M. Chivington led a force of Colorado militiamen into the reservation, and when they finished their work of counter-retaliation, five hundred Indians—men, women, and children—lay dead, many savagely mutilated.

The horror of the "Chivington Massacre" shocked white men the country over, and incited the tribes of every region of the Plains. The following year, the Sioux perpetrated the massacre of Captain W. J. Fetterman and his entire detachment at Fort Phil Kearny, in what is now northern Wyoming.

And so the wars dragged on for another decade and more. To the Plains Indian, the government's policy of removal meant far more than simply exchanging one hunting ground for another—even when the land he relinquished was his ancestral heritage. As soon as he left the old hunting ground, the white hunters moved in, and their methods of destroying the buffalo were far more efficient and intensive than his own. When the white man first came to America, the buffalo (properly, the American bison) was known as far east as the Alleghenies, but by 1850 the species had disappeared east of the Mississippi and flourished only on the Plains. Now, as the formidable Indian was gradually moving from the scene, the white hunter was moving in for a year-round open season on the bearer of the commercially valuable "buffalo robe." The Indian, in short, was losing not only his land, but his sole means of independent survival. With no talents other than riding, hunting, and fighting, he faced the prospect of becoming utterly dependent on the reservation.

Though there were many wars before it, and fifteen more years of skirmishes after it, the Sioux War of 1875-76 was the last of the large-scale Indian Wars. Custer's defeat and death, along with 264 of his men, on the Little Big Horn River in 1876 was the climax of this darkest period in the history of the Plains. In 1887, the Dawes Severalty Act divided the reservation lands into farms to be allotted to individual Indian families, thus breaking down the last vestiges of tribal organization.

The removal of the Plains Indians was one prerequisite to the spread of the cattle ranges. Another was the laying of railroad tracks across the grasslands. During the Civil War the fact had been brought home to the government that there were many disadvantages to having a far-flung domain lacking transportation facilities (the coast-to-coast telegraph system established in the early days of the war had solved the East-West problem of at least emergency communication). After the war, therefore, railroad-building became a major industry lavishly supported in the West by federal and state governments. Federal grants of the public lands to the Union Pacific and Central Pacific railroads to extend their tracks to the meeting-place in Promontory, Utah, amounted to twenty million acres. Cash loans were extended to the two roads in the amount of from $16,000 to $48,000 for each mile of track laid. Between 1850 and 1871, when land grants were discontinued, railroad corporations received more than 159,000,000 acres from the federal government and 55,000,000 from the state governments (the latter acreage had been given to the states by the federal government for this purpose).

The heavy subsidization of Western railroads between 1850 and 1871 was necessary because no market for railroad service existed in the Plains sufficient to cover the tremendous investment involved. There were no cities—no industries to utilize a freight service, except, of course, the range cattle industry. But the experience of the war had proved that railroads were vital to the defense of a nation which spanned a continent. Union victory was to a great degree attributable to the adequacy of the Northeastern railroad system.

The rapid growth of the railroads was a boon to the cattle industry of the Plains in that access to the eastern markets became possible from various Western depots; also, the trains brought in the profiteering buffalo hunters, and where the buffalo vanished, the Indian vanished. This "boon" to the cattle kings was, however, in conjunction with certain other factors, to lead directly to the decline and fall of their kingdom.

In order to touch on some of these other factors, we must recall that American settlements of the Plains was deterred, from 1840 until nearly 1890, by the fact that the farming methods used in the East could not be applied to the semiarid grasslands. The simple tools and techniques which could make a forty-acre farm productive in a well-watered area could not be used on land that required irrigation, because irrigation was so costly that considerable acreage—more than the average northern farmer could handle—was needed to make the investment worthwhile. We must also recall—from discussion in an earlier chapter—that in 1862 Congress passed the Homestead Act, which made quarter-sections of unoccupied public land available free to settlers. Without the proper tools, the settler could not turn to the Plains for farmlands; under the terms of the Homestead Act, he could not get enough of the land to have made irrigating it profitable even if he had had the tools. This state of affairs in the 1860's was all to the good from the cattleman's point of view. The open range—an unfenced domain over which cattle roamed freely—flourished under an improvised system of unwritten law which decreed that a cattleman automatically gained "range rights" as soon as he took possession, as a firstcomer, of the bank of a stream. Streams were so few in proportion to Plains acreage that a range might run to 50,000 acres. The system worked beautifully for about ten years, and then, as in the case of the Western railroads, a new "boon" came to the cattleman as a second fruit of the Industrial Revolution. This boon was to be another factor in the decline of the cattle kingdom.

Cattle ranches in the West enjoyed unlimited expansion until 1873, the year of the first nationwide economic panic to be felt in the cattle country. Early indications of the depression had appeared in 1871, when the practice of raising cattle in Texas and moving them to the northern ranges for fattening began, but in 1873 the Texas cattlemen lost heavily. This was not the end—yet. The demand for high-grade cattle grew enormously in the period of economic expansion which began in 1876 and continued into the early 1880's, and at the height of this upturn came a "cattle boom" that resulted in an overstocking of the ranges and a consequent crowding and hustling of the animals for the available grass. Now came the second "boon" to the cattleman: barbed-wire fencing. In order to compete in a glutted market, it was necessary to produce superior beeves; this goal required a segregation of fine breeders from the scrub cattle. Wooden fencing was an impossibility on the Plains, but barbed wire served admirably (except for the fact that until the animals learned to be wary of it they suffered many a serious laceration).

The "backfiring" of this boon was attributable to the expansion of settlements westward under the Homestead Act. It was expensive to fence in a 40-acre tract even in the East, where timber was still plentiful though becoming steadily less so. When, under the Homestead Act, four times that area became available free, the appearance of the cheap, easily erected barbed-wire fencing was a great encouragement to westward-looking farmers. For the settlers who moved into the Prairie Plains, between the Mississippi Valley and the Plains proper, little else was necessary for successful farming except Cyrus McCormick's recent invention, the reaper—which had begun to appear on the eastern market before the Civil War but really came into its own on the flat, rock-free prairies.

The farmer who settled in the "fertile belt"—the Prairie Plains—had passed the timber line but stopped short of the semiarid region. In this tall-grass land he escaped the drudgeries of stump-pulling and rock-hauling, and still enjoyed the benefit of ample rainfall. With his 160 acres of fine, fertile soil cheaply and efficiently fenced in, and with his reaper and the other modern machinery available—a cultivator, a twine binder, a steam thresher, and perhaps a few other recent inventions—the prairie farmer enjoyed an enviable combination of natural and mechanical advantages.

Though the Homestead Act could not be applied at all realistically to the semiarid Plains (historians today maintain that no really adequate land law has ever been devised for this region), there were ways of utilizing the law to get much larger tracts of the public lands than the federal government intended. The cattlemen had devised their "range rights" within a realistic framework: without water, 640 acres, or ten times that much, was valueless, so land rights hinged on possession of a source of water and included all the land which that water could support. With no other claimants to the land, the cattle barons were free to administer it in the way that suited the circumstances best.

A shrewd farmer, however, had the law behind him when—finding the prairie lands quickly taken up—he began to move into the grazing lands to the West. Under the Preemption Act of 1841 he could claim 160 acres and pay $1.25 an acre for it, then take out a homestead of another 160. The Timber Culture Act of 1873 enabled him to get 160 acres more by agreeing to allot 40 acres to timber, and by the Desert Land Act of 1877 he could acquire 640 acres at $1.25 an acre—provided he improved the land with a means of irrigation. (The Preemption Act was used freely by speculators, who hired preemptors; the Timber Culture Act was also an invitation to fraud, and was widely abused. Both were repealed in 1891.)

By 1877, then, it was possible for a farmer to come by a tract of 1,120 acres within the semiarid region. All the land laws were made with a view to promoting the farmer's, rather than the cattleman's, opportunity to acquire the

public lands legally. Ironically, the Easterners who enacted this legislation misunderstood the nature of the
Plains region so completely that instead of benefiting the
Western farmer, they put an insupportable burden on him
by requiring that he accomplish the impossible before the
land could legally become his.

Though the laws were poor, and were necessarily
flaunted on all sides, the fact remained that they began to
bring settlers into the cattle country as soon as the necessary tools and fencing became available. The influx of
farmers became especially heavy during a succession of
"wet years" in the early 1880's, when many Easterners were
deluded into thinking that the climate of the Plains had
undergone a permanent change for the better. Many single
160-acre homesteads were taken up well within the semiarid region at that time. The railroads, with government
loans to repay, had begun their own campaigns to promote
settlement—and therefore business—along the Plains routes.
With the cooperation of real estate men and other speculators, they offered free transportation and other induce-
ments to Easterners to come West and buy large tracts of
choice railroad lands on apparently liberal terms.

So the "farms" multiplied, and much of the once-open
grazing land was taken up and fenced in. In self-defense,
many cattlemen reluctantly began to fence their grazing
lands, and to take out homesteads; to acquire enough
acreage for grazing, all the cowboys employed on a cattleman's range would stake out adjoining homesteads. At the
same time, speculators were abroad selling range rights to
desert lands they had acquired under the act of 1877,
bringing in immigrants from the British Isles eager to cash
in on the "cattle boom."

The Plains population trebled between 1870 and 1880, rising from about a half-million to more than one and a half, and was to treble again by 1890. This twenty-year period saw an immigration of eight million into the United States. Land appropriation within the same period came to 430,000,000 acres, 225,000,000 of which were placed under cultivation.

The year 1885 marked the beginning of a long bleak period in the history of ranching. A drought in 1883, and a financial disaster resulting from wild speculation in railroading in 1884, brought about the collapse of the cattle market in 1885. The panic spread wildly as cattlemen "dumped" their stock on the market and sold their acreage to try to realize some return. Recovery followed within the next five years, but the old-time cattleman had by then passed from the scene forever. The open range was gone, replaced by stock ranches devoted partly to farming, or to farms where imported hardy grains were raised by dry-farming methods. Windmills for drawing up enough ground water to irrigate limited pasture areas had become as commonplace on the scene as crisscrossing barbed-wire fences.

The Great Plains region, which forms the northwestern part of Texas, the western parts of the Dakotas, Nebraska, Kansas, and Oklahoma, and the eastern parts of Montana, Wyoming, Colorado, and New Mexico, was gradually incorporated into the family of states between 1845 and 1912. The development of Texas, a state since 1845, and of Kansas, since 1861, has already been discussed. Nebraska, which followed Kansas into the Union as a Plains state in 1867, was, like Kansas and the Dakotas, settled chiefly by farmers. Even in the late 1860's, when the railroads first made these lands accessible to settlers in any numbers, the picture presented by these states-to-be was a vast panorama of grasslands being broken by the plow and planted to wheat. By 1880, the states of Kansas and Nebraska were fully settled, with populations of 850,000 and 450,000 respectively. The stream of pioneers then turning northward brought a population of half a million settlers into the Dakota Territory east of the Missouri River by 1885, and four years later—after more than a decade of agitation for separation—the states of North and South Dakota were admitted into the Union. Oklahoma's rise to statehood was delayed until 1907 because of her status as Indian territory.

Across the Plains, the states which spread into the Rockies followed a different pattern of settlement. "Pike's Peak or bust" was the catchword that drew 50,000 men from East and West into Colorado in the spring of 1859; thousands who had started from the East turned back, but experienced prospectors from California stayed on. As permanent settlements developed, which was soon afterward, their demand for status as a separate territory became so vociferous that Congress constituted the Territory of Colorado in February of 1861. Not until March of 1875 was an enabling act passed, though many attempts had failed over the years, which resulted in a constitutional convention and a ratification of this instrument by the people. Colorado at last became a state on August 1, 1876.

Montana also owed her first great wave of settlers to the discovery of gold in the Civil War years. Chiefly to bring order into a wild, lawless area—typified by the mining towns of Bannack and Virginia City—the federal government set off Montana as a territory separate from the Idaho Territory in 1864. Its first governor was forced to flee, and its second died mysteriously. Cow towns later sprang up in the grassy eastern region, but mining remained of first importance. Silver was discovered at Butte in 1875, and the discovery of copper in 1880 led to a period of miners' wars. By 1889, the region had become so prosperous—as well as possessing transcontinental service via the Northern Pacific railroad—that Congress authorized the election of a convention to draw up a state constitution. In November of 1889, President Harrison proclaimed the admission to statehood of Montana. The Dakotas and Washington came in in the same month.

Wyoming, location of the South Pass, a rendezvous point for the Mountain Men and the gateway to the Far West for California gold-seekers and Oregon settlers, began its history as a fur-trading center after the Louisiana Purchase, and eventually came to epitomize the highest development of the cattle industry. Cattle rustling and train robberies were rampant in the 1870's, before the quieting effect of the farmers was felt, but even after barbed wire hemmed in the open range there were wars between sheep and cattle men. Homesteaders, in their turn, had to battle these prior claimants to the grasslands, but it wasn't long before the small-farm settlers realized that Wyoming was not suited to their needs. The Territory of Wyoming, formed from "the southwest portion of Dakota, together with a small portion from the Territories of Utah and Colorado," was formally organized on May 10, 1869, and its constitution provided for full political rights for women. Twenty years elapsed, then a constitution adopted in November of 1889 was accepted by Congress. On July 10, 1890, Wyoming was admitted into the Union. Her constitution was unique in that it gave women equal suffrage rights with men. Not until 1920, with the passage of the Nineteenth Amendment, was this law to be applied to the entire nation.

Wyoming was not unique among the Plains states in the "radicalism" of its constitution and early legislation. A quarter-century later, Colorado and Utah also gave women the vote; by 1920, when it became federal law, New York and Michigan were the only states east of the Plains which already had such a state law, while North Dakota, Nebraska, New Mexico, and Texas were the only Western states *not* to have legislated for woman suffrage. The Granger movement, an organization of the Western farmers to promote their best interests, began its existence in 1866 with a declaration that women were to be given membership and position in the organization.

This movement, while it did not achieve a great deal in the way of legislation against such abuses as the railroads' free hand in charging excessive rates, did pave the way for farmers' alliances. These, in turn, became the foundation of the Populist party in 1892. Its platform represented the "radical" interests of the West: free coinage of silver; a flexible currency system controlled by the government rather than by the banks; a graduated income tax; public ownership and operation of railroads, telegraph, and telephones; the eight-hour day; the direct election of Senators; the initiative and referendum. South Dakota in 1898 was the first state to adopt the initiative in the proposal of ordinary laws. Laws authorizing the proposal of constitutional amendments by popular petition were first passed by Western states.

The radical nature of the Western states' laws was

deplored in the East—though in time the rest of the nation was to adopt many of the West's innovations. Ironically, it was the "lawless" West—that part of the nation where Eastern laws could in many ways never be applied—which thus provided the United States with the seeds of its most progressive and democratic social legislation.

CHAPTER X

Alaska

From 1912 until 1959 there were forty-eight states in the Union. Then two territories—one at the edge of the Arctic Sea and the other in the heart of the Pacific Ocean some 2,400 miles southwest of the American mainland—became the forty-ninth and fiftieth members of the United States.

Alaska, the forty-ninth, has more than twice the area of Texas and is nearly one fifth as large as the entire continental United States. Siberia could be reached by a fifty-five-mile boat ride westward across the Bering Strait.

Alaska's proximity to Russian soil accounts for the fact that she was once called Russian America. In 1724, a Dane —Captain Vitus Bering—was commissioned by Peter the Great to explore northeastern Siberia to find out whether Asia and America were joined. Peter died before the expedition got under way, but Bering carried out his mission and returned to St. Petersburg in 1730. His findings were not conclusive—he had sighted land to the east, but was it an island or part of a mainland?—and at his request the

Empress Catherine I (Peter's widow and successor) sent him on a second expedition in 1733. Seven years of personal and official wrangling over details of the expedition delayed its embarkation until June 4, 1741, when at last the ships *St. Peter* and *St. Paul*—with Bering in command of the *St. Peter*—set sail from Petropavlovsk, Siberia. It was on this journey that Bering discovered the northwest coast of America. He was taken ill on the return voyage, shipwrecked, and died on an uninhabited island—later named Bering Island—in December. Renewed interest in the northern Pacific (the search for a northwest passage was never long abandoned) now brought European explorers: the Spaniard Bodega y Quadra, La Pérouse of France, Captain James Cook and George Vancouver from Britain.

Survivors of Bering's second expedition provided Russia with some knowledge of the northwest coast of the American continent and the Aleutian Islands. The information of greatest immediate interest was that the islands were rich in fur-bearing animals. This news naturally brought a stream of fur traders, who moved eastward through the Aleutians and entrenched themselves in Alaska during the next twenty years.

The Russians depended upon the Aleut Indians, a branch of the Eskimo family, for guidance in exploring the mysteries of the fur-laden islands. These savages, dressed in garments made of seal intestines and parkas of bird skins and feathers, were willing to trade with the Russians on their own terms. They understood the philosophy of "might makes right." To the natives, the pistols and cutlasses dangling from the tunics of the Slavs were insignias of an almighty power. The Russians demanded as hostages children and wives of Indians to insure good conduct from the braves. This conduct was not reciprocated, however. The women were retained as slaves and the men were subjected to cruel abuse. Deprived of their families, their furs, their hunting grounds, the Aleuts bided their time for revenge.

In the fall of 1763, a ship commanded by a Cossack, Alexei Drusenin, entered Captain Harbor, in the extreme northeast Aleutians, for the winter hunt. Drusenin felt lucky. Not only had he evaded the ships of his competitors by coming this far north, but in the otter-rich islands of Unalaska and Unimak he had discovered untapped wealth. And the Indians here were so friendly that they voluntarily brought hostages to him. This was a surprise to Drusenin, who had heard tales of Indian restlessness elsewhere.

While the men were building huts and making plans for the winter's hunt, the Aleuts were busy too. The chief of every tribe received a bunch of faggots with instructions to burn one each day. A general attack was to take place on the day the last stick was burned. Bands of Aleuts quietly surrounded the Russians' huts. An Indian lured the unsuspecting Drusenin and two of his officers into visiting his underground home. (In the wintertime the Aleuts lived in cellars dug three or four feet deep in the earth.) The moment Drusenin set foot in the dwelling, he was struck a blow that sent him reeling to the ground. The next Cossack, stumbling over Drusenin's body, was slashed by knives traded to the Indians only the day before.

The third Cossack beat his way back to the entrance with the ax he was carrying. Then he turned and fled under a shower of arrows. He reached his hut, tripping over the dead body of a sentinel. The door swung open and a Russian, under protection of musket fire from the window, dashed out and dragged him inside to safety.

There were only four men within the hut, all that were left of the fifty-five hunters Drusenin had stationed at Captain Harbor. For four days they held off the Indians with their muskets. They were alone, twenty miles from their ship, and surrounded by Indians. But without water they could not last. Their choice was either to surrender or to try making a dash for the ship. At night, while their muskets kept the watchful Aleuts at a distance, the Russians carried their skin boat to the water, loaded it with supplies and ammunition, and set out in the pitch darkness to cross the sea.

Rowing with all their strength they managed to reach the main shore of Unalaska. In the blackness of the night there was no sign or sound of life. Following a previously dug trail through the snow, the fugitives headed toward the village of Kalekhta, where a second detachment of hunters was stationed. They reached the village before dawn and shot a musket to signal their countrymen. Instantly a hundred Aleuts leaped up. It was too late to do anything but make a dash for a nearby rock. Here, with a sharp drop on all sides and the sea behind them, the Russians made their stand. Indians attempting to scale the height were beaten off with swords. A barrage from the Russians' muskets forced the natives to retreat, and under cover of night, the four Russians descended from their safe perch and sprinted for the harbor, where a ship was supposed to be anchored.

They succeeded in reaching the port at dawn, only to discover that the shore was strewn with the wreckage of the ship and the mutilated bodies of its crew. The four terror-struck men picked their way toward the mountains of the interior and found a hiding place deep in a ravine. That night they returned to the shore to salvage what they could of planking and other supplies.

From December of 1763 until February, 1764, they hid in the mountains. By February they had managed to put together a skiff made of leather flour sacks they had salvaged, oiled to prevent leaking. One night they launched their craft and, stealing away, rounded the north coast of Unalaska, on the search for Russian trading ships.

For weeks they coasted at night among the sheltering rocks of the shore, hiding by day. As they rounded snow-covered Makushin Volcano, towering five thousand feet above the Bering Sea, they were spotted by an Indian who gave the alarm. The refugees headed for a cave in the volcano. Here they resisted a siege of five weeks' duration. Their only food was the shellfish gathered at night, their only water the snow scooped out of gutters of the cavern. Eventually the Indians wearied of watching, and one dark night the Russians succeeded in launching their skiff un-detected. At daybreak their odyssey ended. They sighted a Russian trading vessel and reached it safely.

During this time the Russian government, which came under the reign of Catherine II (Catherine the Great) in 1762, took little interest in securing to itself the new lands, though its claim to them was unquestioned. Alaska was, in fact, a "white elephant." Men lured into private enterprise on the islands and mainland would be more useful to Russia at home, developing Siberia, and if Russia's territorial claim were challenged to the point of a fight she would find herself hamstrung by the weakness of her navy. In 1769 Catherine wrote, in regard to offers from foreign adventurers to exploit Russian interests in America:

> It is for traders to traffic where they please. I will furnish neither men, nor ships, nor money, and I renounce forever all lands and possessions in the East Indies and in America.

In 1787, however, she agreed to subsidize a monopoly of trade and industry in all Russian discoveries in the North Pacific. Three years after her death in 1796, her son Paul, emperor and czar of Russia, confirmed the consolidation of the Russian American Company by imperial ukase. Managing agent under the company charter was Aleksandr Andreyevich Baranov, who was virtual governor of his country's American possessions until, at the age of seventy, he was retired in 1817.

For eighteen years Baranov was the Czar's strong man in the Pacific. Establishing himself in his capital at Sitka (then called New Archangel), he built a baronial empire in a primitive wilderness. His "castle" was set on the top of a hill overlooking the sound. A light was kept burning at the summit as a signal to ships sailing the coast. Priceless paintings and furnishings were transported six thousand miles across Siberia and then across the Pacific to decorate the enormous rooms of the castle. The walls of one room were lined with books in French, English, Russian, and German. Baranov's great dining hall could accommodate as many as two hundred guests. But the noblemen, sailors, and hunters who accepted his hospitality were forced to keep pace with his prodigious capacity for raw rum. His strength was as notorious as his thirst. He once strangled with his bare hands the powerfully-built

leader of an insurrectionist group who had attempted to
knife him.

Surprisingly enough, Baranov was a little man, bald except for a fringe of red hair. On important occasions he
wore a black wig anchored to his head with a handkerchief.

There were sixty officers on his staff, and two hundred
colonists lived inside the fort. Below the fort lived the
Indians. Baranov trusted neither them nor his own people. A mammoth cannon was mounted by the castle, and
night and day a seven-man guard tramped the rocky trails
for signs of an uprising. On one occasion, however, the
Indians massacred a number of Russian settlers at Sitka.

Slowly, Sitka's fame grew; it became known as the "Paris
of the New World." To its harbor came most of the trading vessels that entered the Pacific. In those days San Francisco was still a fledgling frontier town, and Los Angeles
had not yet been born. On the streets of Sitka promenaded
naval officers and adventurers from all over the world—
from fur traders on the payroll of the American John
Jacob Astor to titled princes of the Russian court with
their elegantly dressed ladies.

Sitka's shipyards supplied many of the vessels that sailed
the coast. Cannons and bells were cast in her foundries.
Brickyards, tanneries, and sawmills brought money into
the treasury. Here was a center of curious contrasts, old-
world luxuries in a setting of pioneer crudity.

Cargoes of furs—land otter, sea otter, sable—lifted from
the Indians in exchange for worthless trinkets were stored
in Sitka's warehouses. The slaughter of the animals was
ceaseless and wasteful; male and female puppies of sea
otters were killed, thus cutting off new generations of the
species. In 1804 the Russians took fifteen thousand skins

from the Sitka waters alone. Thirty years later only eighty skins were gathered from the exhausted beds. (Today the huge Pribilof seals may be killed only by federal employees under government supervision.)

This Russian colony was as much a menace as a showcase. Under Baranov's "rule," which lasted nearly as long as the twenty years granted the company by its charter from Paul I, Russian influence was extended to nearly the whole of our present Alaska, and southward along the West Coast almost as far as San Francisco.

Although the Russian influence in Alaska declined after Baranov's retirement in 1817—he died two years later on his way home to Russia—and Sitka lost its position as chief port of the Pacific, traces of Russian hegemony still exist today. About twenty of every hundred Alaskans are of Russian extraction, and the Slavic names of cities, islands, and mountains give added evidence of the tenure of these early settlers.

After Baranov's passing, Russia attempted to stave off the encroachment of foreign traders along these already badly depleted shores by means of a ukase barring all foreign navigators from sailing within one hundred miles of the North American coast above the fifty-first parallel. Both Britain and the United States protested, and on December 2, 1823, President James Monroe delivered in his message to Congress the famous Monroe Doctrine:

> . . . that the American continents, by the free and independent condition which they have assumed and maintain, are henceforth not to be considered as subjects for future colonization by any European powers.

The Doctrine was also aimed at European designs on

South America, but was, in effect, a general declaration. Though not "official" as United States policy, this implied warning was effective: a treaty was quickly arrived at according to which Russian colonization was not to extend below latitude 54° 40′.

The Imperial Council at St. Petersburg renewed the Russian American Company's charter for the last time in 1841, though Alaska had clearly become more a burden than a prize. When Russia became involved in the Crimean War in 1854 it became very clear to her that she must relinquish this colony, since she did not have the power to defend it and could not afford to maintain it.

The possibilities opened to America by these circumstances were completely lost on most citizens to the south. But there was one American with a different attitude. He was William H. Seward, Secretary of State in the post-Civil War administration of Andrew Johnson. Seward was convinced that the United States should buy Alaska if the Russians could be persuaded to sell.

For the reasons mentioned above, as well as the fact that she needed money, Russia was more than receptive, and negotiations were not long in getting under way. Seward first offered five million dollars for the territory, and was met with a counter-request for ten million. A compromise of $7,200,000 in gold was arrived at.

The terms of the treaty—which stipulated that the cession be "free and unencumbered by any reservations, privileges, franchises, grants, or possessions by any associated companies, whether corporate or incorporate, Russian, or any other, or by any parties except merely private, individual property holders"—were wired to St. Petersburg over the Atlantic Cable, which had only started to operate successfully the previous year. Russia had balked at the provision just quoted above, but Seward stood firm; now he anxiously awaited her reply. He feared it would come too late for Congress, which was meeting in special session, to take action. His worry was groundless.

On the evening of March 29, 1867, the Secretary was at home with his family when Baron Edoard de Stoeckl, Russian minister in Washington, knocked at his door to inform him that his government's permission had been obtained. "I will come to your office in the morning for the signing."

"Why wait? Let's draw it up tonight," suggested Seward. De Stoeckl dispatched messengers to summon his secretaries. At four o'clock on the morning of March 30, the treaty by which Alaska and the Aleutian Islands were ceded to the United States was signed.

President Johnson presented it to the Senate on the same day. Fortunately, in Charles Sumner, Chairman of the Committee on Foreign Relations, Seward had a powerful ally. Although Sumner was amazed to learn of the treaty, and was privately opposed to the idea, he promised to work for its passage. He wrote to a friend:

> This Russian treaty tried me severely. . . . I am against further accessions of territory, unless by the free choice of the inhabitants. But this question was perplexed by considerations of politics . . . and the engagements already entered into by the Government. I hesitated to take the responsibilities of defeating it.

Others expressed their hostility vigorously. Criticism poured into Washington from all over the country. Alaska was called "a frozen, valueless region" where only "tundra abounded." The purchase was dubbed "Seward's Folly."

But the Secretary of State remained unperturbed. He entertained his friends by reading to them old newspapers which had criticized Jefferson's purchase of the "sandy waste" of Louisiana and the later acquisition of the "poisonous swamps" of Florida.

In the meantime, Sumner worked on a speech advocating the ratification of the treaty. On April 9 he delivered it in the Senate. He speculated on the reasons why Russia had parted with her holdings. He suggested that the war between Russia and Great Britain in the Crimea had led Russia to doubt the advisability of holding on to possessions "so little within the sphere of her empire" and from which, so far, she had "obtained no income commensurate with her expenses."

Then Sumner spoke of the reasons why the United States should accept Alaska. He scoffed at the notion that Alaska consisted only of "icebergs and polar bears." He cited the valuable metals, timberlands, and fisheries to be found there. At the conclusion of the speech, the Senate ratified the treaty by an overwhelming vote of 37 to 2.

Rougher sledding was encountered in the House of Representatives. The House felt it should have been consulted beforehand on a matter involving the payment of money. In the end, however, Seward won. For the rest of his days he considered the acquisition of Alaska the major accomplishment of his life.

On October 18, 1867, Alaska was transferred in ceremonies at Sitka. General Lovell H. Rousseau took possession in the name of the United States government. The ceremonies were impressive, with salutes of artillery accompanying the lowering of the Russian flag and the raising of the American, but poor provision was made for American administration of its new acquisition. The Alaska Commercial Company took over the commercial rights of the Russian American Company, but made little use of them. No civil and judicial government was provided until 1884 (this was modeled on the laws of Oregon), and in the meantime Alaska was first under jurisdiction of the United States Army, then became a customs district, and then, in 1879, was made a ward of the Navy.

The Secretary of the Treasury in Washington made the laws for revenue regulations, and a single United States warship provided the only harbor defense, its crew sometimes being called on to act as a land police force.

The first civil government, set up in 1884, was elaborated upon by act of Congress in 1900, but it wasn't until six years later that Alaska was given an elected territorial representative in Congress, and another six years passed before she was actually organized into a territory. Her capital was then moved officially from Sitka to Juneau.

Constitutionally, the territory resembled a ward of Washington to a greater degree than had any other territory. Its bicameral legislature, which first met on March 3, 1913, had no authority to dispose of any of the public domain, and its borrowing power was limited to administrative expenses. All legislation passed in the territory had to be sent to the President, who would submit the bills to Congress for approval. Alaska was, in practice, governed by a series of government bureaus in Washington which issued confusing and frequently conflicting regulations.

With the purchase of Alaska, the national domain—that is, land under the political jurisdiction of the United

States government—had been increased by about 580,000 square miles, including the Aleutian archipelago. Very nearly all of this territory was also *public,* or federal, domain—meaning it was owned by the federal government. While, for example, the thirteen original states are in the national domain, none of their land became public domain except that which was ceded to the federal government after the Revolution. As the federal government acquired new territory by purchase and cession—some three million square miles of it in all—the process was reversed and it became customary to grant to each new state a half-million acres to be used in the public interest; universities, canals, and railroads generally received grants of public lands. It was not until the Homestead Act of 1862, however, that settlers could acquire public lands free of charge; before that time these lands had been looked on primarily as a source of revenue.

In 1903 the Homestead Law was applied to Alaska—the regular system of land surveys had gone into effect in 1889 —and when the remaining public lands were withdrawn from "settlement, location, sale, or entry" in 1934 and 1935, the Territory of Alaska was excepted. The Homestead Law still applies in Alaska today.

The early growth of the Territory of Alaska did not, however, hinge on the Homestead Law. In July of 1879, a party of men had debarked in Seattle, Washington, from a steamer that had arrived from Alaska. They were miners lugging a fortune in bundles and satchels; they reported how they had stumbled across more than $800,000 worth of gold from the creeks and valleys of the Klondike, just east of the Alaskan border.

The United States was then in the throes of a depression, and news of a gold strike electrified the land. More than fifty thousand people poured their savings into weighty mining equipment which they had to carry for thousands of miles.

Most of these miners were bush-leaguers, with no experience whatever in outdoor living. Yet they rushed heedlessly into a territory noted for its severe winters. All summer long a procession of steamers docked at Dyea and Skagway, north of Sitka, the two chief ports of arrival. From there the miners followed the winding mountain trails which led to the Klondike gold creeks.

The blizzards and rains of the mountain passes deterred many from making the Klondike trip. Instead, they decided to stop and look for gold around Nome—where the sun shone for twenty-one hours a day—and at Fairbanks, 120 miles south of the Arctic Circle.

The "new frontier" attracted some unsavory characters who didn't bother to go all the way to the gold fields but settled at the ports of entry to prey on new arrivals. One of the most notorious was "Soapy" Smith. Landing at Skagway, he and his henchmen ran the community with their six-shooters. "Soapy" was on hand to greet each new boatload from the states with a shell game at the dock. Many of the newcomers were lured into his game and swindled of their savings. In the gold fields themselves, communities sprang up haphazardly. Along the muddy streets log cabins were erected with stovepipes protruding at raffish angles. Groceries were hastily stored on platforms built on stilts nine feet high, beyond the jaws of ravenous dogs roaming the streets. In the dance halls, "sourdoughs" —as the miners were nicknamed—danced with girls and paid for their favors with nuggets of gold.

Newspapers were in short supply. The cooped-up sour-doughs were so hungry for reports from home that when one newcomer brought in a newspaper, a miner bought it for one hundred and eighty dollars, and distributed post-ers advertising that he would hold a public reading. He got a dollar admission per person and filled the hall five times.

While fortunes were made by some prospectors, hun-dreds of others suffered tragedy. Many a man, having reached the gold fields after incredible hardship, set up his equipment and sluiced tons of gravel without finding a grain of valuable metal. The effort necessary to extract gold from the frozen tundra was enormous. Pits had to be dug and fires built to burn all night. Each dawn the pros-pector would sift through the thawed-out gravel and sepa-rate the ore by panning. Sometimes it took weeks, even months, to extract an ounce of gold.

Jack London was one migrant who found a different kind of treasure. Coming up to the Yukon to pick up local color for his stories, he collected material for the books that made him famous.

While many of the miners moved out after the gold strike, other, more permanent, settlers moved in. They were attracted by the vastness, the scenic splendor, and the untapped bounty of Alaska's soil. In the southern part of Alaska, American entrepreneurs established salmon can-neries, destined to become the largest in the world. These attracted white labor as well as providing work for the Eskimos and Indians. Often enough, sportsmen who came for a holiday decided to stay on permanently. Mountain climbers, lured by the abundance of challenging peaks—especially Mount McKinley, the highest in North America

—returned regularly to Alaska to try their skill. Other immigrants from distant parts worked as government officials and hotel-keepers. They settled, for the most part, along Alaska's southern coast, where the salmon canneries and most of the larger towns were located. Here a climate that was no colder than that of Oregon and Washington permitted ships to enter and depart all year round.

But to the old-timers, descendants of the original "sourdoughs" of the interior, this southern portion was not the real Alaska. To them, Alaska could be reached only by dog team or by flying over tundra dotted with lakes and laced with big curling rivers. They preferred a freezing winter to the milder temperatures of the south, and lived in towns called Purgatory, Coldfoot, Calamity Gulch—names pregnant with meaning to an Alaskan frontiersman.

Survival in the interior depended on courage as well as health. Much also depended on the Alaskan malamute and Siberian husky which made up the sled teams in areas where no other transportation was available.

Many legends have grown around these extraordinary animals. In 1925 a dog team saved a whole community from death. Diphtheria—called the "black death" in the north—struck at Nome. Only one doctor from the United States Public Health Service and a handful of nurses were on hand to care for a territory containing twelve thousand people and stretching one thousand frigid miles eastward and as far north as the Arctic Circle. The Eskimos were particularly susceptible to this disease, and many were marked for certain death unless antitoxin serum could reach Nome in time. The epidemic struck in the dead of winter. Airplanes could not be relied upon because of a furious blizzard. The only other way to reach Nome in winter was by the traditional sled and "mushers."

The journey of a package of antitoxin serum to Nome was a dramatic one indeed. Men and dogs fought against a 40-below-zero blizzard which brought a groundswell from the Bering Sea miles inland. The rescue team somehow covered more than 650 miles in a record-breaking five and a half days. This trail had never before been traveled in less than nine days.

The inhabitants of stricken Nome sent up a prayer of thanksgiving when, on a black, howling morning, the exhausted dogs staggered into town with the badly needed antitoxin.

The ambiguous boundary line separating the Territory of Alaska from British possessions in Canada—a line that had never been staked out, or even officially surveyed, in the transfer of Alaska from Russia to the United States— was finally settled by arbitration between America and Great Britain in 1903. The actual survey, along the agreed line of 141° west longitude, was completed in 1914.

That same year Congress authorized a bond issue of $35,000,000 to build a federal railroad in the territory. Nine years later (the First World War badly disrupted all railroad building) the 529-mile road was completed, running from the Gulf city of Seward to Fairbanks, and the Alaska interior was brought closer to the "outside" world.

The territory was moving toward statehood, but slowly. She suffered from the stringent conservation laws passed under Theodore Roosevelt's administration, laws which hampered the use of her vast natural resources. Her progress was halted by the war—in which she supplied three thousand men to the services, led all the states in per

capita purchase of war stamps, and was second only to
Delaware in subscriptions to war bonds. There were obstacles to settlement: pioneers could be drawn in by gold,
but not by the prospect of life in an arctic climate where
transportation was a formidable problem.

It was evident from the work of her first territorial legislature, however, that her aim was statehood, and that she
intended to follow a broadly social course in constructing
a government for her citizens. The first enactments of this
legislature gave women the vote, limited hours of labor
in mining and public works to eight hours a day, made
school attendance compulsory, and provided for arbitration of labor disputes. Two years later she adopted the
most far-reaching workmen's compensation law in the
country, and in 1917 she passed a general eight-hour-day
law and made homesteads available to non-residents of the
land.

Not until the Second World War, however, was this
"worthless land of icebergs" recognized as "the most important strategic place in the world for the defense of the
United States." Only two miles of water separate the So-
viet Union's Big Diomede Island and the United States'
Little Diomede, which became—aside from the Philippines
—the American base closest to Japan. The route from Chicago, by way of Edmonton, Fairbanks, Nome, and Siberia,
to Vladivostok was invaluable in the transport of arma-
ments to northeast Asia.

To transform Alaska into a military stronghold was an
immense and costly undertaking. When the GI's arrived,
less than half of Alaska had even been mapped. The Alaska
garrison, pitifully unprepared for its strategic role, had
only three hundred soldiers. The population numbered

less than eighty thousand. There wasn't an airfield large
enough to accommodate a modern-type heavy bomber.

Lack of transportation facilities was, as always, the biggest problem in Alaska. Although flights from Seattle to
Juneau took only five and a half hours, no more than one
hundred passengers a week could be transported with their
equipment. Military personnel, construction workers, and
all supplies had to be conveyed by ship. There was only
one major road and—running alongside it—one important
railroad.

The difficulty of laying railroad tracks over Alaska's expanse of snow-covered mountain ranges and arctic coastal
plains led to the conclusion by American military experts
that the usefulness of Alaska depended upon aviation.
Work was centered on the construction of air bases. Air-
fields and radio and weather stations connecting with new
fields in Canada were built. Accurate weather reports were
of paramount importance, since rain, fog, and wind made
flying perilous. From necessity Alaskan flyers became
among the best in the world. The federal government
spent almost two billion dollars to develop military bases,
and Alaska played a vital part in bringing the war against
Japan to a successful conclusion.

After V-J Day, thousands of new residents took up life
in the "new frontier" of Alaska. The population in 1950
was 128,643, including military personnel. In 1910 it had
been 64,356.

Several bills for Alaskan statehood had been introduced
into Congress after the First World War—the first in 1916—
but had been defeated. Some leaders of the salmon industry feared an unfavorable economic climate if Alaska
became a state run by local politicians. They were joined

by the Alaska Steamship Line, operating from Seattle to the territory, which felt that it would be hampered by federal commercial regulation once statehood was achieved.

Other business interests, however, pressed for statehood. Wherever people gathered, Washington's remote control of their internal affairs was heatedly discussed. At one point the rates charged on the Alaska Railroad—which were devised in Washington and were higher than those in the states—angered some Alaskan business men so much that in protest they boycotted the railroad and trucked their goods up Alaska's single highway. When the government set a toll of $9.27 a ton at the highway ferry, the truckers locked up the toll collector and ran the ferry themselves. The grand jury refused to hand up an indictment.

Alaskans found their leading sponsor for statehood in Ernest Gruening, a former newspaper editor and author whom President Roosevelt appointed territorial governor in 1939. Gruening pressed vigorously for this final act of acceptance. By 1945, when Alaska's strategic position was fully appreciated and thousands of former military and civilian personnel stationed there during the war had begun to inquire about settlement and homesteading, agitation for statehood reached a high pitch. Early in 1945 the Alaskan legislature provided for a referendum on the subject at the 1946 general elections. On January 22, President Truman urged Congress to admit Alaska as a state, but no action was taken. The territorial referendum resulted in a vote of 9,630 to 6,812 in favor of statehood, and in 1947 Alaska's delegate to Congress introduced a statehood bill. In February of the following year, the first hearing ever given any bill to make Alaska a state came about through a statehood recommendation by a subcommittee of the House Committee on Public Lands. The Committee almost unanimously approved the necessary legislation, and the election of Harry Truman seemed to assure passage of a bill at the next session of Congress. In 1949, however, the House Rules Committee blocked bringing the measure on the floor before adjournment.

For the next nine years the proponents of statehood worked while they waited. In April of 1956 a state constitution was submitted to the voters of Alaska, who ratified it. In October they elected two provisional senators and a provisional representative to take office as soon as the statehood bill should pass—and who would in the meantime work to influence Congress toward its passage.

Secretary of the Interior Fred Seaton was one of the staunchest allies of the statehood-seekers. Joined by the senators from Washington and California, he did his utmost to get the bill through. In opposition was a bloc of Southern congressmen who resisted the entrance of a new Northern state.

Finally, in January of 1958, President Eisenhower proposed Alaskan statehood, and on March 28 the House of Representatives voted in favor of it 208 to 166. On June 30 the bill passed the Senate by a vote of 64 to 20, and on July 7 the President signed it. On August 26, in a special election, 35,000 Alaskans voted 5 to 1 for statehood. Democratic candidates won all major offices in the election held on November 25.

On January 3, 1959, by Presidential proclamation, Alaska officially became a state. A thirteen-year-old schoolboy of Seward, named Benjamin Benson, designed the state flag. It features stars forming the Big Dipper, and in the northwest corner of the field is a single star, representing Alaska.

The statehood celebration was lavish indeed. Gold dye was poured into rivers, huge bonfires were set, and in the sky above Fairbanks two weather balloons carried a fifty-foot star.

The 1960 census tallied the population of Alaska at 226,167, which includes some 30,000 natives: Eskimo, Aleut, Tlingit, Tsimshian, Athaparcan. The Homestead Law, which provides a 160-acre tract free except for administrative fees, still applies to millions of acres of land in this young state. The land must be made productive, however, before a Homesteader receives title to it. In March of 1959, forty-two Homesteaders set out from Detroit to take advantage of this opportunity. They called themselves the "Fifty-niners," and settled in cabins, trailers, and quonset huts about eighty miles north of Anchorage. Nine months later only ten adults and three children were left. Of the rest, some went home to Detroit and some moved south to Anchorage. They were dismayed not only by the cold climate, but by the primitive living conditions —no electricity, and no water unless a settler dug his own well.

Perhaps the old Homestead Law, which requires that land be cleared and crops planted, is too severe for a land abounding in tundra and wilderness. At any rate, the problem of revising the law is being considered in the state legislature. An extension of this problem is that even when a Homesteader has succeeded in clearing and planting his land, transportation is still so slow and undependable that the farmer may not be able to dispose of his produce.

Despite the fact that homesteading is a difficult art indeed, thousands are still attracted to it, judging by the number of entries on file with the Bureau of Land Management in Alaska. True pioneer spirits can "stick it out" in Alaska as they did in Oregon, Arizona, and Utah, but the present need is for better farming and marketing methods rather than for more farmers.

Canned salmon is still—as it has been for years—Alaska's principal product, and woodpulp ranks second in exportable goods. As a source of revenue to the state, the defense program ranks highest, though precious metals are mined and valuable furs produced.

As a state, Alaska now manages her own resources after more than fifty years of federal management. Only the fur-seal herd of the Pribilof Islands continues to be under the jurisdiction of the United States Fish and Wildlife Service.

The most extensive federal land grant ever made to a new state was the 103 million acres Alaska received. (Her total acreage is 375 million acres.) This grant—the state was given its choice of locations—is roughly the size of California. Mineral lands may be leased by the state, but not sold outright.

Alaska today is truly a "new frontier." Many opportunities exist; in 1957 the territorial legislature adopted a tax-incentive plan providing relief from territorial and certain local (but not federal) taxes for as long as ten years to enterprising business firms locating in Alaska. Fishing and gold mining are still sources of wealth, but today tourism, building materials, wood-using industries, repair services, consumer goods, financial institutions, and —perhaps most important to the overall picture—the prospect of locating new oil resources are the state's present hopes for future economic expansion.

Alaska's rise to statehood has been difficult, even heroic, but the indications are that her future will be prosperous.

CHAPTER XI

Hawaii

AMERICA'S WESTWARD EXPANSION culminated in March, 1959, with the entrance of Hawaii as the fiftieth state of the Union. In three respects, Hawaii is different from all the other states: She is separated from the continent by more than two thousand miles of Pacific Ocean; her Caucasian population makes up only twenty-five percent of the total figure (exclusive of some 50,000 military personnel) of over 580,000; and more than half her population in 1958 was under twenty-four years of age.

The entire Hawaii story is, in fact, unlike that of any of the other states. Here there was no slavery issue, no gold rush, no burgeoning network of railroads, no cattle baron. There was a dynasty of kings by "divine right," a taboo system which marked off the people into castes; here the coming of democracy worked from the top down, rather than from the bottom up, by reason of the enlightenment of a superior breed of kings and queens.

Surely the creators of the Constitution of the United

States could not have dreamed that the fabric of government they had made would be strong and supple enough to reach a quarter of the way around the world to embrace a predominantly Oriental people. And yet, despite Hawaii's exotic origins and Eastern traditions, our new state is as essentially American as any other.

The existence of the Hawaiian Islands was, so far as can be determined, unknown to white men until the year 1778. The United States of America had already been born when Captain James Cook, British explorer, discovered the Islands, which he named the Sandwich Islands in honor of Lord Sandwich, First Lord of the Admiralty. Cook figures in the annals of seafaring as an adventurer, but he was also an outstanding man of science. He set out on his explorations with high aims. "I not only had ambition to go farther than any man had been before, but as far as it was possible for a man to go."

During his three voyages to the South Pacific, which were undertaken by the English Admiralty at the instance of the Royal Society of London for Improving Natural Knowledge, Cook kept a journal that, for its keen description of the native islanders he met, constitutes a major document in anthropology.

His experiences were truly memorable. On his second voyage—in search of a "great southern continent"—he came upon Easter Island, and islands in the Southwest Pacific. The Englishman was alert to the fact that physically and linguistically the natives closely resembled the aborigines of the South American coast, who were located thousands of miles eastward. He wondered how these people, if they had come from South America, had managed to navigate about a quarter of the earth's circumference in their primitive vessels. Cook's speculations have been echoed or argued by all subsequent visitors to the island.

Tahiti was among Cook's other stopping-off places on this second voyage. Here he spent two very agreeable weeks. Such rapport developed between the natives and the white men that the chief asked Cook where he planned to be buried when he passed on. Cook said he hoped his remains would be put in the family vault in the parish of Stepney, London. The chief explained that knowing the last resting place of his white brother would make it easier to locate him in the next world.

Among these Polynesians, life was a constantly seductive experience. On another expedition to this lotus country, a party of British sailors launched the celebrated mutiny against Captain William Bligh of the *Bounty*. Bligh, incidentally, had sailed under Captain Cook as an officer.

Cook's voyages took him as far south as the Antarctic, and north to the Arctic Sea. He visited New Zealand and the New Hebrides. But the climax of his explorations, in terms of historical significance, was his discovery of the Hawaiian Islands on his third and last voyage—this one undertaken in search of the ever-sought Northwest Passage. Cook had set out on this trip from Plymouth, England, in July, 1776. He sailed southward to round the Cape of Good Hope and thus, by way of the Indian Ocean, enter the Pacific. From Tasmania to New Zealand to the Society Islands to Tahiti, he sailed northeastward until he entered the Bering Strait.

It was after he left Tahiti that he made his momentous discovery of the "Sandwich Islands," but he stopped there only briefly before continuing northward. Passing through the Bering Strait—in the middle of which the Arctic Circle is crossed—he went on as far as 70° 41'. Here he found his way blocked by a mass of ice which rose twelve feet out of the water and stretched northward as far as the eye could see. Once again, all hope was abandoned of crossing from the Pacific to the Atlantic Ocean over the northern boundary of the American continent, but Cook kept a journal of his explorations for the benefit of future explorers.

There was nothing to do but turn back. Heading southward, he stopped at points in Alaska known only to the Russians. In January of 1779 he arrived again in Hawaii. The expedition landed at Waimea, Kauai Island. The natives professed to be delighted. So tumultuous was the welcoming party that clambered aboard the flagship that the vessel listed to its shoreward side.

The first sign of trouble appeared one dawn when Hawaiian swimmers were discovered under the British ships, stealing parts of the rigging. The ringleader was seized and whipped with a cat-o'-nine-tails. Shortly after this, a cutter was stolen by the natives. Cook went ashore with nine armed men. His purpose was to seize the tribal chief and hold him as hostage until the cutter was returned, but he would have to be subtle. He invited the chief to spend the day aboard the British ship. Just as the Hawaiian was about to accept the invitation, however, a messenger rushed up and reported that one of his tribesmen had been shot and killed by a white sailor. Instantly the tribe attacked the Englishmen. Cook was murdered, mutilated beyond recognition.

The stunned survivors of this ill-fated expedition, who remained aboard ship, made a truce with the natives. In the dead of night messengers climbed aboard and offered the white men a bundle. In it were the remains of Captain Cook. Both hands were intact, identifiable by a scar. With these remains, the white men hoisted anchor and sailed home.

Cook's trip, though it cost him his life, was not wasted. Others following him to the islands he had mapped were to civilize and Christianize the descendants of the people who had murdered him.

But meanwhile, the Islanders engaged in a succession of intertribal bloodlettings. Three years after Cook's death, there occurred the first of the internecine clashes from which a single, all-powerful chieftain, Kamehameha I, was to emerge, and ultimately to unite the Islands under his rule. In 1790, after becoming king of half of the island of Hawaii, Kamehameha invaded Maui Island with a fleet of canoes. Upon landing, he ordered the canoes dismantled and buried in the sand. Thus cut off from retreat, his army stood their ground and overwhelmed the Mauians in a savage battle. The site of the engagement, Wailuku, meaning "Waters of Annihilation," later became the capital of Maui.

Next Kamehameha maneuvered to gain sole control of Hawaii Island. To do so, he had to eliminate Keoua, ruler of the other half. Kamehameha's good luck kept pace with his ambition: a volcanic eruption virtually wiped out Keoua's army. The ruler still lived, however, and here Kamehameha resorted to trickery. He invited Keoua to a peace conference, and plunged a spear into him when he appeared.

In quick succession Kamehameha now brought Molokai, Lanai, and Oahu under control. Then, by cession, he absorbed the islands of Kauai and Niihau to the north. After two decades of warfare, this remarkable statesman and warrior became, in 1810, sole ruler of all the Hawaiian Islands.

Social conditions continued to be primitive. Kamehameha's empire was based on a feudal land-tenure system, but his dealings with foreign traders were shrewd. He was courteous to the American traders who brought the Islands' sandalwood to China at a good profit to him, but he routed the Spanish pirates and the Russians who, inspired by Baranov's success in Alaska, sought to use the Islands as a profitable base for themselves.

In Kamehameha's day chiefs and their families had arrogated rights and privileges from the gods, who they claimed were their ancestors. These included not only property rights but political and social rights as well. The lower classes were obliged to offer a degree of worship ordinarily reserved for gods, and to follow an elaborate etiquette system based on complicated social gradations. The people were required to prostrate themselves before some of the chiefs; others pronounced their persons too sacred to be touched. Lineage was as important in this community as under the caste system in India, and the taboo became the major instrument for control of the labor and wealth of the society.

Despite the autocracy of his rule, Kamehameha behaved with surprising benevolence in his later years. He established a code of humane laws and sent heralds throughout the islands to announce them verbally, since there was no written language. At the approach of death, he refused the sacrifices of human life offered to persuade the deities to prolong his own.

Shortly after the death of this powerful king, in 1819, two of his widowed queens destroyed the old religious system. Foreign influence had already done much to undermine the old faith, and when the women committed two major sacrileges in public (one ate forbidden coconut; the other dined in public with her son Liholiho, who became king as Kamehameha II) and lightning did not strike nor any other calamity ensue, the Hawaiians were ready to abandon their religion with a degree of equanimity. A bloody battle ensued between progressives and conservatives, but the high priest, who sympathized with the progressives, proclaimed the "death of the ancient gods" and set fire to his own temple.

First to step into the void created by the demise of the taboo system was a small company of New England Protestants. News of the "godlessness" of the Islanders had reached Boston through American whalers returning home from the Pacific. At revival meetings, volunteers were asked to bring the Christian faith to Hawaii.

A group of these missionaries and their wives set sail from Boston in 1819 under the leadership of two clergymen, Hiram Bingham and Asa Thurston. The voyage took seventeen months. The young missionaries—in addition to the Bingham and Thurston couples there were two male teachers, a physician, a printer, a farmer, and their wives —were agreeably surprised, upon landing, by the delightful climate and the hospitality of the natives. For their part, the native women were enchanted by the sedate dress of the white ladies. The *holokus* of today were, in fact, developed in emulation of the "Mother Hubbards" worn by the evangelists' wives.

Although Liholiho urged his people to embrace the

teachings of the missionaries—several thousands of the Islanders were taught to read and write—he postponed conversion for himself. After five more years of pleasure, he told the missionaries, he would take up Christianity. However, he and his wife died on a trip to London in 1824, before the five years were up.

The Protestant missionaries placed as much emphasis on education as on religion. It was they who taught the Hawaiians to commit their spoken language to writing, and printed the first Hawaiian textbook. It was they who achieved a Hawaiian translation of the Bible in 1839. Hiram Bingham founded the Punahou Academy in Honolulu, which, later renamed Oahu College, received the children of California pioneers who could not yet obtain such a high quality of education in the American West.

The American missionaries brought political as well as cultural and religious enlightenment. During the farsighted reign of Kamehameha III—which began in 1824 and lasted thirty years—the Islands were granted significant democratic rights. In 1829 this good king proclaimed the creation of the Islands' first law-making body. A bill of rights was proclaimed in 1839, followed almost immediately by an edict of toleration covering religious sects. In 1840 the king bestowed upon his people a constitution, one of the provisions of which was that a representative legislature be elected by the people.

Beginning in 1845, the social-minded king abolished the *mahele,* the feudal system of land tenure under which the crown, the government, the chiefs, and certain landholders had held title to sizable tracts, and changed over to the allodial—or independent ownership—tenure system. New constitutions were adopted in 1852, 1864, and 1887. Not until the last one—which was framed by the people—did the citizens get the right to elect the House of Nobles as well as the House of Representatives. Until this time, the Nobles—including female chiefs—had been elected by the nobles themselves or appointed by the king.

Missionary influence in Hawaii was not exclusively Protestant. Seven years after the arrival of the Bingham party, three Catholic priests arrived in Honolulu on a ship from Bordeaux. They were not warmly received, and in 1831 were banished as "idolaters." In 1839 the French government demanded the release of imprisoned Catholics and the free practice of the faith, and agreement was reached with the Hawaiian government.

In 1864, a Belgian Picpus Father arrived, and in that same year he was ordained in Honolulu. Father Damien (born Joseph de Veuster) came to the Hawaiian Islands, it might be said, by accident. During his novitiate at the Monastery of the Sacred Heart in Louvain, Belgium, his brother Auguste, an ordained priest, had been chosen to go to the Hawaiian Islands. Then typhus broke out and Auguste was infected. He recuperated, but was left too weak to take the Hawaiian assignment.

The young novice wrote a letter to the Superior-General requesting that he be assigned to the Islands in place of his brother Auguste, and permission was given.

After his ordination in Honolulu and missionary training in several outlying parishes, Father Damien asked to be sent to the island of Molokai, on which the government of Kamehameha V had established a leper colony in 1865. He had heard about the plight of natives sent there to rot away, without spiritual consolation or medical assistance.

Though he knew that the risk of infection would be great, Father Damien pleaded with his superiors for the privilege of living out his life among the doomed, and, if God willed it, becoming one of them. When his request was reluctantly granted, he boarded a ship along with fifty lepers.

The island of Molokai is shaped like the leaf of a willow. The two leper settlements—spaced a few miles apart —were sunk in a crater formed by volcanic forces. Mountains soared over a thousand feet above the settlements, creating what amounted to a prison for the lepers.

Upon landing at Molokai—on May 11, 1873—the thirty-three-year-old priest was shocked by the sight of these people. Sixty percent of the two thousand lepers who had originally been sent to the Island were dead. The remainder were in various stages of disintegration. Faces that were nothing but a mass of tubercules, hands without fingers, paralyzed features, blind men, madmen, men without voices—these were the things Father Damien saw. Worse than the sight of these people, however, was the air of hopelessness that pervaded the colony.

Immediately the missionary set about to improve conditions in every way he could. He had picked up fragments of medical knowledge here and there from textbooks, and he had the courage to put this to use, amputating the gangrenous limbs of victims who were no longer able to feel pain.

Faced with an unsatisfactory supply of water—the lepers were constantly thirsty, and there was never a drop to spare for bathing or housecleaning—the priest bombarded the board of health in Honolulu with requests for new pipelines. But the Hawaiian government, beset with numerous other problems, was indifferent to the welfare of men who were for all practical purposes among the dead. Reluctantly, and only after Father Damien had written many times, was a shipment of piping sent.

The priest persisted in his role of gadfly, and gradually he wrung concession after concession from the board. He obtained more generous food rations and medical supplies. He persuaded the authorities to build a hospital, and he trained the healthier lepers to nurse the weaker ones. He even had a general store constructed so that his "patients" could buy fruit and other treats.

To take some of the ugliness from death, which was a daily occurrence, Father Damien turned funerals into occasions of pomp. He organized "burial associations," decking out the living in festive finery and encouraging them to strum their guitars and beat their drums with enthusiasm as they accompanied a neighbor on his last journey. And each survivor prayed he would be accorded the same cheerful farewell. Had not this missionary priest promised them that they would enter the Kingdom of Heaven in perfect health?

In the course of his ministrations, Father Damien ceased to look or behave like a white man. He had adopted the food of the natives, and even their way of thinking. And one morning, when he was fifty-five, he discovered that he was sharing their terrible affliction as well. He had upset a kettle of steaming water while shaving. Although it spilled on his bare foot, he felt nothing. This insensitivity of the flesh was a mark of the leper.

Father Damien went quietly about his work. Within a few weeks dark blotches appeared on his arm, and he found he could not feel the prick of a needle. When the priest broke the news to his bishop in Honolulu, it was with the words, "I am calm and resigned and very happy in the midst of my people."

Now, after toiling twenty-one years on Molokai in obscurity, Father Damien became a celebrity. News of his dramatic illness was flashed over the world. Four Good Samaritans, moved by the story of the lepers of Hawaii, volunteered their services and arrived on the island to help the priest.

Clergymen of different faiths raised money for the colony. Doctors arrived with the newest medicines and equipment. Armauer Hansen, a Norwegian scientist, had recently succeeded in isolating the bacillus which causes leprosy. An oil was developed which in some cases arrested the disease.

But all this came too late for the missionary priest. He spent the four remaining years of life happy in the spiritual rewards of his dedication. A half-century after his death, in 1888, his body was removed from its grave on Molokai and brought to Belgium to be reburied with national honors. But the name of Damien remains inseparably associated with that of Molokai.

The political and international experiences of Hawaii during the middle of the nineteenth century—when, because of its strategic position at the "crossroads of the Pacific," it first began to attract the attention of the European powers—constitute another absorbing story of our fiftieth state.

England and France were the first to display interest in Hawaii. Indeed, to prevent the French fleet from seizing the Islands in 1843, England did so herself. The occupation, however, lasted only half a year. The Hawaiian kingdom asserted its independence, and the United States recognized it. The two powers then made a joint declaration recognizing the Sandwich Islands as an independent state, and relinquishing forever all claims to it.

In the meantime, Americans had become attracted to Hawaii. The success of the missionaries had been widely reported in the states, and Yankee business men founded plantations and sugar mills on the island. For a time, the American settlers vied with the British to influence Hawaiian economic policies, but America's cause received something of a setback when Kamehameha IV ascended the throne in 1855. His wife, Queen Emma, who was the granddaughter of an English sailor, had become enamored of the British way of life. On a visit to England she struck up a friendship with Queen Victoria, and determined to pattern the manners of the Hawaiian royal family on those of Buckingham Palace. On their return to the Islands, the royal couple surrounded themselves with British advisers, and brought the Anglican Church to Hawaii.

Into this situation, in the spring of 1863, stepped a remarkable American. He was Dr. James McBride of Oregon, appointed first American minister to Hawaii by President Lincoln. A few days after his arrival, a reception was given in his honor at Iolani Palace, where he met the King and Queen, their relatives, members of the diplomatic corps, and all the prominent citizens of Honolulu. Among those present was the King's brother, Prince Lot, who was destined within the year to succeed to the throne as Kamehameha V.

In the weeks following his arrival, innumerable *luaus* (native banquets) were held in Dr. McBride's honor. The pioneer from Oregon sampled roasted pigs and chickens, raw fish, live shrimp, yams, and *poi*. Despite these honors he was quick to sense the coolness shown him by the British, and their skepticism toward the government he represented. This was the time of the Civil War, and British sympathies were openly on the side of the South. The notion that the Union would not survive much longer was widely held.

These unfriendly relations reached a climax a year later, when a British man-o'-war docked at Honolulu and two young lords came ashore for a spree. What better lark, they thought, than to steal the gilded emblem of the American Eagle from the Legation's gatepost and carry it away as a souvenir? Choosing a time when the Legation was closed, they unfastened the coat of arms and hired a native to carry it to the dock. Here it was smuggled aboard the British ship without attracting attention. When Dr. McBride arrived at his office the next morning, he was astonished to discover the loss. This was an affront to his government.

Armed with a native informant and a search warrant, Dr. McBride called on the captain of the English warship, demanding the return of the insignia. The Englishman protested that he knew nothing of the theft, and claimed that the insignia was not on his ship. Nonetheless Dr. McBride insisted on a search. Eventually the guilty parties confessed and produced the eagle.

To the British commissioner who called at his office to offer his apologies, Dr. McBride announced that this was not sufficient amends. He would consider the matter closed, he told them, only when the young culprits had replaced the insignia with their own hands—just as they had removed it. Despite protestations, Dr. McBride had

his way. On the day appointed for the restoration, a crowd
of natives gathered in front of the Legation to enjoy the
embarrassment of the two Englishmen.

Dr. McBride's four years in Honolulu not only en-
hanced the dignity of the United States government, but
were largely responsible for making Americans back home
aware of the strategic importance of Hawaii. He was the
first to recommend that the United States purchase a tract
of land near Honolulu for the purpose of building a naval
station to protect American commerce in the Pacific. Hawaii was to make this very important cession to the United
States in 1887.

In Dr. McBride's time, Prince Lot succeeded his brother,
Kamehameha IV, to the throne as Kamehameha V. Since
he failed to marry and produce an heir, the royal line of
Hawaiian kings ended with him. His successor, William
C. Lunalilo, was elected by the legislature and ratified by
popular vote. During his reign, Lot had forced the adoption of the Constitution of 1864, which reduced the legislature to one house and limited voting rights by imposing
property and educational qualifications.

After a brief reign (thirteen months), King William
died in 1874, and the throne was again unoccupied. The
ascendancy of American influence over British in Hawaiian affairs became clearly apparent. The Americans favored Chief David Kalakaua to occupy the throne. The
British, on the other hand, were solidly behind Queen
Emma, widow of Kamehameha IV. So high were feelings
that when the pro-American candidate was elected, a riot
incited by British sympathizers broke out in the legislature.

King David Kalakaua, nicknamed the "Merry Monarch," was addicted to having a good time, as his poker and drinking companions could attest. He traveled around the world to observe the splendor in which other monarchs lived, and introduced the first coronation ceremony ever held in the Islands.

Under Kalakaua's rule American and British interests continued to exert pressure on the economy, and Kalakaua played off one against the other. An example of this concerned the disposal of the Hawaiian sugar crop, the Islands' major export. Frustrated by the high American tariff system, Kalakaua channeled an increasing bulk of the cane to the friendlier British colonies—Australia, New Zealand, and British Columbia. Reports circulated in Washington that the entire crop might be diverted into the British orbit. Pro-American residents on the Islands warned that political domination by Great Britain might well follow this economic development. The Grant administration in 1875 was persuaded to negotiate a reciprocity treaty under which Hawaiian sugar and other crops would enter the United States duty free in return for the admission of American manufactured goods into the Islands.

This treaty gave a substantial impetus to American investment and swung the Islands decisively into the economic orbit of the United States. Capital poured into Hawaii for roads, railroads, electricity, retail stores. The sugar industry was a particular beneficiary. Owned by the descendants of American missionaries and Irish and Scandinavian settlers, Hawaii's sugar plantations employed cheap labor from Portugal, Japan, and other countries with a surplus population.

In the meantime, the authority of the native government steadily deteriorated. The American Board of Missions had withdrawn in 1863, leaving their work in local hands, and the old authority of the chiefs was no longer in force. The government became involved in scandals that rocked the Islands. One, involving bribery by opium interests, implicated the King himself.

In 1887 the reciprocity treaty, which had had a seven-year term, was extended for another seven years with the stipulation that the United States be given the exclusive right to Pearl Harbor as a naval coaling and repair station—a right which was not exercised for some time. In this same year—when a low ebb in Hawaii's internal affairs had been reached because of Kalakaua's despotic ambitions and the existence of corruption at high levels—the people firmly but peaceably demanded a new constitution. For the first time the people themselves, through popular representatives, drafted their own blueprint for government. The monarch's function became purely executive; all his legislative powers were taken away. The House of Nobles became elective, and now sat in joint session with the House of Representatives. The legislature was empowered to remove, "upon sufficient cause," any of the four ministers of the king's cabinet, which he himself appointed.

The Constitution of 1887 was to prove more important in its abrogation than in its adoption. Kalakaua died in 1891, and his sister, who succeeded him as Queen Liliuokalani, swore to uphold the constitution. But on January 17, 1893, her government fell because she longed to be a queen in fact, and had, two days earlier, tried to put through a new constitution that would again secure the absolute power of the throne by giving her the right to appoint a new House of Nobles and disfranchising all foreigners. She had already, at the beginning of her reign, rid herself of the existing cabinet. The revolutionary proclamation read, in part:

> We, citizens and residents of the Hawaiian Islands, organized and acting for the public safety and the common good, hereby proclaim as follows:
> 1. The Hawaiian Monarchical system of Government is hereby abrogated.
> 2. A Provisional Government for the control and management of public affairs and the protection of the public peace is hereby established, to exist until terms of union with the United States of America have been agreed upon. . . .

The rebels hoped for immediate union with the United States, but the political climate in Washington was unfavorable. Grover Cleveland, a Democrat, was in the White House. His party was opposed to annexation. In the meantime, then, a republic was set up on July 4, 1894, with Sanford B. Dole, a missionary's son, as president.

Four years later, with a Republican, McKinley, in the White House, and the American nation involved in a war with Spain that focused the people's attention upon the value of Hawaii as an outpost of defense, annexation was finally achieved. But it was not achieved without a struggle. Democrats in Congress and elsewhere throughout the United States argued that the United States did not have the constitutional right to annex territory in these circumstances. Moreover, Japan, acutely aware of the strategic importance of Hawaii, also registered a protest against its annexation to the United States. (She later withdrew the protest.) When the treaty was reported to Congress under the McKinley administration from the Committee on For-

eign Relations, the two-thirds majority needed for its ratification was not forthcoming. The sponsors of annexation
in Congress had to resort to an alternative technique: the
passage of a joint resolution which required only a majority in each house. After a fierce legislative.battle the measure was passed, and was signed by the President on July
7, 1898.

The joint resolution stipulated that the Republic of
Hawaii consented to cede to the United States "all rights
of sovereignty of whatsoever kind in and over the Hawaiian Islands and their dependencies" and "absolute fee and
ownership of all public, Government, or Crown lands,
public buildings or edifices, ports, harbors, military equipment, and all other public property of every kind and
description belonging to the Government of the Hawaiian
Islands. . . ."

The resolution accepted and confirmed the said cession
and the annexation of the Islands. One notable concession
was made by the United States: "The existing laws of the
United States relative to public lands shall not apply to
such lands in the Hawaiian Islands; but the Congress of
the United States shall enact special laws for their management and disposition." The only provision attached
was that the revenue from such lands—except for that in
civil, military, or naval use by the United States or for the
use of the local government—"shall be used solely for the
benefit of the inhabitants of the Hawaiian Islands for educational and other public purposes." The United States
assumed the public debt of the Republic of Hawaii up to
a limit of four million dollars.

One restriction which bears explanation is that curtail-
ing all Chinese immigration into the Islands, as well as all

emigration of Chinese from Hawaii to the United States. The Chinese had begun to arrive, encouraged by the Hawaiian government because they were good workers, in 1852; by 1883 their numbers were so great that the government applied restrictions. Congress had passed an exclusion act for the United States the year before, banning the immigration of Chinese laborers (who had earlier been utilized by the Pacific Coast railroad builders) for ten years. The joint resolution on annexation extended to Hawaii the American law.

President McKinley had, under terms of the annexation resolution, appointed five commissioners to recommend legislation for the government of the islands, and they made their recommendations to Congress in November. Congress then argued for a year over just what the relationship between Hawaii and the United States was to be. It was not until April 30, 1900, that the President signed the "Act to provide a government for the Territory of Hawaii" that Congress finally passed. It was this Act which formally constituted Hawaii a Territory, and Sanford B. Dole was appointed, by the President, its first governor.

For the next fifty-nine years Hawaii remained a Territory of the United States, a remote "outpost in the Pacific." It took an unleashing of bombs to turn her into a "flesh and blood" member of the American family.

Pearl Harbor, ceded to the United States as a coaling and repair station in 1887, became a naval station in 1900, after annexation. Harbor improvements were made, and in 1940, when war was already raging in Europe and Asia and the Berlin Pact was signed by the Axis nations, the station was appropriately fortified.

At 7:58 on the morning of December 7, 1941, while

Japanese representatives were carrying on negotiations in Washington, a swarm of carrier-based Japanese bombers materialized out of nowhere and swept down over Ford Island, in the center of Pearl Harbor. About sixty-five planes were grounded on the airfield there, and almost half were destroyed in the sudden attack. Simultaneously, torpedo planes and dive-bombers closed in on Hickham Field, adjacent to Pearl Harbor, Kaneohe Naval Air Station, and Wheeler Field.

The row of eight battleships and innumerable smaller ships in Pearl Harbor sustained the brunt of the enemy attack for nearly half an hour, and all were hit. Before the "day of infamy" was over, the battleship *Arizona*—with a thousand men trapped in her hold—was a flaming ruin; the *Oklahoma* had capsized; the *West Virginia, Tennessee, Pennsylvania,* and *Nevada* were sinking. When the last Japanese plane headed back to its carrier, located about two hundred miles to the north, nearly twenty-five hundred Navy, Army, and Marine servicemen were dead and fifteen hundred others wounded. One hundred eighty-eight planes were lost and eighteen ships seriously damaged.

At the time of the Japanese attack, America was enjoying a leisurely Sunday. In Des Moines, Iowa, citizens were napping on their sofas after their noonday meal. In Los Angeles, where it was still morning, they were listening to church sermons. In Manhattan, two thousand people were seated in the Radio City Music Hall watching a film when the news of the attack at Pearl Harbor was announced. There was a moment of silence. Then the voice of a Marine rang out, "We'll whale the tar out of them."

Politicians, industrial leaders, spokesmen from all walks

of life were heard. Said Herbert Hoover: "American soil has been attacked. We will fight with all our spiritual and physical resources until we prevail."

The following day, Monday, at 4:10 P.M., the United States declared war on Japan. President Franklin Delano Roosevelt stood before Congress and said: "Yesterday, December 7, 1941—a date which will live in infamy—the United States of America was suddenly and deliberately attacked by naval and air forces of the Empire of Japan. . . . We will not only defend ourselves to the uttermost, but will make it very certain that this form of treachery shall never again endanger us. . . . We will gain the inevitable triumph—so help us God."

During the four years of war no part of America underwent a more profound physical transformation than Hawaii. The beaches of this Paradise were ringed with barbed wire. Familiar landmarks, as well as strategic installations, were camouflaged with paint in zigzag patterns. Mobile barricades, ready to move at a signal, were placed along flower-bordered roads. Barracks sprang up in parks, on plantations, in open fields. Miles of piers, wharves, and warehouses studded the ocean fronts. Tunnels were drilled into the sides of mountains for refuge and storage space. New roads, runways, and radio installations materialized almost overnight.

Hawaii's role in the war made statehood inevitable. For years, opponents of statehood had argued that the preponderance of Asiatic races on the Islands precluded them from ever becoming genuinely "American." However, the war with Japan taught a striking lesson: The Asiatic population of Hawaii remained loyal. Not a single case of sabotage was officially reported. Four fifths of the Hawaiians killed in action against the Axis Powers were of Japanese origin. Over a thousand Nisei (American-born Japanese) took part in the invasion of Italy as the 442nd Regimental Combat Team, winning more decorations than any other unit in the war. Upon the conclusion of World War II, the Truman Administration actively espoused Hawaiian statehood; legislation was actually passed in the House of Representatives in 1947. However, despite strong newspaper support, especially in the West, the bill was killed in the Senate. The issue had become a political football. Since Hawaii was predominantly Republican, the Democrats refused to vote for its admission unless Alaska, a Democratic stronghold, was granted statehood also.

When Alaska entered the Union in 1959, the way was clear for the Islands. On March 12, 1959, Congress passed the Hawaii statehood bill, and President Eisenhower signed it on March 18. At a primary election on June 27, 1959, Hawaii's voters answered an overwhelming *Yes* to the proposition: "Shall Hawaii immediately be admitted into the Union as a State?" There was a turnout of 94% of Hawaii's registered voters to elect as one of their senators Hiram L. Fong, a Republican of Chinese ancestry, and as Representative, Daniel K. Inouye, a Democrat of Japanese blood. Inouye was the first individual of Japanese lineage ever to take his seat in the United States Congress.

Today more than half a million souls reside on Hawaii's eight inhabited islands. (A dozen or so smaller ones are uninhabited.) The largest group identifiable along racial lines, amounting to almost 40% of the population, is of Japanese origin. Americans and white Europeans make up 20%; 18% are full- or part-breed Hawaiian natives; 14% are Filipino by origin and 7% are Chinese. This community, heterogeneous as it is, has a notably high literacy rate, and more than nine tenths of its citizens vote in the elections.

With the admission of Hawaii to the Union, no more organized territories wait at the gate. The Virgin Islands, purchased from Denmark in 1917, form an unorganized territory administered by a governor appointed by the President and a unicameral elected legislature. Control of the islands rests with the Department of the Interior.

Guam, ceded to the United States by Spain in 1898, is also an unorganized territory. Its governor and legislature take office in the same manner as in the Virgin Islands. Under the jurisdiction of the Interior Department, its people are American citizens but do not vote for President.

American Samoa, about two thousand miles southwest of Hawaii, is a possession of the United States administered by the Department of the Interior, and its governor is appointed by the Department. Its legislature is bicameral, its population chiefly Polynesian.

The Canal Zone is a military reservation of the United States under the jurisdiction of this country and the Panama Canal Company, whose president is also governor of the zone. The governor reports to the American Secretary of the Army.

Wake Island, about two thousand miles west of Hawaii, and the Midway Islands, twelve hundred miles northeast of this new state, are possessions under the jurisdiction of the Secretary of the Navy.

Other islands in the Pacific are administered by the Navy, the Department of the Interior, or—in the case of the Caroline, Marshall, and Mariana Islands (except

Guam)—by the United States under a United Nations trusteeship.

Puerto Rico is, of course, the closest and the most populous of all the outlying regions of America. She is the easternmost island of the Greater Antilles, which include Cuba, Hispaniola, and Jamaica. On August 5, 1947, President Truman signed an act giving Puerto Rico the right to elect her chief executive by popular vote, and on June 4, 1951, she won the right to draft her own constitution.

The constitution devised is very similar to that of the United States, and after it had been ratified by popular vote on March 3, 1952, Congress passed a resolution approving the constitution and giving Puerto Rico the status of a free commonwealth associated with the United States. This was signed by President Truman on July 3, and became effective July 25, 1952.

The governor of Puerto Rico is elected by direct ballot every four years, as are the members of the bicameral legislative assembly. A Supreme Court and such other courts as are established by law comprise the judiciary.

Puerto Rico has a Resident Commissioner in the United States Congress, but he does not have a vote. The original Organic Act of 1917 gave American citizenship to Puerto Ricans, but while they may vote for President of the United States if they live here, they may not do so as residents of the commonwealth.

So far as the future of American statehood is concerned, Puerto Rico is as close to it as her voters ultimately decide. At any time, ten percent of the electorate has a right to call for a referendum on whether the commonwealth shall become independent, become a state, or remain a commonwealth. All three possibilities have their supporters, but Governor Luis Muñoz Marín, who has recently been reelected to his fourth term, is a member of the Popular Democrats; this is the party which opposes statehood, largely on economic grounds.

As for the rest of "overseas America," the unincorporated territories of the Virgin Islands and Guam have open to them the possibility of becoming incorporated territories. During the 1960 Presidential election, this opportunity was suggested.

The story of American statehood is, in all probability, yet unfinished. Its power lies not in the fact that new states have been entering this Union for nearly two centuries, but that in every case they have done so voluntarily, by a majority vote of their citizens—and that they could in no case have done so if their state constitutions did not uphold the tenets of that far-reaching document of human rights: the Constitution of the United States.

DATES OF ADMISSION

Alabama	December 14, 1819	(22)
Alaska	January 3, 1959	(49)
Arizona	February 14, 1912	(48)
Arkansas	June 15, 1836	(25)
California	September 9, 1850	(31)
Colorado	August 1, 1876	(38)
Connecticut	January 9, 1788	(5)
Delaware	December 7, 1787	(1)
Florida	March 3, 1845	(27)
Georgia	January 2, 1788	(4)
Hawaii	August 21, 1959	(50)
Idaho	July 3, 1890	(43)
Illinois	December 3, 1818	(21)
Indiana	December 11, 1816	(19)
Iowa	December 28, 1846	(29)
Kansas	January 29, 1861	(34)
Kentucky	June 1, 1792	(15)
Louisiana	April 30, 1812	(18)
Maine	March 15, 1820	(23)
Maryland	April 28, 1788	(7)

Massachusetts	February 6, 1788	(6)
Michigan	January 26, 1837	(26)
Minnesota	May 11, 1858	(32)
Mississippi	December 10, 1817	(20)
Missouri	August 10, 1821	(24)
Montana	November 8, 1889	(41)
Nebraska	March 1, 1867	(37)
Nevada	October 31, 1864	(36)
New Hampshire	June 21, 1788	(9)
New Jersey	December 18, 1787	(3)
New Mexico	January 6, 1912	(47)
New York	July 26, 1788	(11)
North Carolina	November 21, 1789	(12)
North Dakota	November 2, 1889	(39)
Ohio	March 1, 1803	(17)
Oklahoma	November 16, 1907	(46)
Oregon	February 14, 1859	(33)
Pennsylvania	December 12, 1787	(2)
Rhode Island	May 29, 1790	(13)
South Carolina	May 23, 1788	(8)
South Dakota	November 2, 1889	(40)
Tennessee	June 1, 1796	(16)
Texas	December 29, 1845	(28)
Utah	January 4, 1896	(45)
Vermont	March 4, 1791	(14)
Virginia	June 25, 1788	(10)
Washington	November 11, 1889	(42)
West Virginia	June 20, 1863	(35)
Wisconsin	May 29, 1848	(30)
Wyoming	July 10, 1890	(44)

BIBLIOGRAPHY

Adams, James Truslow, *The Epic of America*. Boston, Little, Brown & Company, 1941.

Bancroft, George, *History of the United States From the Discovery of the American Continent* . . . New York, Appleton-Century-Crofts, Inc., 1928.

Beard, Charles A. and Mary R., *The Rise of American Civilization*. New York, The Macmillan Company, 1939.

Berger, J. and D., *Diary of America*. New York, Simon & Schuster, Inc., 1957.

Billington, Ray Allen, and Hedges, J. B., *Westward Expansion: A History of the American Frontier*. New York, The Macmillan Company, 1949.

Botkin, B. A., *A Treasury of American Folklore*. New York, Crown Publishers, Inc., 1944.

Bracke, William B., *Wheat Country*. New York, Duell, Sloan & Pearce, Inc., 1950.

Bryce, James, *The American Commonwealth*, 2 vols. New York, The Macmillan Company, 1888.

Butler, Evelyn I., and Dale, George A., *Alaska: The Land and the People*. New York, Viking Press, 1957.

Clark, Thomas D., *The Kentucky*. New York, Rinehart & Co., Inc., 1942.

Clugston, W. G., *Facts You Should Know About Kansas*. Girard, Kansas, Haldeman-Julius Co., 1945.

Colby, Merle, *Guide to Alaska, Last American Frontier*. American Guide Series. New York, The Macmillan Company, 1939.

Commager, Henry Steele, *Documents of American History*. New York, Appleton-Century-Crofts, Inc., 1935.

Dale, Edward E., and Wardell, Morris L., *History of Oklahoma*. New York, Prentice-Hall, Inc., 1948.

Dobie, J. Frank, *Coronado's Children*. Dallas, The Southwest Press, 1930.

Faulkner, Harold Underwood, *American Political and Social History*. New York, Appleton-Century-Crofts, Inc., 1937.

Fergusson, Erna, *Our Southwest*. New York, Alfred A. Knopf, Inc., 1940.

Fox, Charles D., *The Truth About Florida*. New York, Simon & Schuster, Inc., 1925.

Gould, Charles Newton, *Oklahoma Place Names*. Norman, University of Oklahoma Press, 1933.

Gray, James, *The Illinois*. New York, Farrar & Rinehart, Inc., 1940.

Gruening, Ernest, *The State of Alaska*. New York, Random House, 1954.

Hacker, Louis M., *The Shaping of the American Tradition*. New York, Columbia University Press, 1947.

Hanna, Phil T., *California Through Four Centuries*. New York, Farrar & Rinehart, Inc., 1935.

Hatcher, Harlan, *The Great Lakes*. New York, Oxford University Press, 1944.

Hebard, Grace R., *The Pathbreakers from River to Ocean*. Glendale, Arthur H. Clark Co., 1940.

Hill, Ralph Nading, *Contrary Country: A Chronicle of Vermont*. New York, Rinehart & Company, 1950.

Howard, Joseph K., *Montana: High, Wide, and Handsome*. New Haven, Yale University Press, 1943.

McReynolds, Edwin C., *Oklahoma: A History of the "Sooner" State*. Norman, University of Oklahoma Press, 1954.

Morison, Samuel Eliot, and Commager, Henry Steele, *The Growth of the American Republic*, 4th ed. New York, Oxford University Press, 1950.

Muzzey, David S., *Readings in American History*. Boston, Ginn and Company, 1915.

Myrdal, Gunnar, *An American Dilemma*. New York, Harper and Brothers, 1944.

Nevins, Allan, and Commager, Henry Steele, *America: The Story of a Free People*. Boston, Little, Brown & Company, 1942.

Pierson, George Wilson, *Tocqueville and Beaumont in America*. New York, Oxford University Press, 1938.

Pollard, Lancaster, *A History of the State of Washington*. Portland, Binfords & Mort, 1941.

Richardson, Rupert Norval, *Texas, the Lone Star State*. New York, Prentice-Hall, Inc., 1943.

Sanchez, Nellie, *Stories of the States*. New York, Thomas Y. Crowell Company, 1931.

Saxon, Lyle, *Fabulous New Orleans*. New York, D. Appleton & Company, 1928.

Sherman, William Tecumseh, *Memoir of William Tecumseh Sherman*. New York. D. Appleton & Company, 1889.

Shotwell, James T., *The United States in History*. New York, Simon & Schuster, Inc., 1956.

Smith, Lucy, *Biographical Sketches of Joseph Smith, the Prophet, and his Progenitors* . . . Lamoni, Iowa, Reorganized Church of J. C. of Latter-Day Saints, 1912.

Stegner, Wallace, *Mormon Country*. New York, Duell, Sloan & Pearce, Inc., 1942.

Thompson, Charles M., *Independent Vermont*. Boston, Houghton Mifflin Company, 1942.

Tocqueville, Alexis de, *Democracy in America*. New York, Alfred A. Knopf, Inc., 1945.

Turner, Frederick Jackson, *The Frontier in American History*. New York, Henry Holt & Company, 1920.

Webb, Walter Prescott, *The Great Plains*. Universal Library. New York, Grosset & Dunlap, 1957.

Whipple, Maurine, *This is the Place: Utah*. New York, Alfred A. Knopf, Inc., 1945.

Wissler, Clark, *Indians of the United States: Four Centuries of Their History and Culture*. New York, Doubleday, Doran & Company, Inc., 1940.

Wood, Elizabeth, *Arizona Hoof Trails*. Portland, Binfords & Mort, 1956.

Writers' Project, *Arizona*, rev. ed. American Guide Series. New York, Hastings House, 1955.

——, *California*, rev. ed. American Guide Series. New York, Hastings House, 1954.

——, *Utah*, rev. ed. American Guide Series. New York, Hastings House, 1954.

Index

A

Adams-Onís treaty, 151
Addison, Don James, 182-186
Alabama, creation of Territory of, 152; secession, 166; statehood, 66, 152
Alamo, 77, 79
Alaska, boundary, 227; capital of, 222; civil government, 222; diphtheria in, 226-227; gold in, 223-226; Homestead Law, 223; homesteading in, 232-233; laws, 228; salmon canneries, 225; statehood, 229-232; as Territory, 223-231; in World War II, 228-229, 230
Alaska Commercial Company, 222
Alaska Railroad, 230
Alaska Steamship Line, 230
Aleuts, relations with Russians, 212-215
Alexander VI, Pope, 20
Allen, Ethan, 27
allodial tenure, 243
American Fur Company, 112-113, 116, 117
American Revolution, beginning of, 11
American Samoa, 258

American Society for Encouraging the Settlement of the Oregon Territory, 122
Annapolis Convention, 15
Anza, Don Juan Bautista de, 96
Arizona, admission to Union, 187, 190; creation of Territory of, 173; gold in, 181-182; newspapers in, 174; picture money in, 173; Spanish ownership, 70
Arkansas, creation from Territory of Missouri, 63; early reconstruction, 168; secession, 166
Articles of Confederation, 1, 12, 14-15, 16, 17
assembly, first legislative in America, 3
Astor, John Jacob, 112-113
Atchison, Topeka, and Santa Fe, 189
Atlantic Cable, 219
Austin, Stephen F., 71, 75, 76

B

Baranov, Aleksandr Andreyevich, 216-218, 240
Barbé-Marbois, François de, 50, 51-52

267

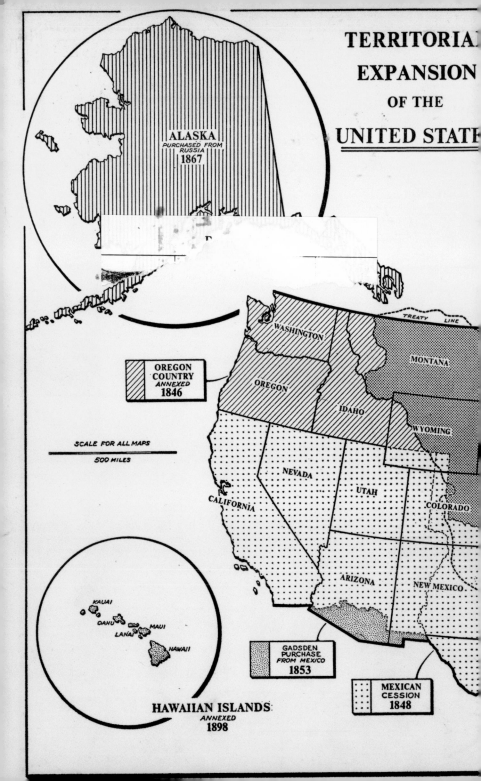

TERRITORIAL EXPANSION OF THE UNITED STATES

ALASKA
PURCHASED FROM RUSSIA
1867

WASHINGTON

OREGON

MONTANA

IDAHO

WYOMING

OREGON COUNTRY
ANNEXED
1846

NEVADA

UTAH

CALIFORNIA

COLORADO

SCALE FOR ALL MAPS

500 MILES

ARIZONA

NEW MEXICO

TREATY LINE

KAUAI

OAHU

MAUI

LANAI

HAWAII

GADSDEN PURCHASE
FROM MEXICO
1853

MEXICAN CESSION
1848

HAWAIIAN ISLANDS
ANNEXED
1898